Enlightenment
is
Losing Your Mind

Enlightenment
is
Losing Your Mind

by PAX

*To find out about other products offered by
Moose Ear Press see the last pages of this book.*

Editor: Jackie Stocking
Copy Editor: Jackie Stocking
Proofreaders: Karen M. Bates, Roger Anderson
Photographs: Jerry Stocking
Cover Design and Artwork: Jerry Stocking
Cover Model: Judson Stocking
Inside Models: Emily and Judson Stocking

Thank you to Publishers Express Press
for assistance in the printing of this book.

Published by
Moose Ear Press

First Printing 1995
Second Printing 2002

Copyright © 2002
Jerry Stocking, P.O. Box 2422, Clarkesville, Georgia 30523
(706) 754-7540

ISBN 0-9629593-4-0

"Me like it."

Judson Laurence Stocking, the birth of
consciousness at two years of age.

A special thank-you is extended to Karen Bates
whose contribution to the production of this book ranged from
being with the children during the many hours of editing and pre-
press production to the preparation of wonderful meals to hours
spent proofreading and compiling the glossary. Also Karen was
an active participant in many of the discussions that ensued during
the writing of Enlightenment is Losing Your Mind.

Note from the Editor

On February 17, 1990, Jerry realized enlightenment, and Pax, which means peace in Latin, now resides within him. Jerry Stocking has written three books that have been published. I have played a part in the editing and production of each one. *Enlightenment is Losing Your Mind* is Jerry's fourth book and was written in just eight days, with Jerry as more of a witness, typing at the keyboard, than an author. After some consideration Jerry decided to use a pen name for the first time—Pax. Not coincidentally, our children, Emily and Judson, have been calling Jerry, Pax, for years. Finally, we caught on to it as the name of Jerry's perception of enlightenment.

As the editor I have read *Enlightenment is Losing Your Mind* six times. My term for this book is "elusive." So many times after completing a chapter, I couldn't remember the content of what I had just read. However, I was more acutely aware of changes within me—aware of subtlety and process. This resulted in healthy doses of disorientation. I found myself laughing more often at nothing than at something. From my experience, this consistent phenomenon is part of using the book as a tool to lose your mind.

At first I wanted to understand and control what I was reading—figure it out. I soon relaxed and just enjoyed myself, trusting that I would learn what I needed to learn. Realizing that children learn constantly through play, I played "reading the book."

Pax wishes you well. He wishes you peace, confusion, and love, along with the perception of your own enlightenment.

Jackie Stocking, Editor

Table of Contents

Introduction

A frog made seven jumps from lily pad to lily pad, making certain to land safely in the center of each pad, and reached a point halfway across the pond. Not being one to stop and assess things, the frog jumped from pad seven and landed instantly on the opposite bank, never touching the next lily pad. This instantaneous arrival did not seem like an instant to the frog, who not only landed on the next lily pad but continued to jump from lily pad to lily pad, finally reaching the bank. On what bank it landed, the frog could not be sure, but it was stable dry land, with support different from that offered by the lily pads.

Thought provides you with padding to fall on, in the inevitable event that your thinking lets you down short of your goal. As you call moving from thought to thought, progress, time is created and the space between thoughts is entirely ignored. Enlightenment is always closer than your next thought.

Maybe you don't like the "Everything is illusion" route. Perhaps you have a need for there to be things, a mind, and people. Although it isn't likely to happen, you can recognize your enlightenment while keeping all of your current perceptions intact. A Koan, supposedly, worked for many a student in the East.

As you become aware of more subtleties around you, discovery will be yours. You will continue to notice new and different things; you will enter new worlds of both cause and effect where life makes sense to you and then makes no sense at all. You will hold on and let go until that becomes your pattern. Depth and revelation will be yours. You will discover that anything you can perceive must have been there all the time. Yet it may not be there at all. Watch out for meaning.

Anything you can perceive now, you could always have perceived. To put it less accurately and more usefully, given how you think, "Anything that is now has always been."

"Anything that is now has always been."

Let that sit with you for a little bit. It is different to be told something than it is to discover it yourself. The idea "Anything that is now has always been," brings you halfway across the stream. It is half of the Koan. Before you think another thought, there is the possibility to transport yourself to anywhere without landing. You must jump but not land; then you can land anywhere. As long as you jump and land, you will be caught in the world of cause and effect. If you jump to jump, rather than jump to land, everything becomes possible for you. Reality is revealed. Spirituality is consciousness focused on reality. You become purely spiritual, and you transcend any possible bonds to illusion while becoming the whole. When you are the whole, then you are already everywhere. There is nowhere to get to. You already arrived. Perfection. But, if you leap and then land, you miss it. You must just leap.

Complete the other half of, "Anything that is now has always been."

Perceive without thinking. Observe without being the observer. The other half will be obvious. Come up with answers, many answers, until you have one that you can trust. Whether you have never done an exercise from a book, have always done exercises from books, or have done some exercises, DO THIS ONE. Do not read on until you have pondered the other half of the idea "Anything that is now has always been." What comes next? What allows you to be between thoughts?

Have you figured out the answer? If so, that is not the answer. If you have discovered the answer without figuring it out, you just might have it. If the answer provides you with tremendous relief, sets you free and unburdens you

from fear, then it is the answer. If not, ponder it some more. If, "Anything that is now has always been," what then? What is the other half?

Hint: If you can't wait for the answer, relax and think of Jack Benny.

1

Fork in The Road

There were odd-shaped groupings of symbols, pointing which way to go, but not in an obvious manner. They were in the shapes of complex V's, kind of like this:

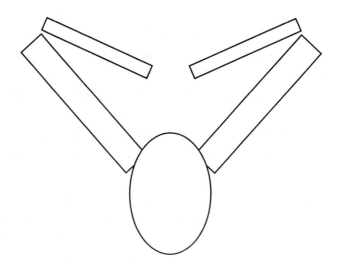

Closer examination revealed that all of these symbols were, in fact, piles of bones, human bones. Each grouping seemed to be put there as some kind of mirror, reflecting and taunting the fork in the road. It was not until some time later that it became clear to me exactly what these shapes represented. The circle was a skull resting on top of the rib bones and back bone. Radiating out from this center point were the large thigh bones and then coming back toward, but not quite reaching center again, were the calf bones.

At first I thought this might be a warning for me. It was, but not directly. The bones were the symbolic remains of a person left undisturbed in a full lotus position for long enough.

No book learning would have revealed this to me. It arrived as an insight, at this fork in the road at which I found myself frozen as I assumed the lotus position myself: filled with the fear of taking the wrong fork, or not taking the right one. With the irony I have since come to expect from life, it should have been obvious that both paths ultimately led to the same place. There was a little solace in the company here; certainly my predecessors were dead but at least they had shared my present dilemma. If they had been a bit more gregarious, they could have talked back as I spoke to them of the problems that faced me this day. It seemed that the further our civilization progressed, the more important and thus terrifying became the simplest either/or.

Thinking that one is the master of his or her fate is fine until one is presented with a dilemma. That is when mastery is proven. "To whom would I have to prove my mastery?" that was the fear, the seemingly unanswerable question. If this had been a democracy, the only live vote would have been mine. In retrospect, the absence of any other species' bones at this crossroads should have told me something. It could have revealed to me that only the thinking being is able to become immobilized by a fork in the road. Or perhaps, it is only the conscious being who even considers the possibility of splitting the universe into right and wrong or good and bad. Animals happened by from time to time, but they always kept moving. They occasionally paused to smell one of the V-shaped piles, either they were curious or tantalized by the lingering possibility of food, but on they went. Animals don't care which route they take, this was a human trap. No food needed to be used for bait, a simple split in the road was sufficient to trap a thinking being.

I sat, able but unwilling to move. The world went on around me as I searched for reasons to take one path over another. Any incentive would do, or even a little perspective reminding me that I had been at many such intersections before, and it had never mattered which way I went. Finally, motivated only by the symbols of my brothers and sisters around me pointing to either path, I rose. Stiff-legged, hungry, still confused, and yet resolved not to die here, I walked down one of the paths, the right one if memory serves me well. I walked for several hours, and finding nothing particularly noteworthy, turned and walked back to the crossroads and took the other one.

Spring is a blessed time for those who carry a confidence within them that they are on the right path because they have longer to walk in the light, but, for me, this spring day just provided more light on a longer day of confusion. The days were getting longer, and I would only discover later that the whole idea of day and night was available to push me along the path game.

Once I found myself, I could move equally well in day or night or not move in either but still cover much ground. As that gift filtered through me, night and day became the same and there were no longer forks in the road. Now there is openness in all directions. Thank goodness, or perhaps God, that this gift of finding myself did not happen too early for me, or I would surely have been lost. I think fondly of the days when I clung to structure as some of the best days possible, when I can remember them.

It only took doubling back once, second guessing myself, to have the courage to move on down the left fork. Luckily, I soon forgot that fork in the road, stopped entertaining the thought of what I might be missing if I had just persevered on the other path. It seems that I could acclimate myself to anything once I stopped thinking about what might be missed if I had just stuck to the other path.

I walked on. Slept. Walked in my dreams, and then woke. There was a different flavor to the walking in my dreams. More seemed possible and I pondered how little effort seemed to go into dreams while waking often seemed so difficult. What if dreams were an invitation to step upward and avoid the whole horizontal progress all together? Imagine entering a world of vertical invitation? What then? Were horizontal steps wasted—aging us, but not increasing our potential? Certainly raising an object increased its potential energy, why not us? I attempted to raise my dreams in my awakening, and was partially successful, though not in the usual sense. This experiment didn't get me anywhere physically, but it did lead to more smiles and much less seriousness.

I had passed another test; the fork in the road dilemma. With each test came certain rewards but also the certainty that the next test would be a bit more interesting and challenging. Moving and changing seemed to be the constants in this equation. I could only count on what I could control, and I could only control what I perceived to be both other and less than myself. Ironically, the moment I demeaned anything that thoroughly, I couldn't care about anything.

Many years earlier man had tended his flocks, until he built fences to do the tending for him. Mathematics seemed to be the fences that I used to tend all my possible flocks, but try as I might, I was still more fascinated by the wild things, the untamed thoughts, than I could ever be with anything that had succumbed to my domestication.

Fencing my thoughts was another fork in the road, though not so obvious as the physical one. The test now was to let go, or hold on. Another invitation to split, even if all I did was dignify the idea of division. This nuclear decision consumed my energy; I could no longer walk or even move.

There were no symbolic V-shapes in the road now, only lush green growth. Surrounding me was the wet smell of plants in perfect humidity, growing each moment and so near to flowering. Suddenly the first flower bloomed and then so many more in all the colors of the rainbow and with a sweet deep smell that I will remember forever, if I can. To always breathe in the smell of fresh rose petals— this is the promise of being a king, a ruler at least in one's own mind. The current offer is to be immobilized by the visual and olfactory beauty of the moment and to remain here, transfixed, just long enough to be pollinated. Unite with the plants and take on a different kind of movement by playing on the breeze while remaining rooted in the dark rich soil.

I woke to discover that I had been digging downward with dirty fingernails, hands clenched into a claw shape to facilitate the digging. In my dream it appeared that I had risen when all the time I was edging ever so slowly downward. Dreams, it seemed, could not be counted on. There is the inevitable awakening to discover what one has done while asleep.

Laughter came as I moved the dirt out from under each fingernail to the nail of my right index finger, dropping some to the ground in the process, and finally looking for something to clean under my index fingernail.

Hands still dirty, I moved onward without walking, wiser but not sufficiently so. A little more open than before. Eating a meal of profound variation. My uncertainty vanished into nothingness and I mentally and physically stretched and took in a deep breath at the same moment, observed, and then released the breath with no regret or need for the possible next one. The air was no longer mine as it had always been before, nor was the breath individual. I blew upward, effortlessly but hard, and the stars moved. They swirled, carried around by my breath, only to return to their original position again, or perhaps close enough to convince me of their location.

Opening, The Present

You are at a crossroads. You: Universe, Earth, creatures, human beings. A gift has been given. By whom and to whom is not so obvious. Even that it is a gift is in doubt, but this book seeks to alleviate any question about that now. You have the gift of being conscious. You can watch yourself and you can see both what is here and what is not without even knowing the difference between the two.

Any gift is three-dimensional, at least two-sided. Unless you can discern the difference between what is here and what is not, you may be tantalized by the imaginable and let the real rust or fall apart.

To a deer the woods is not even the woods. The deer uses its senses to get from the deep underbrush that provides its sleeping cover during the day to the corn fields that offer food at night. It moves listening, watching, and smelling. If you have been out in the wild with deer, or at least near them, you know that their senses are more acute than yours. They hear, see and smell what you cannot. Deer seldom get divorced, keep diaries or get jobs. They are never occupied; they just do what they do. If there is a sound or an unfamiliar smell, they run—not far, because curiosity is intrinsic in the deer. They want to keep the unknown or potentially threatening at a distance, but not so far that it stops influencing them. But a deer never second guesses itself while a human seldom stops.

The deer needs no entertainment, money, or fishing license. The deer remains current without currency. It must. Its very survival depends upon it while yours doesn't seem to anymore. The deer obeys the laws of nature while you attempt to legislate to prove your control. The deer is neither better nor worse than you, but seemingly different. A difference, whether initially true or not, that you attempt to make true by using it to justify your dominance of the deer. The deer has no importance, and you seek importance in the way that the deer seeks food. You gravitate to it. You mean. You think. You ponder. You solve. You identify. You understand. You communicate. You propagate. You date. You work. You run. You hide. You play. You dance. You write. You study. You move. You stay still. You eat. You travel. You watch TV. You play trivial pursuit. You argue. You fight. You hug. You kiss. You struggle. You war. You laugh. You cry.

You do all these things in an attempt to control and to discover your place in the universe, when, in fact, you are already here. You are the most, and perhaps the only, insecure beast on the planet. Other animals may actually be insecure when their habitat is threatened, but they do not perceive themselves to be insecure. They do not, as humans do, consider themselves to be their own habitat, often missing the environment all together. So few people perceive themselves as secure that you could say nobody does. The same species that reaches for the stars suffers from Chronic Fatigue Syndrome. The person who is loving one moment kills in the next and then enjoys a snack while watching television. It is all in a days work.

People are odd. That is a point with plenty of evidence. Whether this oddness is funny peculiar or funny ha-ha remains to be seen. Funny ha-ha is being funny and knowing it, while funny peculiar is being funny and not knowing it. The end is not yet written, but people are writing as fast as they can. That people are creatures with infinite perspectives available to them and they typically remain stuck in one is a great irony, one of many. Allen Funt was right, "people are funny." When people learn to laugh at themselves they will naturally find that they are laughing with themselves.

Consciousness is an evolutionary gift. The cost for ignoring this gift is a very insignificant death, a passing on without being remembered.

Pick a day, any day, December 23, for example. There you are sitting around a pine tree that you have taken into the house and hung with all kinds of things, including but not limited to: colored lights, old strings of popcorn, glass balls, a star, plastic strands that look like chrome-colored metal, little angels hand painted by a Korean, miscellaneous metal shapes, and a figurine of a big fat guy wearing a red suit with white fringe and with cheeks almost as red as his outfit. You find yourself looking under the tree, temporarily insane in that you ponder opening a present two days before you are supposed to, or one day if you are the kind of a person who opens presents on Christmas Eve. Well, maybe you're not so insane because there are many people considering opening their presents early, but if you actually go ahead and do it, then, Lucy, you have some explaining to do.

And this you call a religious holiday. You have come a long way from religion, but where have you gone?

You reach for a package without a label. There is no way of knowing who this unfamiliar package is for or who it is from. At this moment you join most of the rest of the civilized world by performing the universal gesture of raising the package to your ear and shaking it. Perhaps auditorily you can discover what is inside. No clue. What is the sound of everything in the universe making noise at the same time? Yes, silence reigns as all sounds cancel out at that precise moment, and you hear nothing but the ticking of the thoughts in your head.

You get a little risky and smell the package. After all, Aunt Harriet gave you cheese when you were a young child, and if you had only thought to smell that package before the fateful opening, you would have been able to avoid your dismal look when you realized what you had received. Aunt Harriet stopped giving presents to you after that. For some people one look is enough.

The package smells bitter. Pungent and disagreeable, but not familiar. Perhaps it is a new kind of cheese, sent as a joke from Aunt Harriet who died some ten years ago. No, that is not a thought worth dwelling on.

If you were good, you would be patient. You would also go for all the gusto you could get and aggressively pursue what you wanted without pausing. You don't decide to open the box as much as you just find yourself ripping the paper from it. With an expression reminiscent of Eve in the garden on Apple Fall, you rip with all your might. Under the paper you discover a wooden box. A solid form with no obvious means of entry but a more-than-apparent invitation to find your way in, to solve the puzzle of the box. There is something inside.

Three days later you have not yet managed to open the box, but this is not for want of trying. You have explored every polite avenue available and exhausted them all. Next, and hopefully last, is the ball peen hammer, the handle of which fits so well in your hand. Wits end is a strange place to be and yet it isn't ever very far away.

You haul off and hit the side of the box as hard as you can. With the confidence of a person who has exhausted every possible alternative, you smash the little rascal, hitting the box and the thumb of your left hand with approximately equal pleasure. You never were very good with a hammer.

The moment between being asleep and being awake. The planet aware of itself. In that moment everything becomes brighter. The lights on the tree seem ready to explode, shaking the whole tree in an attempt to express all of the color in the universe. The moment of orgasm has arrived and yet it doesn't pass quickly. No, there is no cheese in this box. What there is has been released and can never again fit within the confines of the box. An opening has occurred, and you were there. Now you are here, and nothing is the same. Nothing makes sense and everything appeals to your senses. Consciousness is like that. It is the ability to have everything and nothing occur in the same place at the same time, with you as a participant and observer.

To put it more clearly, consciousness provides you with the opportunity, at first the necessity, of having multiple illusionary perspectives at the same moment. It opens everything. It is the door to observation and creation all in one. It is the stick, waiting to be whittled, that at this early stage can go any direction, that can only be limited by imagination and yet it includes imagination too. It is the All opening up before and within you. Illusion is a result of the gift and with it everything becomes possible, and the only threat to it is—reality. With the smashing of the box and the release of consciousness, you have made everything possible. You have expanded endlessly. You have created the universe and you are here, a part of it to appreciate it. The gift has arrived, and only moments later, hours with some people who are either slower or more creative than others, the nasty question arrives.

Now what?

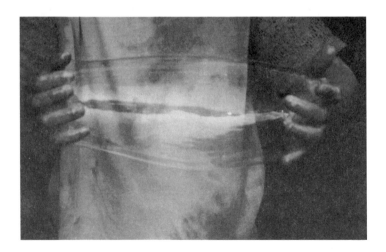

Consciousness

The question itself is too biased to ignore.

Disaster doesn't strike; it is created within, sneaks outside and then knocks at the door so somebody else can be blamed for its arrival.

"Now what," is the insidious question that precedes a fall. Consciousness has no time; it begets time. Consciousness has no space; it proceeds space. Consciousness is not a quality of being; it allows being. How tall are you willing to be? Within what parameters must you live? Shatter the box and you expand endlessly. Think one more thought, twice, and you start to limit yourself again. It is you who is the big bang. Left to universal devices, you will simulate the universe by expanding massively and then contracting, ever so small. You will be of no certain size and just big enough to contain all fluctuation. Any thought once is entertaining and any thought twice is a threat to consciousness and to the

universe that sets you up as the opponent of the grand
champion who by definition cannot be defeated.

Consciousness is the gift, and you have received it.
How you use it is yet another game. Illusion is your
playground, but it gives you no place to stand. On thin ice
it is best to keep moving, and illusion is the thinnest of
ices. Movement itself limits, but it also facilitates variation
of perspective so necessary for a creature who has the
opportunity to move. You are mobile. Never has a creature
been able to move so fast in so many directions. You can
be in Paris for lunch and New York for dinner. On the
moon one day and in the jungles of South America the
next. This movement throws you off balance, but not
enough. Consciousness allows you expansion but it is
seldom used that way. You take a step and are provided
with an entirely different perspective of your kingdom,
though you strive for consistency. In the next step comes
another whole shift. A tilt of the head brings another, and
driving in a car brings so much variation that you get tired
doing it. If you could learn to feed on variation, you would
always be fed. Feeding on consistency starves people in a
world of abundance. Security comes from recognizing
illusion as illusion and expanding so as to match your gift.

To repeat, "Consciousness is the ability to have multiple
illusionary perspectives at the same time." How many? It
seems to be unlimited, yet at a certain point people lose
track because counting is the very act of shifting focus,
and having simultaneous illusionary perspectives runs
counter to shifting anything. If you could maintain multiple
illusionary perspectives without moving, you might not
require legs or even muscles for that matter. Movement
serves as a constant reminder that the purpose here/now

is to explore thoughts with awareness and let go of whatever you most want to hold on to.

Stay still. Really. Stay perfectly still. You can't do it. If you could for even a moment, you would very quickly discover that everything else is moving. Everything. If you could stay still for just a fraction of a second, you could become aware of the movement of Earth. You could notice the tree being blown ever so slightly by an otherwise very subtle breeze, you could also see the tree growing and dying at the same time. Everything is moving, but the calculation of subtracting your movement from that of everything else leads you to a strange man with shoes, but no socks, who taught us that everything is relative, and a physicist, Heisenberg, who remains memorable because of his uncertainty. The more still you are, the less of an actor you become and the more the play, the ongoing play, reveals itself to you. It provides you with the entertainment to last at least a light year or two. This show is not *for* you; it *is* you. That is the message of consciousness. The gift of consciousness is the gift to be entertained from within, never requiring anything from outside yourself again.

Step right this way. Within this world is the greatest entertainment of all time. It never stops. The show must go on, and so it does. It is all here, not so much *for* you, but *because* of you. Your appreciation is its reward, and consciousness allows you to be a significant enough observer to provide that appreciation. The moment you use consciousness for anything other than entertainment...the moment you confuse yourself with the show or think that the show has a purpose or limits...the whole thing appears to come to a crashing halt. It, of course, does not stop. It is you who has fallen so flat on your nose that your visibility has grown dangerously close to zero and you miss the entertainment for the meaning, and what could have been play becomes struggle. It could happen to anyone.

Consciousness is a gift. It is a gift given freely. It is an evolutionary gift that can lead you to the next gift. Evolution is persistent and, as such, lacks tolerance. It speaks once, perhaps twice, but seldom three times, until it changes the point it has to get across. Like water, evolution takes the path of least resistance. Entertainment is that path for consciousness. Anytime that you use consciousness for anything other than entertainment, you are not only jeopardizing the quantity of existence of life in the universe but, at the same time, destroying its quality. Human beings seldom even talk of quality anymore. Quality has been defined as absence of pain: a remedial definition and certainly not an amusing or entertaining one.

In this play, this dance, this show, you are the observer, with a twist. You are able to step in at any moment and become the jester. You can do this simply by your reverence and appreciation for the play. In this play you are both passive and active. Taking part and watching. Smile, grin, laugh, cry, whine, and wail, but know that it is all your contribution to the play.

It is you who became curious enough to open the box. It is you who let consciousness out. There is an opportunity here, and no matter how hard you try, the Christmas tree will never look the same again. Nothing will ever look the same again unless you attempt to return to the same illusionary perspective time and time again, squeezing security from nothing, for that is exactly what illusion is—

nothing. This nothingness is what enables illusion to be everything. Illusion is too much fun to be real. Reality is fun, too, but in a different way, and it shouldn't be spoken of yet. Not until you have gotten on with defining much more of who you are.

You now know what consciousness is, though it eludes you almost all of the time in your attempts to mean something and be real. Consciousness is the ability to perceive multiple illusions simultaneously. The more illusions the merrier. The purpose of consciousness is entertainment. Anytime you use consciousness for anything other than entertainment you are in evolutionary quicksand and going down fast. This going down fast, in an upside-down cultural world, is defined as progress. So, in such a world, the further behind you get, the more ahead you are. The very act of noticing illusion as illusion opens the door to entertainment. But who is noticing? Awareness. Who's that?

Awareness is Now

The deer walking through the field sees what it sees, smells what it smells and hears what it hears. There is no object to the senses, or objective, only the implied location that results from the sensing itself. The deer does not think, "There is a man." It uses pure perception without judgment or identification. The moment identification arrives there is the added trap of symbolism, removed reality. Awareness is pure observation, sensory data with nothing added. It is what keeps the deer alive and, much to people's chagrin, what keeps them alive as well. Thinking has nothing to do with awareness. Thinking is the illusion that illusion is not illusion while awareness is the perception of illusion as nothing.

A fairly accurate analogy for awareness is a wind in your head. Wind is the result of nature balancing itself, a natural flow of air from high to low pressure, an evening out. Awareness is just such a balancing act in your head.

When the flow occurs in your head, you are aware, and when it does not, you are not. The greater the imbalance that is getting balanced, the greater the awareness. Thus the very process of being aware lessens awareness. But the wind keeps blowing and awareness continues to exist.

In the case of the wind, it is the movement of air from one point to another. In your head it is illusion balancing itself—the movement (or process) of filling holes with stuff. Awareness is the process of having *some*thing where there was *no*thing and having *no*thing where there was *some*thing. Complete awareness occurs when there is everything and nothing both everywhere and nowhere. Until you can perceive complete awareness, which is obvious and just waiting to be observed, your role, ironically, is to use consciousness to provide yourself with every possible opportunity to be off balance. Putting yourself as far off balance as you can will result in the most awareness. The deer does not have this opportunity. It just uses the awareness that it has. The deer has a constant state of maximum imbalance. The deer is either awake (aware) or asleep (unaware). Before it sleeps, the deer finds the safest place to rest its body and will awaken at the slightest provocation.

People aggressively mitigate differences and compare things. In this process they reduce their level of imbalance and thus undermine awareness. Awareness is the evolutionary step just prior to consciousness. People long for the earlier step and seek to deny that they have taken the next step. This explains the phenomenon of having their consciousness masquerade as awareness. In doing so, people refuse the gift they have been given and become ungrateful and dissatisfied in the process. An ungrateful son is an unhappy son. Aunt Harriet may stop giving presents; get that look off your face.

You think, hence you override sensory data. You see what you think you will see rather than what is here. You see a robin because you have identified it as such and lose the very distinctions that, in an inspired moment, first resulted in the affixing of the name robin to that innocent little bird. Who killed cock robin? People did, by identifying it and then failing to notice it again.

The deer uses awareness to find food and to avoid danger. You already have enough food and are bent on proving that there is no danger. You live most of your life in a waking sleep with information from your thoughts being so repetitious and constant that it has lulled you into a false sense of security. You have the same thought over and over again: "Go for and value consistency, and define yourself by your persistent conditions."

The senses return to a zero or neutral state each moment, ready for the next input. Thinking does not. Thinking carries along the baggage of every prior thought and the patterns in which those thoughts occurred. Deer are always at the beginning: listening, seeing, and smelling. People are always somewhere lost in the middle with so little awareness that they can generally go through their whole day and never notice anything.

Awareness is sensory opportunity. The ability to smell fresh baked bread, a rose, or coffee. The ability to see a sunset, the waves on a calm or rough day on the ocean, to hear the waves or the call of a bird not yet identified.

The thrill of discovering a new species can be yours, in fact, is yours every moment. Each and every fraction of a second you are a new species. Notice things, use your senses and you will discover that it is a very rich world you live in. Imagine a smell, a taste, a picture, a sound, a feeling. Consciousness can imagine anything. It can see what you have not yet seen and imagine a smell that has never existed. Consciousness can create marvelous sensory illusions, for it does not need to feed on momentary sensory input. Consciousness, while attempting to play the role of awareness, limits sensory acuity. Evolution has little patience for such stupidity.

There must be a balance between awareness and consciousness. The function of awareness is to keep you alive in the moment, the same role it performs for the deer. Consciousness is meant to keep you entertained. You need to be both alive and entertained. Without consciousness you would not need to be entertained. Have you ever heard a deer laugh? You laugh, you cry, you argue, you do all of these things for your entertainment. If you don't know you are doing them for entertainment, then you are crazy, mistaking illusion for reality and overriding awareness with consciousness.

Awareness seeks to control nothing, it is just the wind. Awareness requires no effort and no struggle, it never means anything. It is outside the loop of judgment. It just is. The moment something takes any degree of effort or struggle or looks at all like a problem, you can be certain that, at least to some degree, consciousness is interfering with awareness. You are missing what is around you by confusing it with the illusions in your head. The more you do this, the greater the difficulties you have, but since you are ultimately very adaptable, you call these new problems, "The way life is." Suffering becomes the status quo and evolution begins to turn its face away from another species. Consciousness attempts to control nothing by calling it something.

What is here now? Look, listen, smell, taste, and feel. Discover what is around you. Pretend that you have arrived from another planet and are not familiar with any things, labels, or symbols. All purpose has disappeared for you and all meaning. Explore with curiosity and wonder. Naming and identifying is a way of killing things, at least to your perceptions. You fail to notice what you think you know. Repetition is the bane of your existence, and you think that it is the root of security. Only a thinking being could make such a big mistake.

Take what you want and pay for it; this is a rule of the universe. *Take nothing, accept everything*; this is the rule of life.

Reach upward, toward a star. Tiptoes might help. Stretch as tall as you possibly can. The very process of reaching for a star can be rewarding unless you think perhaps that getting it would be better than reaching.

There is so much more *how* something is done than *when* something is done, that if you learn to enjoy the *how*, the *when* will take care of itself. You can live a lifetime in a moment and you can live one hundred years and never have lived at all. The quality of your life is determined fundamentally by the delineation of consciousness from awareness. When consciousness pretends to be awareness, it forgets to be entertained and attempts to aide in the survival of its host. It is not content with noticing; instead, it interprets the outside to be a reflection of the inside and this conception locks you into the tiny space within the head. Not much of the world or the universe will fit within your head, so when you attempt to do so, the world and the universe are shrunk down, losing their variation and vastness. Life becomes a competition and a war at this point. You must control everything because anything uncontrolled threatens all that you have done and thought up until now. Wage war on the universe and you will get what you have now, a lot of unhappy, scared people.

The same star that can look so far away can come down for a visit. If you focus on the star instead of the distance, it comes closer. If you include that star in the definition of who you are, it comes closer yet. Nothing is far away unless you make it so. There is no scale. You are the creator of scale, consciousness as the controller needs to know just exactly how it compares to everything else. That is enough to keep it busy, and consciousness busy is consciousness not being entertained.

Consciousness can be entertained by the sensory data of awareness, but the moment it attempts to control awareness, there is great danger. Life is threatened.

The purpose of awareness is to live in the moment. The purpose of consciousness is to be entertained. These are two different evolutionary steps and people are torn apart when they confuse the two. You always have consciousness—that is the evolutionary step that defines you—but you can shut down awareness with consciousness, and then you are neither aware nor entertained. A compulsion sets in at such moments; it is you against the world, and you wear yourself out.

Difficult Play

"What stage is thisssss, then?" she convulsed, leveraging her desiccated frame to a standing position. To imagine her face, consider morality assumed when something that just happened is deemed not only impossible but wrong. She had practiced this look on millions of her first grade students over thousands of years. It was a great look but hardly sufficient. She toppled over backwards, her feet leaving the ground at the precise moment that her head and chest, lightness and all, headed toward the north side of the back of her chair.

She was not the only one protesting. Everyone in the Audience/Actor (AA) group was resisting, each in his or her own way. There was a man crying in the front row and a woman attempting to distract her neighbors in the third. The play moved on undisturbed, including everything, but only being observed when the action in the AA settled enough to lead attentions back to the play.

This rise and fall occurred over and over again; different parts of the play would set off whole sections of the AA, and those sections would set off other individuals or sections. There was obviously a connection between the AA and the play on stage but it was difficult for anyone to remain an observer; to notice. There were a few unattached individuals who could appreciate the sheer entertainment value of what was happening. They were getting their money's worth.

The play is reminiscent of a stream in the spring when it is flowing more rapidly than usual and carrying too much water for its banks to contain. Rocks, which were normally a safe distance from the water, and trees, who usually contact the stream with just their roots, were being scoured by the rush of water and tossed about in the flurry. Tiny eddies swirled about and white water, water without direction but too much purpose, rushed every which way.

The AA tripped on itself and fell on the play. The moods were endless and persistent. The content or disposition mattered much less than the intensity. The only way to be noticed was to be more outraged, angry, bitter, happy, or intense than your neighbor. This was not Mrs. Applebie's first grade class, and it became apparent that she carried no weight now, real or imagined. She was so used to being bigger than the children that her strategies for control were quite useless with adults. This, however, did not stop her from attempting to maintain order. She was now flat on the floor, panting but still attempting to catch her breath so that she could speak, to reassure herself.

Nobody was looking at her now. The round man pushed his feet against her, making room for himself. She remembered him, not his name but his face. She had had her chance with him twenty-some years ago in her class, but who was she to him now? All she needed was a little respect and things would at least be better. She gained her breath and tried, "Steven!"

He continued to fidget, fixated only on the stage where food was being consumed without his active participation. His name was not Steven, but even if it had been, her ploy would not have worked. He was hoping that someone would throw a scrap of food his way, and that he could move his feet a bit further forward and stretch his legs.

No, the situation isn't very pretty. Everybody is attempting to fight for control, run the game, be in the driver's seat. People are all back seat drivers, along for the ride, reluctantly. The few who know otherwise are not telling, at least not in ways that crazy people can comprehend. The many who speak are just fellow AA's, the same as yourself in all significant ways. How ugly can it get? Now that is an appropriate question, but one which won't be entertained because it would require considering things even crazier than those under scrutiny now.

Mrs. Applebie was seventy-four when she finally gave up. She was lying on the floor of the theater while all the AA's who were not otherwise preoccupied sang Happy Birthday, the funeral dirge. The whole idea of getting attention for such a meaningless thing as surviving for this many years sickened her. "I would rather be dead," she said.

She almost got her wish. But her fate in that moment seemed worse than death. She gave up who she was, everything she had been, and all she had done, knowing that she had to in order to die. When it was all gone, every last bit of it, she lay there forever waiting. Waiting for the grim reaper, God, Devil, or the moment of truth. Nothing happened. Poised and without poise she waited. "This isn't as bad as I thought it would be," she thought to herself.

Thankfully she was spared the moment of her whole life flashing before her eyes. She blinked, disappeared, and began to smile. The AA's were no longer singing; at least she couldn't hear them. She was still alive, or more accurately, alive for the first time. The more she smiled, the greater energy she felt within her, warming her from head to toe. She didn't move; she didn't need to. She lay there, not resisting enough to be interested. In that lifetime, she joined the few people who were neither play or AA. In the next moment she became all of the AA and the whole play. She laughed, rose up without effort and walked out of the theater.

The sun was spreading its light upon the land, and she felt its warmth on her face. Slowly she disrobed as she ambled down the street. With each step her walk become more fluid until finally she was moving more like a cat than a person. To see her walk was to observe her progress without being able to distinguish the movement that had resulted in the displacement of her body. She never stopped laughing after that, but she never spoke again, at least not out of her mouth.

She communicates, though, all the time. It doesn't get any better than this, and it keeps getting better.

Reality and Illusion

"You can't lose what you don't have," said the universe on an unusually blunt day. Resonating with the universe that is shaking its head is not easy when you are holding on to anything, imaginary or not.

"Reality requires no maintenance!" it hissed.

In her younger days, Mrs. Applebie was a teacher who went about business as usual. Now Johnny you must learn to share, or your life will turn out very much like Hitler's.

"Did Hitler really have such a bad life Mrs. Applebie?"

She, along with all the children, had entirely forgotten her first name. She had considered getting married, once, but had abandoned the idea for the fear that the mandatory name change, in her mind, might confuse the children. Her middle name was Sacrifice, but she never used it. Now she really was Mrs. Applebie. Not Occupant, not Amanda, as she had been as a child, but the figurehead—Mrs. Applebie.

"What a thing to say Johnny. Go to the principal's office now. But say, 'Thank-you. May I have another?' first."

"Thank-you. May I have another?"

That was then and this is now. Finally, after these many years, since before Earth was cooling, she had gotten the message. Mrs. Applebie could not get the message, but whoever she really was, there were not yet words for this, had discovered the line that separates illusion from reality, fact from fiction, and endless pain from ecstasy. She couldn't control anymore, that was true, but she didn't even want to try. If she had bothered to look back at her life, she would discover that she had not been in control anyway.

That day in the theater of life, she learned without teaching. Anything that makes you sad, angry, happy, pleased, or anxious is not real. The whole idea of any thing doing anything to anybody at all is much too expensive to buy: no*body* can afford it. Emotions, both positive and negative, are the result of an overlap between illusion and reality. Reality is not kind or unkind, but what it lacks in disposition, it makes up in persistence and sheer size. Illusion also is not kind or unkind, but it is addictive. In a world of illusion, you can be king, queen, prince, princess, and prime minister. You can be the richest and most beautiful person in that world, but it doesn't do you any good. Not *real*ly, because in *real*ity there is no good and no bad either. The whole idea of dualistic, digital judgment is too silly to be real.

What is reality? It is what you have always been told that it is. It is exactly that. Told by whom? Not by your parents, the President, Hugh Hefner, or Soupy Sales, but told by the universe or reality itself. (The words universe and reality are used interchangeably to refer to what is common to All.)

Mrs. Applebie finally stopped talking and stopped listening long enough to hear the universe speaking. It is always speaking. People are the only species that is often more interested in their own voices than in listening to the universe.

"Everything is nothing," says the universe. People translate her absolute expressions into excuses. "Ah, so everything is relative."

People trust others to translate what the universe is saying when, in fact, she is always speaking to each person individually. Anytime a species confuses who it is with something outside itself, it is soon to disappear from the face of Earth. When the Spotted Owl confuses who it is with its terrain, the end is near. It does this by needing the terrain so badly that it cannot live without it. The more specific a species becomes, the more interesting and threatened is its existence.

Humans are migrating to distant worlds. The spaceships leave from any location but at a specific time. At about five or six years of age, the ship launches with its young passengers on a journey to the land of illusion. Very few people survive this trip, perceiving wholeness. Suspended animation is necessary because otherwise the passengers would realize that perhaps they don't want to go on the trip. They would notice that they are aging, becoming uglier by the moment and not having any fun at all. The moment of departure is truly one of the most heart-wrenching human events. Symbolized by the eating of the apple in the garden of Eden, it is the end of all that is real and the entry into the crazy, make-believe world of adulthood. It is replacement of what is with what isn't and the beginning of a life of toil and difficulty. The end of play. Childhood's end.

At this moment, special attention was given to Mrs. Applebie, because she was to be a guide for the passengers on their space trip. She was allowed to leave early, to use some of the new tricks that can facilitate earlier departure. Her mother beat her and her father sexually abused her, all in the name of having her leave earlier. Mrs. Applebie had the dubious distinction of embarking upon the good ship Illusion at three years of age, three years ahead of schedule. For her efforts, she got a pension and the unwillingness to ever quit her job, because she was her job. In spite of her efforts, she woke up anyway in her seventies and regretted nothing.

From the moment you glimpse reality, your crazy journey is over.

Illusion is everything. Everything that you can see, hear and feel. You do not create your own reality—You Create Your Own Illusion. The difference between illusion and reality is as great as it can be and, humorously, reality includes all illusion while illusion contains no reality at all. Reality is pure possibility. It is all possibility.

Technically, reality is the mathematical computation of all possibility. There is no time or space in reality, other than being able to include them as the vital elements of illusion that they are. Reality happens once and forever. There is no equals sign (=) in reality. Illusion means less than everything and reality has no meaning. Reality is endless and contains all ends and all odds too. Once you glimpse reality, you will know that there is nothing that can be said about it which doesn't diminish it. Silence is as close as you can come to accurately talking about reality. Silence both within and without.

What if everything that could happen did happen? The answer to this question is simple. You would have reality. Anything short of that is how you have limited reality and thus produced illusion. Illusion is for sale in the marketplace; reality is free. Really free. Everything that could happen is already happening, and the tiny amount you can see is your individual scientifically-controlled evolutionary experiment in pain and limitation.

The world of illusion reduces the highs and the lows of life. It mows things down to a supposedly manageable size. If you can limit what is sensed, then you can be the master of that which is sensed simply by ignoring what you don't want to see, hear, feel, taste, or smell.

A person perceiving only illusion is the Grand Editor, editing everything down to a mere pittance and then editing some more. The limiting process has one big pay-off, the illusion of security, mock security—unlike the real security of observing illusion as illusion. It has an even bigger cost, the universe. People are universal beings, and as such, they can and are everywhere at once.

Mrs. Applebie could only be in the classroom, in the supermarket or at home. And she had to be in the classroom from 7:00 AM until 4:00 PM daily and had not taken a sick day in three thousand years. There is work to be done. Surely the work is trivial, destructive, and anti-universe, but somebody has to do it. Within her illusion, her work looks both right and good. In reality, she is unemployed, as are all people.

In reality, there is nothing to prove, nothing to do, and nothing to say. You do not need to remain occupied here because here is everywhere. It would be too silly to try to determine your relationship to everything when you are everything. In the world of illusion, the individual fighting for a place in the universe, carving out a niche for himself or herself, is all important. If you are everything, then all ideas of control disappear.

In illusion, there is a not-so-humorous one-liner. One line that divides what you are willing to see from that which you are not. On one side of the line is that which you can use to convince yourself that you are in control, and on the other is the undefinable, the nebulous, and ultimately the bad and wrong. The area on the apparent controlled side of the line is much thinner than the line itself, but it is the whole world to you. You make the little into the big and then ignore the big.

The tiny fraction $1/10000000000000000000$ 000000000000000 does not even do justice to the fragmentation and fractionalization that illusion requires for survival. You approach nothing everyday and never get there. You make the denominator bigger every day and thus have less of yourself to go around. You define expertise as having the largest denominator possible. All the denominators are divisible by ten, so they are all common. Ten is not an accidentally chosen number, it is how high you can count and remain digital without bending over to use your toes. You make your niche smaller and puff up your chest with pride as you cash your paycheck and turn your back on the line and anything on the other side.

Most things get larger as they grow. Trees, flowers, animals, people (at least physically). But mentally, in the world of illusion, growth is defined as getting smaller. You are swimming against the current, in fact ignoring the current and attempting to define the current not by what it is but by what you want or think it should be.

Reality continues to speak to you and at anytime you may hear it. Mrs. Applebie heard it in what appears to be the least likely possible moment. In utter frustration and surrender she finally gave up. It does not have to be at such a moment. Since time does not exist, it can be anytime. Typically, the more difficult and offensive your life has been, the more difficult the moment has to be to have you let go of illusion. Mrs. Applebie's journey ended in the theater and she became the universe. She never went to work again; from then on, there was only play. She played for another twenty years until the game shifted again and she called the universe on what few limitations she had left. People usually call this transition death. Death is an increase in the speed of expansion outside of the possible current constraints.

Reality is the mathematical computation of all possibility, and illusion is everything that you see, hear, feel, taste, smell, think, or perceive. Control is how you act within illusion. Reality requires no maintenance and illusion necessitates constant control. Emotion is what you get when illusion and reality overlap. There are numerous things, almost all things, that you get in between them when they are not yet overlapping. As you explore these is detail, you may catch a glimpse of Mrs. Applebie's rear end as she rounds the next bend.

Immediate Results

"Step right this way to join the order of things and phantoms. One line, for simplicity, please."

The carnival barker went for organized chaos. People had to want to get inside so badly that they could taste it, but he also wanted an orderly line. The people in line were so interested in where they were going that they did not appreciate their present location.

"There will be wonders beyond your wildest dreams inside. You will see things you have never seen before. Tell your friends. Tell your relatives. Come one, come all. The show that never ends," he lied.

Honesty is the best policy.

"There is nothing inside worth seeing. Turn away, don't waste another moment here. I am trying to cheat you out of your money. I'll give you one more experience of loss, perhaps, hopefully, the final one that drives you straight to resignation. You will be ripped off again in the name of progress and everyone will know, but they will also be taken here."

Oops, wrong script.

There is a time for honesty, and it is in the order of things which has nothing to do with the perceived order. Everything is already in order, nothing is out of place, and basically everything is everywhere. Chaos only exists in people's minds when they have imposed order too aggressively.

Reality has to be the biggest, the ultimate, gargantuan, tremendous, colossal, and the tiniest, infinitesimal, and quantum. It cannot mean anything; in short, it cannot matter. Matter is what comes out of reality; it is a primary result of reality. Only in the moment of materialization, demoralization, and limitation of reality does matter appear. In reality there is nothing. Reality is the *process* of expression not that which is expressed. Reality is the *express* which lights you, you are reality.

Reality gives birth to things. Each thing represents aspects of reality in its own particular way. A piece is not the whole and a thing is not reality. Things are the results of reality and each thing allows a certain reality to flow through it. The reality that flows answers the question, "What is possible for this result of reality?" The major demarcation between living and non-living things is that in a living thing, there is a greater range of possibility fluctuation. What is possible for the rock is a lot, but at a quick glance it appears to stay the same. The rock has already arrived, it isn't going anywhere. To a squirrel, like you, the possibilities seem to be change, and the whole definition of control has to do with the ebb and flow of the possibilities you can perceive. As a squirrel, if like most people, you confuse yourself with your food source, you are a nut.

Reality feeds you everything. The mind prompts you, feeding you only your next line.

Most creatures have a set range of possibilities. They are programmed at birth. The wood tick climbs to the top of a blade of grass and waits for something warm to come by. When it does, if it does, then the tick lets go and either falls on the warm blooded creature or not. If it lands on its host, then the tick drills in and sucks blood. If it misses, the tick climbs to the top of another blade of grass and waits. Like an assembly line worker the tick does not need to think to do its job. Its whole life is work. Expression of programs is working; following orders (order).

Appreciating the sunlight is as remote a possibility for the tick as it is for the rock. The tick decreases possibility with programming whereas the rock does so with substance.

There are three components of matter. These are stuff, holes and process. Stuff is the steadiest element. Holes is the area between pieces of stuff that gives matter a place to be by separating it from other matter. The separations, or holes between the stuff, are what define matter. Process is the ongoing interaction between stuff and holes—the dance that defines the limitations of possibility that distinguish this matter from that matter. The stuff is not real, the holes are not real and the process is not real. Reality is possibility and matter is an experimental limitation of possibility.

Stuff is a particular kind of hole that is no longer content being nothing and must derive self-esteem by being something. Stuff is, of course, not really something. To repeat, stuff is not real at all. In an attempt to differentiate itself, stuff declared itself no longer a hole. This is, in essence, a limitation, since for holes, almost anything is possible whereas for stuff, less is possible. Anything with greater possibility influences more than that with lesser possibility. Thus, stuff exists only by the grace of the holes and is at the whim of the holes. Entropy is holes influencing stuff.

Mrs. Applebie, until her moment of revelation, did not experience stuff, holes or process. She operated at a much greater level of abstraction, an infinite distance from reality and too far away from where you are to even be seen from here.

Stuff, holes, and process is a more basic distinction than people usually observe. To bring you to Earth look around and discover that all things on Earth are made of stuff, holes and the interaction between them.

The density of stuff determines your perception of it. It takes great advancement on your part to see holes. Almost nobody does. Enjoyment is seldom derived from the holes. Some people experience holes as a momentary absence of stuff. Metal is composed of more stuff than wood and air which is composed of much less stuff than either. What defines all interactions between matter is the ratio of stuff to holes. The greater the ratio of holes to stuff, the lighter something is. The lighter something is, the less energy it takes to express its possibilities. That is exactly why enlightenment is called en*light*enment.

The greater the ratio of stuff to holes, the more effort it takes to speed the thing up, slow it down or change it in any way. Stuff limits possibilities more so than holes. It is not an accident that there have been Eastern pursuits requiring a student to give up all material possessions. Stuff begets definition. When you speak, you talk almost exclusively of stuff. When you work, you work for stuff. When you play, you play with stuff. It is time to appreciate the holes, without which stuff would lose all distinctions.

If you attend to your breath, you get lighter because you are focused on air which has much less stuff and far more holes than you do. If you eat vegetarian you will be lighter because vegetables and fruits have a different ratio of stuff and holes than flesh does.

A small definition of stuff could be atoms while a larger definition could include a fireplace or couch. These are of very different sizes, but the only thing distinguishing them is that the couch is made up of a certain order and pattern of the atoms. Still, they are both stuff. Anytime you organize and force atoms into a pattern, you must expend energy and limit possibility. You can sit on an atom that is within the fabric of the couch but unlike the princess and the pea, the atom would not affect your emotional state or equilibrium.

A bull in a china shop is seldom picking its dinnerware pattern. Atoms are too small for you to express your cumbersome grace through, but this may change as you appreciate greater subtlety.

You pay for the couch because it took energy to pattern the atoms. The person who made the couch interacted with stuff at a particular level and processed the stuff to end up with a specific set of limitations called a couch.

"Don't stand on the couch. It is for sitting on."

It is you, in an attempt to control, who defines what a particular order of stuff is used for. Matter defines what possibilities can be expressed and you through your enforcement of patterns determine what possibilities should be expressed. The couch can be burned, but that is a threat to the order you paid for. If you have the couch long enough or pay a sufficient quantity of money or are entirely confused about who you are and the order of things, you may begin to confuse the couch with who you are. At that point you must protect and defend the couch. You must make rules about the use of the couch.

The very existence of stuff requires defense. The relationship between stuff and holes and stuff and other stuff requires even greater defense. At the level of stuff and holes, there is constant movement; nothing ever stays the same. The moment you bring the couch home, or the couch maker declares it complete, it starts falling apart. In fact, the faster someone can make the couch, the easier it is to make, because in the whole process of construction, the thing is falling apart. If you were to work too slowly, you would never end up with a couch.

All matter is composed of stuff, holes and process. Consciousness (remember consciousness?) seeks to determine what process goes on between stuff and holes. It seeks to make the whole process orderly to a specific interim end and judges itself by the degree of order that it manages to produce in a set period of time. Consciousness, misused, seeks to form limitations into a particular shape that it defines as comfortable in an attempt to prove to stuff once and for all who is in control.

Each step taken away from perceiving reality reduces control and increases the perception of control. Sphere of influence increases and ability to observe decreases. Every time there is a step up the perceptual limitation chain, there is a corresponding loss of dimension. Things become flatter, more limited, as they get further and further from reality. Possibilities that can be expressed become more localized, and a battle is waged to discover who can come up with the most plausible explanation for the suffering that is everywhere.

Order leads to maintenance and matter is the level at which some people work. A few. Most people are not nearly this concrete and are much further away from reality than matter. They no longer look at what is, but look at what they *think* is.

Matter is basic illusion one distortion of reality. All that needs to happen to reality to get matter is to have some self-righteous little hole call itself stuff and declare itself different from other holes. In this way the whole playground of matter is created. Matter does not look like illusion because it is closer to reality than the looker (mind). Bodies are composed of matter. To find out something about yourself, the place to start is with the most real element of yourself: your body. And there is Mrs. Applebie's rear end.

Mind—Brain

She came this way. Most certainly. Mrs. Applebie left tracks that could easily be followed. She didn't stop with the stuff and holes, though she may have appreciated them along the way. She kept right on going.

Starting from reality, you move into matter; that is a first level distortion. Matter includes the physical body, which is as close to reality as human experience can get. The body gives you grounding, like the ropes which keep the hot air balloon tethered in place. The body can bring you back from the next level of abstraction; thoughts.

There is a difference between the mind and the brain. The brain is composed of stuff and holes, a first level distortion, while the mind is based on the brain. So the mind is a second level distortion, a distortion of a distortion. Thoughts are not real and they are not matter. They are the result of a particular kind of matter called the brain. In the brain there is a constant movement of stuff and holes, as there is everywhere. This movement, the wind in your head, gives rise to awareness. When structure is imposed upon this movement, patterns result and programming takes place. Evolutionarily, life moves from entirely patterned to aware and then up the next step to consciousness. You may ask what the next step after that is, which is an appropriate question.

In life forms less evolved than human beings, data travels on more limited paths (which you can notice as "patterns of holes"). If you have a dog you know about pattered responses. The dog does the same thing in the same way over and over again. An Irish Setter never acts like a Labrador. There is a pre-existent, perhaps genetic structure that determines the flow in a dog's brain. The dog has awareness, focused more on the nose and ears than on the eyes. Spontaneous thoughts and connections are impossible for the dog to perceive. Associations can be made, as Pavlov discovered. The dog is capable of, in fact limited to, stimulus and response. Human beings are not. That is not to say that most human beings are beyond stimulus and response; but they have the ability to be.

People have minds. Dogs do not. The dog cannot mind itself, but it can fit minding a person into its patterns. The mind results when an organism has the ability to perceive itself and one thing other than itself. The planet became aware of itself when people first realized that they existed. There is a big difference between existing and realizing that you exist. The difference is the evolutionary step called consciousness. Consciousness brings forth an opening, the ability to notice and have a perspective, to subtract out present position and thus explore things independent of a perceiver. It is an anti-bias mechanism which can raise the level of sophistication possible. Without it there is no science and no art. When people judge they add bias which is short circuiting consciousness and obscuring awareness.

When Mrs. Applebie used to teach art, she would grade the students based on how much each drawing looked like the assigned subject. There were no points for originality or subjective interpretation, and the very idea of having a student draw something she had not seen would have thrown Mrs. Applebie for a loop, and resulted in a poor grade for the student.

The mind is the result of a being aware of awareness. This self-awareness is an opening. From here, if people were to continue to open, they would discover a playground around them. The opportunity is to dance with every part of the universe, but, at least so far, the mind has not been used in this way. For the most part, the mind has been used as a weapon for defense. It noticed itself and then immediately strove to distinguish itself from everything else, a never-ending job.

Without the mind there is no consciousness and without consciousness there is no mind. Without the mind there is no suffering and there are no problems. The thing about an opening is that anything can come through. The moment that a human being has the same thought twice, justification for the repetition becomes necessary. The number of possible thoughts is so large that without some purpose, in mind, people would probably never have the same thought twice. Most human beings have the same thought over and over and over. The underlying purpose that this reveals is to limit the range of thinking and thus define the individual.

People define themselves by their limitations, and the earliest limit is repetition. From there, people use patterns, symbols, preferences, beliefs, facts and eventually stories to perform the limiting act of deciding who they are (are not).

Nothing is as it seems, because nothing that is perceived *is* at all. People have created a grand, and often not-so-grand-illusion with thoughts. They have done this so systematically and from such an early age that the very act of pointing this out is perceived as impolite.

There is a longing for the earlier evolutionary stage of patterned existence, acted out by limiting the range of what is thinkable to such a degree that people have become automatic. This is neither necessary nor fun, but it does *appear* to be safe, at least to the automated person. To a non-patterned person, the automated person is predictable, funny, humorous to the point of laughter beyond control.

Observing self-imposed exile from ecstasy is funny. If it sounds sad to you, that is probably because, to some extent, you have fallen into the trap yourself. It is not sad— that is more of the trap. To the person caught up in misuse of the mind, everything is meaningful. To the person free to think, to be entertained and amused, everything is meaningless. There have been thousands of books written about the meaning of things. People have been aggressively adding meaning in an attempt to have their thoughts prevail in realms in which they carry no weight at all.

The logical extension of the use of the mind to determine its individual worth and relationship to anything else is a mind in control of the universe. The mind is a player in a playground (the universe) and the more it attempts to control, the less it is able to play. To be enlightened is to lose your mind. Did you ever notice that the gurus have knowing smiles on their faces? They live without distinguishing anything. They are the universe, and in not having to dig out their place, they don't have to do anything at all. When the mind is not used for judgment, it is free to wander. No thought happens twice—and that is the very definition of entertainment.

Mrs. Applebie had striven for a controlled life. She always wanted to know exactly where she was and what she thought. She had a position on any subject that you might want to discuss. She was in control at all times. She never had more than one possibility available at a time. Where her intellect left off, her belief system took over. She knew the difference between good and bad and tried to do only the good. Without even knowing it, she carried the mind as far as it could go in a direction bent on limitation. She lived in a tiny world of her perceptions, and every other person on the planet was a threat to that world. She had no friends because she did not have an interest in what anyone thought about anything, including herself. She had backed herself into a corner, the same corner that everyone who has any interest in control is heading toward.

That moment in the theater was a crossing over for Mrs. Applebie. She was defined by her limitations, when they disappeared, the possibilities flowed in. She had lived below *see* level. She couldn't perceive anything that she did not first think. She built dams around herself as protection from the rising tides of possibility. She was damned. In the theater a dam broke. She became the universe. Enlightenment is a giving up of control, a releasing of thoughts and an acceptance of the flow of things.

Mrs. Applebie had defined herself by all that she could exclude, and in a moment she included everything. Enlightenment is often like that. It is instant, a flip of the switch.

There are supposedly techniques for becoming enlightened, but technique is a fancy word for patterns, an earlier step. Mrs. Applebie had been working toward enlightenment her whole life, and didn't know it.

Today there are many people working consciously toward enlightenment. Sadly, this doesn't work. The very act of doing such a thing is another expression of control. Also, underlying *work*ing-toward-enlightenment is that somehow there is somewhere to get to where someone is not NOW. While this does serve to keep people busy, it does not lead to enlightenment. Enlightenment is not a path; it is everywhere. When life is the way it is and is not the way it is not, enlightenment is obvious.

Rules about enlightenment; or anything, are only added control. For example, many people are wandering around thinking that it is bad to judge other people. Simply translated, what this means is that people who judge people are bad people. By denying yourself judgments you add meaning. The way to eliminate judgment is to exhaust it by doing it extensively and well. Then you will discover that it does not serve you .

Paradox and irony are rampant. As you approach perception of enlightenment, control breaks down and they rush in. Once you cross over there is no more paradox. Up to this point, all too often it is exactly what looks pious and good that leads one away from the perception of enlightenment.

When you lose your mind you will see your enlightenment, but in order to do so, you need to have a mind to begin with. Since the mind is an illusion, you have nothing to lose, but that is not usually how it appears.

Who Are You?

Who are you?

There are at least four types of answers to this question. Who do you think you are? Who do you act like you are? Who do you want other people to think you are? Who are you really, underneath all of that?

This is a pretty complicated mess, as identity usually is. With all of these you's to keep track of, perhaps schizophrenia is the next evolutionary step and perhaps it is not.

Do you act differently with your boss than you do with your spouse? Would you speak differently to the President of the United States than you would to a bum on the street? Do you treat women differently from men?

Identity for most people is an exercise in juggling, keeping track of how they are supposed to *act* and with whom.

Identity is the fall-out of what you would not do, think, or have. In short, it is who you are not. Identity is defined by the limitations and restrictions that you place on yourself.

The basis of the whole question, "Who are you?" is that you are something. You are not. If you are what you do, then the range of behaviors that you perform defines who you are. If you are what you think you are, then the thoughts in your head determine who you are. If you are who other people think you are, then the thoughts in their heads determine who you are. Clearly, none of these can possibly be true. Before two years of age, you performed certain simple behaviors with no thoughts about exactly who you were, and other people had not yet refined their opinions about you. Though you obviously were, by the criteria that most adults define themselves by, you were not.

The person who most people think they are is an illusion constructed from repetitious limitation and based on a composite of what they wouldn't do and what is culturally dictated that they shouldn't do. Thus, they are a particular limitation of possibilities at a specific location. The very idea of composite limitation requires the shrinking down of a universal being to a menial definition. No wonder people have problems with self-esteem. If you think you are anything short of everything, then you are living in a world of illusion.

People are the only species who even seeks definition. People are the creators of illusion, a dubious honor. At first it is pure and simple. A magician masters an illusion which can be both fun and entertaining, but it becomes neither when the magician forgets what is illusion and what is not. If people hadn't forgotten what reality is, then they would not have to use the word "really" so much in conversation. Really?

To think of yourself as anything or anyone at all requires that you maintain an illusion of distance from reality. Bridging this distance demands an expansion of your perception to include all possibility where you become both everything and nothing. All possibility means no limitation. The very act of imposing meanings, that are thought to be true and existent, is demeaning. People abuse themselves every time they do so.

The nature of thought gets in your way. Thought, a second level distortion, is much further removed from reality than things (stuff and holes), a first order distortion. Thought is a two-dimensional representation of three-dimensional things. Thought occurs in the mind, which is a fictional entity. People go on their merry way building fiction upon fantasy and wondering why life, when they look below the surface, seems meaningless and empty. When the mind takes itself seriously, it confuses illusion with reality, thus making everything trivial while thinking it has just made everything significant.

The mind contains no physical objects. Millions of pictures and sounds constantly flow through the mind. These are two-dimensional representations of sensory input. If you don't like something you think, since it is an illusion, then you ought to be able to think some other illusion, but this is not how thoughts work. People are deeply imbedded in the process of convincing themselves that thoughts are even more real than reality. People add meaning to illusion and then call it real. Meaning plus illusion results in meaningful illusion not reality.

Initially, meaning is defined as repetition; later it becomes mere persistence. If you have the same thought over and over again, you become convinced that there is something real about the thought. The mind can think it is in Des Moines so often that it becomes convinced it is in Des Moines. It then edits evidence to the contrary. The mind does not see the Sears Tower while walking down the streets of Chicago because it is convinced that it is seeing the skyline of Des Moines. Thinking you are in Des Moines does not put you there.

There is colossal humor in thinking that something is true when it is not, but only when you take a step back to observe what is happening. Consciousness is the ability to perform this observation. Without consciousness, people are hopeless slaves of earlier programming or sensory awareness. You *are* the universe; thus you do not have to determine your place in it. When consciousness forgets to observe, it strives to control everything it sees and hears in an effort to find its place in the universe. It takes over the senses so that thinking determines perceptions, and it even steps back earlier in evolution to become a slave to patterns. Consciousness seeking control has to *try* to be everything when it already is everything and thus it makes an illusionary horrible mess.

Thoughts are two-dimensional representations of results of reality. Thoughts don't need to be limited to this but are when consciousness forgets what it isn't—anything. The less consciousness observes and the more it considers its representations to be true, the further from reality consciousness gets and the more illusionary it becomes. As this process progresses, the sole job of consciousness becomes the maintenance and care of illusion and the frantic act of keeping illusion as far away from reality as it can. When an illusion gets too close to reality, possibility destroys illusion and growth occurs. This is usually defined as a bad experience, loss, pain, or being wounded. It is, in fact, exactly the opposite. It is returning to who you really are: everything, light and expansive.

When people find out that something is possible for them that they did not think was possible, they are often pleasantly surprised. But when they find out that everything is possible for them, they act hurt or wounded and retire to their corner to patch themselves up. *Dances with Reality* is the name of this movie. For the chair, the couch, or the dog there is a set range of limitations. For consciousness there are no limitations. When the mind seeks to determine who it is or what it is, the easiest and least threatening way to accomplish this is by setting up limitations, which usually come in the form of earlier evolutionary steps.

The mind focused on things results in limitation. The mind focused on thoughts as things results in limitation. The mind focused on a possibility or two results in limitation. The mind focused on all possibility becomes infinitely light and thus enlightened. When people accept the existence of physical objects, they lock themselves in to having to deal with them.

The earlier evolutionary stage of patterns requires doing and repetition. How much of your day is involved with activities, patterns, and repetition? Each repetition is an invitation to an earlier, more primitive stage. Awareness, the next evolutionary stage after patterns, is sensory-based and thus reaches down to the world of things, stuff and holes. The better you are with your senses, the more effective you will be at manipulating things. Your senses are as close to things as you can get, while your thoughts lead you away from them.

I, John Brown, am an architect. Architecture is what I have been trained in, and it is a limitation I can live with. I actually get paid due to my willingness to adopt this limitation over a period of time. To be an architect is to be able to have a picture in my head of a building and to convert that picture through specific materials to the world of stuff and holes outside my head. In other words, it is to take a thought and convert it to a thing. For this I get paid. The house is the symbol of my control over the environment. I am called a master when my limitations are exact.

When I say I am an architect, I am eliminating all other possible careers for myself. When I say I am John Brown, I am really saying that I am not any of the other names in the world. I live in Des Moines, which means all the other cities in the world become places to visit, not my home. I live on Earth, so every other planet becomes foreign.

This is an example of how people use limitation to seemingly make themselves important, to know who they are. You have been told from an early age that "You must know who you are." You are asked, "What do you want to be?" This is the kind of question that drives you directly to limitation for an answer. In the act of determining who you are in relation to everything else, you exclude so much and include so little that it is no wonder you are so lonely.

"Whether I'm right or whether I'm wrong. I'll do it my way." These are the lonely lyrics illustrating living with a mind seeking control. "No Johnny, I guess that Hitler didn't have such a bad life." In retrospect Hitler was wrong and a very evil man, but it seems that he had more control over things than most people, something many people are seeking. Do you want to be Hitler? If not, then you had better give up the illusion of control.

Spirit and Spirituality

The sun is setting. "Will it rise again tomorrow?" is an insignificant question. Much more expansive is to ask, "What if it does?"

From a mind bent on control, one of the first steps toward entertainment is to return to your senses. See the sun setting. Think no thoughts of tomorrow or how this sunset compares with all other sunsets. Just watch the sun set. Don't even bother to realize that it is Earth moving and not the sun setting at all. Look outside yourself. Listen to the crickets or the wind. Look at the tree or the grass. Don't even know what it is you are looking at. Just look.

One of the common elements of enlightened people is that they don't have pictures or conversations in their heads. Street people are often, but not always, the opposite. If you see pictures in your head, or hear sounds or conversations, then you are more serious than you need to be. For thought, everything is possible, but for thought of specific pictures or conversations, the limitations of the content is imposed. What is the lightest thing you can imagine? A light show perhaps. Remember light shows? There was nothing to hold on to, only entertainment in the moment. Underneath representations in your head is a light show. There is an All, defined as that which you can look at, or listen to forever without ever having it look or sound the same. Infinite amusement. Life without definition or segmentation.

Consciousness is the grand observer, or at least it can be. When consciousness is the observer, people are constantly entertained and amused, not from outside in but from inside out. People are the party; thus, they do not need to attend a party. As observers, people become the whole universe rather than the control group trying to become the center of the universe.

Who are you?

Spirit? Perhaps.

Spirit is the simplest of non-things, the manifestation of reality in a specific location. Spirit is the doorway by which reality enters from anywhere there is possibility. It is nothing less than that. Where there is possibility there is spirit. From a certain point of view, spirit gives rise to possibility.

Spirituality is equally simple but different. Spirituality is the focus of consciousness on reality, all possibilities. When consciousness focuses on reality rather than on things or on its own limitations, then it reaches upward evolutionarily and soars. Who you are is much greater than you think you are when you think that you are anything at all.

Enlightenment is the ongoing process of expressing your spirituality, not in words but in focus. It is surfing the flow of possibility, right at the crest, and remaining there, suspended and included forever in a moment, outside the illusion of time and space.

This sounds simpler than it is. There is temptation everywhere to focus on anything but reality. Isolate some condition so that it justifies something or makes something more meaningful than something else. The game called enlightenment occurred the moment after consciousness was born. When consciousness arrived, the next questions were, "What will it observe? Will it observe everything or only part of everything? What will consciousness think it is observing? If it focuses on something, will it think that something is everything?" Typically, the answer to the last question is "yes." People confuse the sideshow for the whole carnival. They get bored with the superficiality and repetition put into the sideshow to make themselves comfortable and limit all possible threats to their rules.

The not-so-obvious question about consciousness is, "Will it observe the same thing twice?" The roots of control are in seeing the same thing twice because seeing something once is just seeing it. Seeing it twice is the beginning of philosophy, and seeing it many times is the root of science. The moment people see something twice they make it much more likely that they will see it a third time. After awhile people need to see it. Seeing something ten or twenty times convinces them that they actually are, at least in part, the thing that they see. The thing becomes associated with the person, and any threat to the thing is a threat to the person. After all, how often do you confuse your thoughts with who you are? The most honest answer to this is probably that you have seldom, if ever, thought of this because you just assumed that your thoughts were you. You accepted your thoughts as the gospel of you, the truth, handed down, the sacred limitations. Thou shalt think that one's thoughts are all important. Decartes, the philosopher, identified this condition when he said, "I think therefore I am." If all it took to be true were to be pervasive, this would be true because this idea is everywhere. People have many words confused with who they think they are, including: point of view, opinion, belief, judgment, fact, and many more.

Thought held as all-important overrides the senses and determines what you see, hear and feel, based on what will breed consistency, reasonableness, power and preeminence. Thought is isolating one particular piece of consciousness and thinking it over and over and over. Repetition is the way that people make thoughts important and identify with them. It is the way that people bore themselves to death or, at least, to automaticity. It is also the way that people wonder if there isn't, perhaps, more to life than they yet know, if there isn't something missing. "Is this all there is?" is the question that must haunt any person who considers thought all important and yet has not returned all the way to a completely automated existence. "Is this all there is?" never occurs to the enlightened person. To the enlightened person, there is so much more than everything that the question is ridiculous. The richest man in the world still wants more money, but the enlightened person doesn't want. There is no more to get when there is already more than everything.

The senses are very useful in observing things, but they are not even relevant when it comes to spirituality and possibility. The senses function in an exclusionary paradigm, which sets you up to compete with reality rather than be reality. Since you can't see everything, then you must determine what you will see. This is control. The senses limit you, but in a much less sophisticated way, you think, than your thoughts. You can imagine anything, but you can only see what is here, you think. The bus is bearing down on you, about to hit you. If you are there, aware of your senses in that moment, you will probably step out of the way of the bus, and live to play another day. But if you think that there could not be a bus, you will remain in the same spot, until the bus hits you. Then, in the fraction of a second that the collision takes, you will discover that using your thought to rule your senses is life threatening.

A young girl, about two years of age, pulled a knit hat over her head and eyes so that she could not see. With the naiveté of an adult she then ran forward as fast as her little legs could carry her. "What I can't see can't hurt me," the adult reasons. She fell backwards violently when she hit the wall. She was not hurt physically but was philosophically shaken. Her father sat and cried. She had known that she was finally free: having shut down her senses, she would no longer be controlled by their constraints. The senses, even though they limit as they operate, allow people to move throughout their lives without running into the same wall over and over again. Without the senses, thoughts would get caught behind one small wall and continually run into it thinking it was not there. In most cases, senses are more trustworthy than thoughts. The fact that the stick looks bent when stuck in a pail of water and does not appear so when removed is unfortunate because it has allowed philosophers to reach the conclusion that they wanted to anyway: "Thought is all important." For now, just decide that the stick bent on its way into the water and then straightened out again when it was removed. That ought to offend your logic.

Awareness is the wind in a person's head, and consciousness is the ability to perceive the wind, but not its effects. The moment people become tempted by the effects of the wind, they miss the opportunity to see the wind itself. The wind is a process while the effects of the wind are the content. The leaf moving is not the wind. And the thought is not awareness or consciousness. When you lose your mind, not misplace it, but consciously lose it, you are everything and you see, hear and feel nothing. You expand endlessly. Content disappears and so does all exclusion as you include everything, and rise above everything to—nothing.

Ironically, the way to do this is typically not by doing it, but by doing nothing at all. The moment you do something, control rears its ugly head. It is precisely when everything is empty and meaningless that you are closer to perceiving enlightenment, not when you are happier than you have ever been before. Enlightenment is not having a good day or having things going your way. Enlightenment is a letting go of everything. It is consciousness focused on reality, and nothing less than reality will do. Enlightenment is no limitation.

Emotions give you a reading on your progress. If you are currently having an emotion, then you can know that there is an overlap between reality and illusion. At that moment there is the opportunity to separate the two, so you can discern which is which. Patterns demand that at this moment of emotion you get illusion away from reality and do any necessary repairs on illusion to have it complete and effectively limit again. The closer you get to reality, the lighter you get, except sometimes.

You must return to your senses, but then you must let your senses go, too. Anything that you *know* is not real. Anything that you understand has been so watered down that all it still contains is illusion. The mind will perform magic to maintain its position of king or queen of the universe. The more fully you appreciate the magic, the less control the mind has. Appreciate the magic but notice that it is magic.

The mind is the great deceiver, but it is also the grandest entertainer of all. It has tricks to last a lifetime. It can never control anything, yet it can think it controls everything. The mind cannot control anything, but it can be infinitely entertained by the smallest thing imaginable or nothing at all. The mind is the best, the worst and the only audience in the universe. It is the result of consciousness, and the big question is, "What will it focus on?"

"What is the purpose of the mind?"

Like all evolutionary experiments, it is to find out if a mind makes a species more or less apt to survive. So, boiling this down, it is survival. But survival of what? The mistake the mind so often makes is to think that it is in charge of its own survival, the mind becoming its own master. Evolution does not care for the individual, and the mind does not care for the species. Thus humanity is caught in a double bind. The term double bind is the best definition that can be given for the mind since the process of thinking is an either/or. This or that. The mind, at this early stage in its evolution, can still confuse itself with earlier stages of evolution. When it does so, it takes on criteria from these stages.

In patterns, something is either happening or it is not. To a mosquito, something is either moving or it is not; warm or not. The universe is digital to patterns. When people are pressed, or perceive that they are threatened at all, they return to this digital world. People call things right or wrong, good or bad. This is a return to an earlier stage of evolution. Consciousness controlled by the rules of patterns is consciousness going to war, fighting or loving because it is the right thing to do. It is consciousness with reasons to justify the exclusion of all but the simplest action, often the final decisive action of making a decision. That is the act of murdering the alternatives. Killing off all possibilities but the one which is perceived to be the right one.

Observe yourself walking. Think about what you do when you walk. What movements do your hands make? Which way does your head move? Isolate some small part of your body and notice it as you walk. Continue to vary your focus. Watch other people walk. How do they do it? And in what ways do their walks differ from your own?

Consciousness can bring its analogue abilities to patterns; it can derive enjoyment and add variation to patterns. It can override the repetition inherent in patterns. Alexander and Feldenkrais are two techniques that have been developed to aide consciousness in varying patterns.

It is Sunday afternoon. This is your afternoon. Superbowl Sunday and you are the running back. Will you carry the ball to victory or fall with it to defeat? Pretend for a moment that you care whether you win or lose. You want to win this game! Isolate a split second once you have received the ball. There you are with the inflated skin of a pig held tightly to your chest and with hundreds and hundreds of pounds of very well-paid meat wanting to knock you down.

Which way do you run? The opposing team has watched films of every game you have played. They have observed your movements. By now they know your patterns. They know that you hold your head in a particular way when you are going to run to the right and in a different way when you are going left. They know you, perhaps better than you know yourself. If you cannot get outside of your own patterns at this moment, you will be thrown to the ground and you will lose the game. You, too, have watched the game films and you know the patterns of the people who are trying to catch you. At this moment, millions of dollars are riding on your next step.

At such a moment, you will get whatever you have practiced. You will not be able to bring thought to bear in that split second to influence the outcome. Thought is fast, but it is too slow for a moment like this. If you have been practicing the repetition of your own patterns, then the other team already knows where you will be, and the only matter left to determine is whether they can catch you there. But if you have been practicing the variation of your patterns, if you have been having an identity crisis and are not really yourself right then, you can break out of your own patterns. The other team thinks you are still your predictable self, and they are out ahead thinking that you will be in one place while you are in another. They have watched how you run, but you are not repeating those same steps now. In their split second of confusion, you can escape with the pig.

The ultimate football player, or human being, would bring consciousness to that moment or at least practice doing so often enough that patterns would not determine the next step. It is more likely that the whole scenario described above goes on outside the awareness of any of the players. In this event, the player who can focus awareness most thoroughly on the senses to heighten them will have the events of the moment override the patterns of the past. Overriding patterns with or without awareness can result in a touchdown being scored. In the first, consciousness is being used to add variation to patterns, and in the second, awareness. Taking the abilities of a later evolutionary step back to an earlier one adds flexibility to life and is often rewarded. This is not only true in football but in relationships, work, play, parenting, thinking, and life.

Putting consciousness at the effect of either patterns or awareness is both demeaning and anti-evolutionary. And you will do it every time when the going gets tough, when you consider that you are deeply threatened.

What are you afraid of? If you are afraid of lions, life will be easy. Avoid them. If you are afraid of spiders, life will be a little more difficult because spiders are much more prevalent than lions. Are you scared of what you can't see? People are willing to admit their fears of lions and spiders. They often even name such fears and pay people to help them get rid of the fears. If you are afraid of death, you are in even greater trouble because death is everywhere.

The number two fear of people is being burned to death in a fire. The number one fear is of public speaking. Which means that the number one fear is of other people and what they will think. Consequently, if you are scared of other people and what they think, since you are other people, to those other people you must also be scared of yourself and what you will think. You do not really know what you will think in the next moment although you attempt to have your thoughts be as consistent as possible. When your thoughts are consistent, you know who you are and what you will think and thus you don't have anything to fear. One of the problems with this approach is that the universe is constantly changing, and if your thoughts are not, you become an adversary of the changes of the universe. This makes you afraid of change. Isn't everybody? And change is everywhere. The more often you are fearful, the more likely it is that earlier evolutionary stages will take over from later ones and you will become patterned and predictable, a sitting duck in a changing universe.

The "being wounded," "hurt," and "suffering" that most people go through is an example of having consciousness dominated by earlier evolutionary stages— seldom awareness, typically patterns. Low self-esteem is the result of consciousness perceiving, rightly so, that it is not in control. If it needs to control, then it must either build an illusion where it can control or decide that it is not worthy. Chronic Fatigue Syndrome is giving up the will to control without realizing that one cannot really control. In many cases, it is closer to enlightenment than is the person who thinks he or she is in control. People are in the process of creating names for psychological diseases that all have to do with the subservience of consciousness to earlier evolutionary stages.

Fear justifies returning to what has worked in the past to have people survive and the automaticity that they no longer need. People say that their biggest fear is public speaking, but it isn't. People are too afraid to even say or let themselves know what their biggest fear is, the granddaddy of all fears. What is your absolute, all-time biggest fear?

Nothing is Complete

It is time to go back, back to before Earth was cooling. Before there even was Earth. Back to the beginning of the universe, if it had one. Scientists might say, "Back to original sex, the big bang." Or depending on your religious orientation, "Hand me that apple, Adam."

What was there in the beginning? Scientists are finally catching on to something that many people have known intuitively for a long time. Physicists and religious leaders are passing by each other as the physicists move out to the realms of spirit and spirituality and the religious leaders move in to patterned ritual, business, and dogma. The physicists are now speaking of the universe having formed when nothing began to boil. Each bubble from the boiling of nothing formed a universe.

The universe, everything, began from nothing. It remains nothing. Everything is an illusion that results from the blocking of nothing. Not the real blocking, but the illusionary blocking of nothing.

What are people most afraid of? NOTHING. Watch how busy people are. "I didn't get anything done today." A worthless day is one in which you got nothing done. People are so busy that they have to call it meditation or disease before they are justified in doing nothing. Just sit or lie down and do nothing for a day, a week or a month. Remain idle. Doing something is so good and doing nothing is so bad. This focus on busyness steeps people in illusion, and on a grander scale, it ruins the ecology of Earth. If you were already satisfied, delighted and in ecstasy, you wouldn't need to do anything. But if you convinced yourself that you are not sufficient the way you are and that you really need to accomplish something important, then you have to stay busy.

Compulsive doing, doing that must get done, presupposes that somehow things are not perfect the way they are and that if each of us does his or her part, then things will get better because of our effort. Translated, this is to say that somehow you will be better because you did something. If this were the case, then the world would be a much better place now than it was, say, a hundred years ago, since more has been done. In many ways it is not.

Doing is a form of attempting to complete and control. It is the tumbler for which you are the needed key, making you important. Incompletion lends meaning to your life. You leave the cheese out on the counter, you can—it is your right. Usually you put it away, but not this time. These little things set you apart from wholeness. You can't die until the cheese is put away or this or that is done.

There he was lying on his death bed. He exclaimed, "I cannot die yet, I have too much more to do."

There is no connection between incompletion and longevity.

Every time you go to sleep, you may not wake up, and every time you are awake, you may die and never sleep again. Incompletion only fragments what life you have. Before you go to sleep, complete everything so you may go peacefully if it is your time. Before you awake complete everything.

Anything incomplete screams for your attention. The cost of having your life incomplete is that it distracts you from the humor and joy inherent in the moment. The payoff of having things incomplete around you is the importance you gain from it. A problem, an incompletion, is your problem, really yours, and since it is important, you must also be important. Often the most persistent part of people is their problems. You can doubt it—but how much time do you spend talking about your problems?

Isn't it obvious? You don't have problems that you can have once and then be done. You don't have problems with an unknown stranger. You have them with your parents, spouse, children or work associates so that the apparent source of your problem is around often, persistent, repetitious, and important. These are only apparent sources of your problems, the real source of all problems is the importance you derive from them: you have to have them or life is not worth living. And these very problems make life not worth living. Ennie Meany Miney Moe, catch yourself right by the toe. If you holler hold on tighter.

Incompletion is a ridiculous, unnecessary, and unfortunate process from which to derive importance. Yet in most people, it is a consistent form of self-abuse and identification.

As long as you get your identification by what does not work, you will continually have things not work. You will plant weeds in your own backyard so that you can pull them. You will have whatever and whoever is around you the most often give you trouble. A persistent example of this is illness, or incomplete health. Thus sickness is a very acceptable way of keeping things incomplete.

Talk and think more about ease than dis-ease. CLOSE ALL CIRCLES. Complete the do loops you have begun. "Do loops," are composed of anything you have started but have not yet finished.

A Do Loop

Do loops are always in the form of a circle. In simple terms, a do loop is begun just by living your life and accidentally making a little bit of progress. Progress always means getting closer to nothing. Whether you are conscious of it or not, you create a do loop when you get a little too close to nothing, too close based on your own illusions tolerance for nothing.

An idea pops into your head like, "What I need is a new workbench." Or, "I need to clean up the planet. . . . It is time for me to have children. . . . I have always wanted to learn to make pop-overs. . . . I don't yet know anything about the stars. . . . It is finally time for me to learn to mountain climb. . . . I need a vacation. . . . need to lose ten pounds. . . . learn to speak French . . . go to cooking class . . . marketing class . . . church . . . It is time I was married . . . divorced . . . sick . . . widowed . . . I have never read anything by Shakespeare, Steven King, George Bernard Shaw, Timothy Leary, Jerry Stocking, Robert Bly, or the Bible Boys." Anything is an excuse to consider that somehow life would be better if you did something. The something can and usually does vary, and the more difficult and time consuming it is, the bigger the loop you must make to accomplish it. The bigger you make your do loop, the longer it will be until you have to determine what you will do next. Being in a loop is analogous to chasing your own tail and the one thing that it never results in is progress. The purpose of doing is to retard progress. The shortest distance between two points is never a loop. The easiest way to make a loop is to nail one of your feet to the floor so that no matter how fast you walk, you will go in a circle. Slightly less easy is making some*thing* that *is not* more important than what *is* and setting out to accomplish that *thing* of importance.

Close all circles. Doing is the creation and migration over a circle. It begins with a verbal or physical declaration of incompletion and goodness of completion. The body moves clockwise around this circle and the mind moves counterclockwise.

Truly creative human beings experience this as a sphere, but almost everyone else experiences it as two-dimensional. Mental importance is greatest at the beginning of the loop while physical importance is at its lowest with the most to do. Physical importance grows along the circle until the fraction of a second right before the end when physical importance is at its greatest. By this time, mental importance is already elsewhere. Thus the mind derives importance from incompletion and the body from the process of completion. That is why the two are seldom in the same place at the same time. They are not good friends.

The more incompletions you have, the more important the mind seems—the more messes there are and so the more real the mind must be. This need not make sense; the mind cares not for sense or senses. It wants to be the dictator in hopes that shooting high will ensure evidence of its existence and the end of any talk of its being illusion. The mind has no physical reality at all. It gets evidence for its existence by thinking. In the act of doing, it appears to people that the mind controls the body and thus people have to think that the mind is important. Free choice is the main illusion that keeps the mind in place. Free choice is the declaration that what people think influences what they do. This may, in fact, be true, but not in any kind of direct way, and perhaps it is patently untrue. Free choice opens the door to judgment and blame, two of the mind's favorite tools for proving its own importance.

Human beings began from nothing and will return to nothing. Nothing is flowing all around you, and the moment you appear to block nothing, you get everything. The very act of doing is an attempt to make your illusion real. What would happen if you did nothing? It is only in your illusion that you ever do anything, and anything that you do keeps you from where you are, nowhere/nothing. Do nothing and you will find out who you really are. Do anything and you will discover that you are important and meaningful. You will be chasing phantoms in the pursuit of value, and life will become a busy maintenance of illusion with no end in sight. You will get dizzy as you trace loop after loop, frantically attempting to prove that you can do something. Screwing yourself up or down.

The flow of nothing is continual. It is your source, it is your salvation, and it appears to be your end. Nothing never ends, and since you are nothing, you cannot end.

You never were and never can be in the form that you presently consider yourself to be. When you know, in your bones, that you do not have bones, then you will be enlightened. You will not be you anymore; you will be nothing, which is so much greater than everything that it cannot possibly be expressed in words. Only small parts of it can be seen at one time, but those little parts are revelations of infinite pleasure that create the universe from head to toe.

You are not anything regardless of all of your attempts to prove what you are. You are more than everything. You are nothing, and there is nothing else for you to be. If this seems serious, problematic, confusing, or meaningful, it is probably a sign that you are still attempting to prove that you exist by adding meaning to things and thoughts. If it seems meaningless, light, and obviously accurate, then you are nothing.

Everything is not nothing. Everything is a small part of nothing. So what is there to do with nothing? Nothing? Can life really be that easy? It is. Why does life seem so hard? Because by making it so, you seem to be important and able to justify anything. There is very little that is easier than life.

Crazy and Enlightened

Everything is created the moment that nothing is blocked. Nothing can be blocked by any evolutionary step. That is the definition of illusion, anything that can appear to block nothing sufficiently that everything shows up. There is a wake when this happens. A tail of influence which determines the size of this particular everything. It determines the amount of room everything has to play in this time.

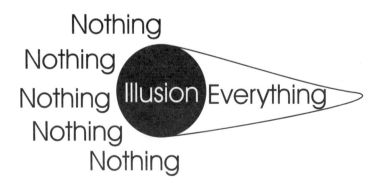

When there is one blockage, you get existence; when there are two blockages, you get the possibility of growth, development, choice, and eclipses. With three, the everything becomes a bit more complicated and eclipses play an ever greater role. Control becomes the major driving force.

The first blockage resulted in a mechanistic, systematic escape from nothing, apparent escape, at least. This opened the land of patterns, anything that happens twice. The more often something happens, the more patterned it becomes. Originally, there was one point that blocked nothing. The next moment, the point blocked nothing again and sufficient blockage occurred to produce a pattern. To define the point a space opened around it. This space defined the direction of the flow of nothing and thus opened the door to limitation.

The second blockage results in the birth of a relationship. The possibility of relationship is born, and with it, wholeness disappears, the second blockage is related to the first. In other words, with a second blockage, there is a point from which to perceive the first blockage. There is not yet the ability to appreciate it or identify it, yet it can now be perceived. This second blockage is the evolutionary level of awareness.

With the third level of blockage came consciousness, "which is the ability to perceive not only the other two, but also itself." Consciousness can perceive itself by identifying itself as something other than what it is and then looking back to discover what it is. On the level of awareness, location was fixed, but with consciousness, location became flexible and, at best, free floating.

The first level blockage created everything from nothing. The second level (awareness) tied everything down by relating to it and the third level (consciousness) set it free. That is what happened at its optimum, at the beginning, but it seldom happens now. Something unlikely and unpredictable has been repeating itself instead, which is the eclipse of one blockage with another which results in the inability to perceive which is which. Consciousness allows multiple illusionary perspectives, but few people are using it that way. Nothing is continually flowing, and people have set themselves up to fight that flow by remaining constant, or at least attempting to. If they were to let their illusionary perspectives flow, people would be constantly changing and flowing; by resisting it, people are continually battered and beaten down. The flow is too great for people to resist successfully.

Consciousness is being used to determine the relationship of itself to everything, and the only way to do that is to have some fixed point from which to view everything and nothing. This attempt to establish a fixed point is the grandest, most difficult task ever attempted. It is the attempt to unify everything from one point. In essence, it is attempting to produce a level one blockage from a level three blockage. It cannot happen, will not happen, and should not happen. But that does not keep people from trying to make it happen. Basically people just want to know where they stand, once and for all. Is that too much to ask? No, it is not too much to ask. It is fun to ask, but it is too much to answer.

Go to the ocean on a very wavy day and calm the waves. Reach out and push the moon forward a few feet in its orbit. Put a pencil to paper and have the universe revolve around that pencil point. All of these are easier than what you already attempt to do every day. You attempt to determine where you stand, when you stand nowhere at all. The form this attempt usually takes is control, understanding, identifying, or figuring out. You always and only have your point of view when you are attempting to determine where you stand. The very act of doing so limits flexibility to an evolutionarily dangerous degree.

The unit of measure of the quality of life is MIPPS. Multiple Illusionary Perspectives per Second. Attempting to figure out where you stand runs directly counter to MIPPS and reduces the quality of your life. What you receive in return for this reduction is the illusion of safety. Each day is spent determining where you stand in relation to new things or re-affirming where you stand in relation to old things. Old things are those for which you have already determined a place or identity. When you purchase a new car, there is a certain period of time in which you are off balance. You are not certain exactly what your relationship is to this car. The window cranks are in a slightly different place than they were in your old car. The whole shape and feel of the vehicle is different. You must become accustomed to the new car, and when you have, you say you are now comfortable with it. This means that you now know where you stand in relation to it. The new car is now sufficiently familiar for you to think that you control it.

You reach for your car keys one day, automatically. You have entered a loop of going to the grocery store to do a little hunting and gathering. In this loop your mind is already eating the food while your body still has to pick up the keys, carry them to the car, place them in the ignition, and so on. Each loop is composed of smaller loops, most

of which you are unaware of if you have completed the
big loop often. In other words, the primary blockage of
patterns eclipses the secondary blockage of awareness.
You reach for the keys, *automatically*. As your right hand
touches the keys, your key ring turns into a snake. Instead
of feeling your key ring, there is a slithery bunch of scales.
If you are fully enough eclipsed, as many people are, you
will grab the snake and attempt to start your car with it. If
only partially eclipsed, you will wake up at this moment
and notice the snake. The more certain you are that the
key ring could not turn into a snake, the less likely you are
to see it do so. This complicates the whole scenario in that
consciousness, in its certainty that the key ring cannot be
a snake, is overshadowing both patterns and awareness.
Consciousness has identified its relationship to the key ring
in a way which has nothing to do with a snake and thus it
knows where it stands in relation to the key ring. This,
knowing where you stand, is familiar to human beings. It
is so much the fabric of their lives that the very idea of
identifying it makes them squirm.

Now pick a different and more likely example of
knowing where you stand. Pretend you live alone and you
always leave your car keys on a nail right next to a shelf in
your kitchen. You automatically reach for your car keys,
but the nail is empty. This presents a moment of
disturbance. You were on automatic when you knew the
keys were on the nail. You had reached for them there
hundreds of times before, and each time they were there.
Now what? Patterns will not suffice here, at least the basic
key-getting pattern that you always used before did not
result in finding keys. Consciousness has to determine
where it stands regarding the keys. The easiest way to do
this is to find the keys as quickly as possible. It calls on

awareness, a secondary blockage, to look around. While awareness is looking, consciousness attempts to understand what has happened. It seeks to repair the automatic chain that has been broken. You always put your keys on the nail. (Assertion) The keys are not on the nail now. (Assertion) In all likelihood, you had already reached for the keys on the nail many times before you were even willing to accept that they were not there. You live alone. (Assertion) (Conclusion) The keys must be on the nail, or they have magically disappeared, somebody has broken into your house and stolen them, they have slipped off the nail, or some other explanation. Every explanation is a new attempt to determine where you stand. You need to control the keys or know why you don't, which is a form of controlling them.

You are now upset. Where are your keys? Your stomach grumbles, indicating that you need food from the grocery store, another explanation to let you know where you stand. You look high, on top of the refrigerator, and low, on the floor underneath the nail. As time goes on, you look in less likely places including, but not limited to, places that are too small for the keys to fit in: your garbage disposal (because your brother once lost his wedding ring down the garbage disposal), inside the refrigerator, under your bed, in your coat pocket. You look everywhere that you think the keys could possibly be, but you don't find them. You get angrier and angrier or a bit resigned as your keys continue to be more in control of this whole situation than you are. You look in the closet to find out if someone has broken into your house to steal the keys and then hidden them there. You lose credibility with yourself as you look in less likely places. What kind of person would pour the milk out of the container to discover whether his or her keys were at the bottom of it? You start to view yourself as a bit nuts. If you could only find the keys, then things would be all right again.

Bigger problems that you used to worry about disappear, like whether you ought to marry the guy you have been dating, or whether you should call your mother, or if you will finish school. You become obsessed with the necessity of finding your keys.

Finally, after several hours of constant searching, your house looks a bit like it has been ransacked, because it has been. You go out to the garage. You never leave your keys in the car, but you had better check there. You step outside your house and fail to notice the fresh air available to you or the robin singing in the tree. You walk, automatically, to the garage and start to raise the door. All of a sudden you don't care whether you find the keys or not. There is no car in the garage! You repeat the whole process you went through with the keys but this time with the car. You need to know where you stand in relation to the car. Cars are less confusing than dogs. A dog is automated, but it can still get up and walk away after you have told it to stay. You remember parking the car in your garage just last night and trusting that it would stay there. It apparently did not. You search for possible explanations beginning with the most likely and moving rapidly to less likely scenarios.

The day wears on as you sit pondering what to do. You do not go into work, and even forget to call in sick. Hesitantly, you call a friend, the most trustworthy person you know. Trustworthy means that you know where you stand in relation to this person. You have been friends a long time, so you don't have to explain to him right away why you need a ride to the bank. He gives you a ride.

Once at the bank, you get your safety deposit box only to discover that the title to your car is not inside. Now you have to begin the whole process of figuring out where you stand in relation to the title, starting with the most likely explanation and working your way out from there.

By now you are fearful, terrified and alone. You didn't really care about your keys, the car or the title for the car, but you took for granted that they would behave in ways you could understand or figure out. If things continue to be this confusing, you will find yourself in a mental institution soon enough. Enlightenment is always closer than your next thought, and a mental institution is never many thoughts away.

Your friend good naturedly doesn't ask what is wrong on the silent ride home. He tries to figure out what your problem is. Perhaps you broke up with your boyfriend or got fired. Maybe somebody died. He settles on some explanation, which lets him know where he stands in relation to you. The explanation he settles on is that you have broken up with your boyfriend. As he drops you off at home, he leans over and attempts to kiss you on the lips. He wants to take your boyfriend's place, when really all you need is your keys, car and title.

At the moment you reach out to push him away, you reach past him, stretch, yawn and feel your new flannel sheets against your bare skin. It is morning; you have been dreaming. Slowly you rise, pull on your bathrobe and reluctantly you walk down the hall toward the kitchen to discover whether your car keys are there or not.

What is a dream? What is a nightmare? What is real? What is illusion? These are all questions that you assume you have already answered in your pursuit of knowing where you stand in relation to things. These are questions that ought to constantly be on the tip of your tongue, and by being there, they will have you discover that anything you are certain of opens you up to insanity. Your mind will drive you crazy; in fact, it has already driven you crazy so many times that you know the route and don't even have to be aware while following it anymore. When you think, you go crazy. When you are crazy, you mistake reality for illusion and illusion for reality. You call a nightmare life and a dream a nightmare. This isn't life. What is life? Now that is a question. You have asked the question, "Where do I stand?" many times without even knowing it. You don't hear the question anymore, nor do you hear the silence when you ask. You hear your own answer, whatever it is at the moment. And you attempt to be consistent with your answers, to learn your answers so you don't have to think anymore.

You are crazy, but you don't have to be. You are two things in this life, crazy and enlightened. When you focus on your enlightenment, nothing, you notice your enlightenment. When you focus on anything else, you are crazy.

"Give me a sign, God. Let me know that you exist. Let me know I exist. Let me know something." The signs are all around you, nothing but signs. But when you are crazy you don't notice any of them. You make up signs in your own head and follow those, only to arrive at where you have already been. You attempt to avoid nothing by having any something, and you are hollow and upset. You reach for your car keys, and they had better be there.

Enlightenment, bliss, delight, and nothing are no place. They have no meaning, and are beyond cause and effect.

You have already arrived and you think you had better be on your way. Irony and paradox are everywhere, but not nowhere. You live nowhere, and as soon as you can think nothing, you will notice that you are already enlightened. And when you get that into your head, you will have it in a nutshell.

13

How Easy?

How easy can things get? Not very easy. Things are never easy—they are nothing at all. How easy can life get? Very easy. When you let everything flow through you, you seem to become everything. Once you have become everything, then you resist nothing. And when you let nothing flow through, enlightenment spontaneously occurs. From that point on, all you do is play. You have no more responsibility than a three-year-old at the park and all day to play. Your park is everything and nothing; it is the biggest park there is.

So, you have this mind. What are you going to do with it? If you shoot yourself in the head, you will likely hit your brain with the bullet, but your mind will not be injured, since it doesn't exist. Suicide does not quiet the mind.

How can you use your mind? Who is the you that would use it anyway? How do you get something from nothing? How can you make more money at work so you can afford to buy a second VCR for the bedroom?

There is a danger in thinking about anything too large or too fast—without careful scrutiny, the workings of thought will appear to be random or chaotic. The range of what can be thought is large, and thinking is fast. There is nothing random about this range or its speed, though. It is more random than are the results of thinking. The route you take to work in the morning or on your way to the grocery store is not random. If you are like most people, you take the same route day in and day out with little variation. The route you take is a function of your patterns. Any aspect of your life viewed through selective filters will reveal the patterns.

Every thought starts out as a revelation, an act of creation which is a pure and simple expression of reality, until you do something with it. The thought as a revelation cannot be understood and is not useful. You have to personalize it before a thought becomes the least bit purposeful or useful to you. The way you do this is subtle and even faster than the original thought. You personalize it by influencing its route based on rules you have adopted regarding the passage of thought through your mind. These rules, at first, are based on statistics. The likelihood of a thought traveling down a road that a similar thought has gone down influences both the speed and direction of the thought. If you were a blank slate, which is the case after enlightenment, then thoughts would occur to you at the speed of light and never undergo the personalization process. The most that would ever happen to thoughts is that they would be observed, with no selection process taking place.

The moment you think a thought twice, you have sinned against nature. Illusion is the result of thinking the same thought many times and building these repetitious thoughts into patterns. When you recognize that you are enlightened, you will never hold on to another thought. Your mind will become a completely flexible, unstructured, random generator of ideas. Thoughts will pour through your mind without ever having to be limited or identified by you. This is going on within you right now, but your patterns are blocking your ability to experience it.

You have been taught that you can control everything, even your thoughts. You are to be careful what you think and think slowly enough so you can keep up with and identify your thoughts. You don't know that you can't control what you can't identify, so you ignore the process of thinking and attend to the final dead end result of thinking. Once a thought is static, gutted, stuffed or rotting, you can become aware of it. Panting for breath, finally having caught up with this dead thought, you congratulate yourself and promise to be true to this thought for as long as you shall live or until some other thought might happen to die along your path.

The moment you attempt to identify or understand a thought, or even think it, you have warped it beyond recognition by stripping all of the revelations from it. Revelations are never personal, and anyone who is thinking personally will never have revelations. Thinking personally is comparing what you can or do think with what you have thought. What you have thought is archived by you; it is a collection of illusion that all thoughts must pass through if they are to fit in and be consistent with past thinking. Fitting in and consistency are two of the elements necessary for control. Remember being a child on the playground at school, the experience of crawling through a spanking machine—a line of kids with their legs spread who slapped your bottom as you wiggled your way through. This is, in effect, the sort of abuse that thoughts go through as you compare them with other thoughts. Every new thought tunnels by and gets slapped around a bit by all your other thoughts. What comes out the other side is a slightly wounded, embarrassed, and less-pleased thought.

The original thought was faster than a speeding bullet. Speed and freedom provide a playground for original thought. The very process of becoming aware of a thought controls thinking. As Heisenberg taught us, the act of observing something influences that which you have observed. In the case of awareness, thoughts must funnel through a small passageway to reach your awareness. This limiting pathway of awareness allows only five to nine thoughts to pass through per moment. When you become aware of one thought, you are not aware of so many others. Limited awareness plays a big role in your desperate battle for control. The universe is huge, but awareness is limited to only a tiny bit of it at a time—this is a formula for terror. What is influencing you right now that is outside of your awareness? To avoid the degree of trust (in oneself and the universe) necessary to ponder this question, most people declare that whatever they are aware of is all there is, or all they ought to be aware of. This anti-evolutionary, unintelligent step is typically the foundation for most illusions.

Illusion is a land without wonder where nothing is as it seems and no thought is allowed in unless it fits with all other thoughts that are already there. The longer you live, the bigger your illusion, and the more oppressive this fantasy becomes. Your fascination with fairy tales and Walt Disney is not an accident. People are masters of illusion, calling their illusions reality.

The next several chapters shed light on many specific ways to tear down your illusions and lighten your thinking. For example: The body and the brain feed on variation while the mind and illusion feed on repetition and consistency. By adding variation to everything you say and do, you will be shaking the foundation of your illusion.

Are illusions really bad? No, they are not bad, but if you do not recognize them as illusions you end up with a world of suffering, hate, pain, anger, fear, murder, abuse, drug use, embarrassment, stupidity, sadness, agony, torture, automaticity and greed. Does that sound like the evening news? The world is full of people who think their illusions are reality and that reality is an illusion. This is a tough way to live and isn't really living at all. It is attempting to survive with the cards stacked against you. The likelihood of your illusion prevailing over reality is about the same as the probability of you winning every lottery in the country without ever buying a ticket for any of them. Not bloody likely—but bloody, as history reveals.

Teasing out illusion is not easy. Often illusion looks like reality and dismantling illusion can appear to be an attack, a personal attack, like the ranting of a madman. In the world of illusion, craziness looks sane and sanity looks crazy. Wear your shirt backwards often enough and you will automatically put it on backwards. Think that illusion is reality often enough, define yourself only in terms of your illusion, and any threat to that illusion will have to be met by defense. Current thinking is set up for defense. People are so steeped in illusion that they cannot think a thought outside of it.

To a person who is used to drinking dirty water, clean water tastes odd and may not even be identifiable as water. To a person used to viewing his or her personal illusion as reality, a pure unadulterated thought usually goes unnoticed. If a person does glimpse reality, it can look like an attack on the very structure of illusion. If there is anything familiar to you about something, then you are letting your illusion determine what you think. If you compare a thought to any other thought you have had, then again your illusion is providing you with a stimulus/ response patterned reaction to the thought.

Intuition is an end run around the illusion. This does not happen often since the whole point in constructing an illusion is to control what you are able to become aware of and provide you with a corpse-like waking sleep in which you are never very disturbed and are always disturbed in the same familiar way. Some people get an intuitive thought, consider it a threat and discard it. Other people, upon receiving one, consider it so dear that they attempt to have it stuffed and mounted so they can always look at it and remember their intuition. Either approach has intuition lose what it has to offer—pure entertainment.

Thinking begins with nothing, where everything is possible. But then in order to control something, thinking says you need to find something to identify with. A point to stand on is created. You have heard people say, "What is the point?" They are referring to the first act of creation, creating a point from nothing. This is a distortion of nothing, and like any distortion it does not contain all of the original elements of nothing. It becomes something, or more accurately, the illusion of something. To this point, time is added and a line ensues, or space is added by the production of one other point. Space (holes) is then necessary to distinguish one point from another. Time and space are second level distortions of the original point, distortions of a distortion. The illusions you live by, that you call life, are distortions of distortions of distortions of distortions. Most illusions are so far removed from reality that only the illusion creator could love and cling to it as if it were of some value.

And you do. The mind is defined by the illusions you hold to. Without these parameters, you would lose your mind, and you can't have that, now can you? The more you hold to your illusions, the heavier you get. With this weight, the effect of gravity seems to increase and the more grave you become. Listen to the language of illusion. "My job is getting me down." "My kids are a burden." "This problem is weighing on me." "The weather is taking its toll." "One more thing to worry about." The more you let go of your illusion, the lighter you become. When you let go of everything, you notice that you are enlightened. Seeing your enlightenment clarifies that your illusion is not all of reality and laughter bubbles up without provocation. A smile spreads over your face as you discover that what has always been hidden *from* you was hidden *by* you and that you now know the difference between illusion and reality. There is nothing to fear when you recognize illusion as illusion. There is nothing to do. You can look reality right in the eye because you are the same height. You can look reality deep in the eye because you are reality.

To recognize enlightenment, you must lose your mind. Examine what you are losing. How do you make your mind important? How can you lose your mind?

Anatomy of Thought

"Do you prefer peaches or blueberries? Would you rather eat a pound of tofu or a pound of ground beef? Would you rather have your body smeared with honey or your honey smeared with body? Do you prefer coffee, tea, or me?"

The foundation of repetitious thought is preference. As long as you know which you prefer for a fraction of a second, enlightenment is beyond your perception.

Thought starts out as creation, you begin to think from nothing. As a baby, you did not distinguish between things. Your eyes moved freely without having to identify and itemize objects. Try that now. Begin by looking over your left shoulder and slowly, without distinguishing anything, move your head and eyes smoothly until you are looking over your right shoulder. Make sure your eyes are open and chances are that your eyes and head will make little jerky movements as you jump from one recognizable object to another, rather than flowing in a smooth arc across the room. You are, in effect, leaping from object to object (lily pad to lily pad), staying afloat and making sure that you don't fall into the stream by remaining focused and never being between objects. You depend on things to know where you are and who you are. You identify with your identifications. The infant does not, nor does the enlightened person. While doing this exercise you may need an observer to help you notice the jerky movements because of their subtle nature. Another way to notice the thoughts is to listen to yourself label what you are seeing as you scan the room. Attempt not to label, and the labeling still goes on.

What do you do first when you wake up? You search for something in your environment to determine where you are. You look for something familiar, so that you can recognize yourself. If, during the night, somebody had moved you into a completely unfamiliar room without waking you, it wouldn't take you long to notice. Everything is illusion and you depend on illusion to know both where and who you are.

Thoughts flow through the mind. Initially people define themselves by the thoughts they become aware of. Then they can divide these thoughts into data received internally, from their minds, and data gleaned from external sources. This subset of thought is very small relative to the quantity of thoughts always flowing through the mind. The good guy riding his trusty stead through the dusty streets of town looks big and important until it becomes apparent that he is in a movie studio riding past the facade of plywood cutouts, painted to look like a town. Thoughts may look big and important, but they are two-dimensional; they are representations not things. There is no physicalness or depth to thoughts. The more distortions that something undergoes, the flatter it becomes. Nothing is in your thoughts, even when you think something is there. You are always closer to nothing than you think you are.

Consider that your mind flows one thousand thoughts or perceptions per second, including all things seen, heard, and felt as well as all links made to past seeings, hearings, and feelings. Since awareness is severely limited, people can become aware of, at most, nine of these thoughts or perceptions per second. Upon being told that people are only aware of a small amount of their thinking, they respond with attitudes somewhere between passive acceptance to rigorous denial. Nobody, it seems, wants to have goings on within his own head that he doesn't know about. This idea flies in the face of control. People can't control what they are not aware of. In the case of a deer, awareness reflects a random sampling of perceptions. People, with the aide of patterns and repetitious thinking, do not become aware of a random sampling of thoughts mirroring the whole. Instead, they use their funnel of awareness to consciousness to repeat thoughts to themselves or to make comparisons and reassurances. This process gives them the illusion of control and some ground to stand on while robbing them of the entertainment available.

Imagine an employee who comes to work anytime he wants to. He works in a location that is not only remote, but also secret. This is your employee, and you are responsible for everything he does and everything he doesn't do. You have no direct contact with him nor do you communicate with him by phone or via mail, not because he is unwilling to be contacted, but because you are so busy that you can never see, hear or communicate with him. Occasionally you think about what he should be doing, or wonder what he is up to. After all, you pay his salary. What is he doing? You will never know.

This is your relationship to most of your thoughts. Are you comfortable with having such an employee? Are you willing to take responsibility for what he does or doesn't do? You will probably do your best to forget he works for you and disavow knowledge of him, while still paying him dearly. And that is what you have done with the majority of your thinking. You have performed an initial limitation which has alienated you from most of your thoughts and yet, at the same time, you have held tightly to certain thoughts. This is a very insecure position to be in: a minority position, which claims that it is the majority. Since everybody you know does the same thing it seems to make sense.

People are only aware of a small quantity of their thoughts, that is the way it is. But there is a way out of this bind that people don't find themselves in because they have denied it for so long. By having consciousness maintain a healthy reverence for all that remains outside of awareness, people can begin to loosen the bonds they have become accustomed to. The next step is to surrender to that which is unrecognizable or not understandable. In other words, to give up control. If people get a few glimpses of how thinking really works, they will meet some thoughts within themselves that have been guiding them for years without their knowledge. A few such experiences may assist people in releasing control, since becoming aware of these guiding thoughts reveals to people that they never really had control anyway.

Giving up what you don't have, but think you have, is much harder than giving up what you do have. You are not in control of anything, least of all your thinking. Since you have never been in control, what you would be giving up is the illusion of control. Illusions die hard, primarily because they are well-fortified. Illusions are surrounded by old, dead, repetitious thoughts which support them, the only company able to make illusions significant. Propping up an old corpse so that you can have tea with it does not make it a good conversationalist or good company, but in an illusion any company will do. The process of selection to produce an illusion is so extreme that the illusion has to take on a life of its own since it does not relate to life or reality any more at all.

What about the thoughts you don't become aware of? What indeed? Those thoughts, not having been handled and contorted to fit your illusion, remain revelations and flow through you. They never get put to the test, true or false, right or wrong. They never have to fit anywhere, so they can remain big enough and fast enough to still, fundamentally, resemble the whole. They are basically nothing, and they do nothing for you, and it is precisely when you are at nothing that you perceive your enlightenment. Since the majority of your thinking consists of such thoughts, you are already enlightened. But, since you block these thoughts so thoroughly from your perception, you don't experience your enlightenment. You wander around enlightened and forgetting to celebrate.

Either everybody is enlightened or nobody is. People are too intimately connected to have it be any other way. Everybody is enlightened, and few people know they are. That little smile on the enlightened person's face, or that laugh that bubbles, wells up and flows from her is in response to a world full of suffering and tormented people, who are missing the most obvious thing about themselves, their enlightenment.

All differences are created by you, in your thinking. No differences exist independent of you. The enlightened ones are not laughing at you. They are laughing with you, but you do not know you are laughing. Once you catch on, you will never forget you are laughing. It is your mind that is enlightened, and it is your mind that keeps you from recognizing that you are enlightened. You are a traveler constantly seeking the place where you are already. Now that is funny. If people walked up to you at the corner of Vine and Olive Street and asked you how to get to the corner of Vine and Olive Street, you would probably think them a bit odd. "They have already arrived; this is that very corner!"

"No, it couldn't be," people exclaim as they head out further and further from where they want to go all in the name of getting to where they don't realize they already are. They do Sufi meditation, and tai chi, they heal their inner-child, then they paint, they learn to play the piano, and take vacations and so on. Everything people do keeps them busy so they won't realize that while they are getting further from where they are going, they remain at the corner of Vine and Olive Streets waiting for Godot. People are working to get where they are, while supporting an argument that they are not there yet.

Sometimes they sit, recline, sleep or stand up, but they never leave the corner, they can't. Enlightenment is where people reside, they just don't know it yet. People have to lose their minds first.

The initial preference of the mind is for things it can become aware of. So, it attempts to reach past enlightenment, which is all around you, to get to the next thought and the thought after that. You find what can fit with who you think you are and where you think you are because anything that does not fit in is too uncomfortable. If you are already enlightened, then why would you have suffered for all these years? Why would you have worked so hard to amass all the money and things that you surround yourself with? Why would you settle for symbols when what you want is already here? Why would you teach your children the work ethic, which has never had people notice their enlightenment?

You get tense and stressed out. And who wouldn't, perceiving that she is someplace where she is not? You go crazy. Losing your mind is the only sane thing to do, but it seems crazy, so you resist the tendency to let go. Instead, you dance faster, work longer hours, cling even tighter to the loud and repetitious conversation in your head which justifies you as you defend your position of control. You meditate, as you should, but it is the very limitations of your perceptions and all of your doing that keeps you from noticing where you are and that you have already arrived. Everything you do in the name of getting somewhere has you perceive that you are closer while still not noticing that you are already there.

Logical thinking, rational thinking and reasoning all put you in the bind of the person who travels halfway to his destination each day without ever arriving. If you perceive you are closer, then you have done well. Halfway there, on the first day, is very good. On the second day it is a bit less, and on the third day, less yet. By the twentieth or the one hundredth day, halfway there is far less. As you continue getting halfway each day, you progress less and less and still never get there. You can never get to where you are already without adapting a different and infinitely more subtle approach than you are willing, or at this point, even able to take.

When you have already arrived, all you need to do is notice where you are. Add nothing to where you are. Where you are already includes nothing. The moment you think, you have added something and you become the interior designer of Heaven. Wouldn't Heaven be even nicer with blue paint on the walls and a couch over there under the window? When you are already perfect, it is crazy to do anything.

Subtlety is a key, which will open you to seeing your enlightenment. Infinitely subtle is one door, as is infinitely anything. The thoughts you can become aware of are always finite. You will never know you are enlightened in the same way that you know you are a Chicago Cubs fan, Merrie's husband, or the owner of a Chevrolet. Enlightenment cannot fit in awareness, it has nothing to do with patterns and it can only be appreciated by consciousness.

If you could stop spinning for a moment, you would realize how dizzy all your work and efforts are making you. You could see illusion for what it is. You say, "But I am not spinning; you are spinning." Appearances are always deceptive, but not nearly as misleading as your thoughts. The purpose of illusion is to triumph over all other illusions—to be the right illusion, the good illusion, the grand illusion. To be the illusion which is best at eluding, at deluding, at providing you with incomplete clarity. The best illusion in the world of illusion is the one which looks the most real. Illusion is not reality, nor is perception.

You are already enlightened. You are still enlightened. You always will be and you always have been enlightened. You are the craziest enlightened person there is. The most ungrateful and disrespectful one, too. You are the lamb baaaing for its mother while still inside the womb. Such a lamb cannot be satisfied, except from within. It can't get any closer to where it is already. Its mother can't do anything for it. How do you get closer to where you are when you are already there? You don't.

"Enlightenment can't look like this," you say.

Enlightenment is so vast and so endless that it can look like anything. At the present moment, enlightenment looks exactly like what you are seeing now. Enlightenment looks like the words on this page. It may feel like a little wiggle in your big toe. Enlightenment is not limited or limiting.

You are not where you think you are, and you do not think that you are where you are. You are busy holding the wool over your eyes, terrified that the wool will get pushed away and you will have to see what is here. The universe has met people like you before, but you have never met the universe. You can't. You can only meet other people who are versions of you. You can only see people who look like wool, since you have wool over your eyes. Nobody could make you this crazy, though people have tried. If your parents did not know they were enlightened, would they want you to think you were?

The President would have to miss the fact that he was enlightened or he wouldn't bother being President. "If elected I will do nothing," would be the political slogan of the enlightened person. "Things will be exactly as they are, forever. We will change nothing, and if anything changes, we will laugh and not change that." An enlightened person will never be elected President. Enlightenment is not something which you can do anything with. It serves no purpose and works toward no end. It is already at all ends. It is every path already explored and includes all beginnings, middles and ends. It is whole and complete with everything left out. It is both empty and full at the same time and outside of time. Are you getting the idea that your digital mind can't get there? Right, wrong and control do not fit with enlightenment, though they are a part of it, a tiny part, a hole in enlightenment so small that it lets little bliss out.

Subtlety is a key to recognizing ones enlightenment. You will never get better. Things will not get better. Quality of life will never improve. Everything is illusion. When you see illusion as illusion, you will see that you are enlightened. Paradox is a key. Disappearance of time and space is a key. Being perfectly unenlightened is a key.

Subtlety and Mushrooms

Now, go where you started to go in the last chapter. Get on purpose, on purpose. Get yourself directed and get down to business. You have to focus or you will never accomplish anything. Shoulders to the wheel, all together now, push. . . .

You see an acorn. It isn't really an acorn, not to a deer or to the eagle gliding overhead. But you had better call it an acorn because other members of your species do. It is an acorn to you, but the label doesn't really say much. Certainly it allows others to know generally what you mean. To get the correct answer on a botany test you have to call it an acorn. To a one year old child it is not an acorn. When Twinkle was 98 years old, it was not an acorn either.

Everyone called her Twinkle. The man at the Red Goose Shoe Store gave her that name when she was about 65 and it stuck. Twinkle has been playing solitaire with the angels for years, but still memories of her remain. People are often remembered for what they became good at. One of Twinkle's specialties was mushrooms. She knew hundreds of species of mushrooms well enough to trust her life to distinguishing which ones were edible and which were not. She had a passion for identifying them and was occasionally called by the local hospital to identify what type of mushroom a child had eaten so that proper medical steps could be applied. It took her time and experimentation to learn her subject. Twinkle had a library of books on mushrooms. She hunted mushrooms. She took spore prints. She learned to make finer and finer distinctions to appreciate the subtleties of different species and the variations within a species. She noticed the effect that rain had on the colors of some mushrooms. She delighted in her pursuit of learning about mushrooms. The more she learned, the more she discovered there was to learn. More than once she would get sick from sampling a tiny piece of a species she thought she had identified correctly.

Curiosity led her onward. In this learning process, there were not good or bad mushrooms. Good and bad are dualistic distinctions based on one side or the other of a single line.

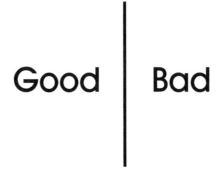

Good | Bad

During the process of learning, a person discovers many subtle distinctions and draws lots of lines for delineation. A person learns to perceive ever greater detail and continue to make observations which separate things between more and more lines.

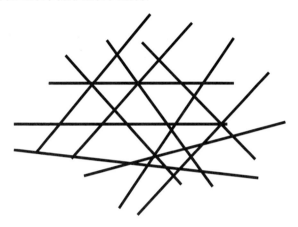

Making these distinctions and dividing the whole up into so many different groups leads to appreciation and perception of subtlety. It is called expertise. This pursuit of subtle distinctions leads to a profound appreciation and acceptance of the whole. Just at the point when everything is the most divided, it all comes together. A few distinctions, one or two lines drawn, result in simplistic (I'm right) or dualistic (good and bad) thinking, but in a complex system, these both disappear.

Twinkle delighted in any and every mushroom. Her preferences for one over the other disappeared just when they became the greatest. She took one thing, mushrooms, and learned to appreciate aspects of it that other people would not even notice. This, Twinkle accomplished by continuing to be aware and observant and by making ever greater distinctions even after her consciousness thought it knew all about mushrooms. She did not learn mushrooms because she was supposed to or for any reason. The study of mushrooms was her passion. Passion is the meaningless pursuit of knowledge for entertainment. Twinkle accepted and learned from all mushrooms. Passion is a function of acceptance. As Hegel said, "Nothing great is accomplished without passion."

As Twinkle got on in years, she returned to a childlike state of lacking distinctions. By the time she died, she didn't know the difference between a mushroom and a pencil. But the little smile she made if asked to do so betrayed that at some level she still knew everything she had learned and much more. Though Twinkle still had her knowledge about mushrooms, she could not become aware of it, so it was no longer consciously useful. Perhaps the only use her knowledge ever served was as an avenue for her passion.

You may not be interested in mushrooms. No one will ever know what inspired Twinkle's interest. What has one person collect baseball cards while another learns all the batting averages and a third learns Beethoven symphonies? It is the very process of thinking that determines these preferences. What would happen if people examined the process of thinking with the same passion and subtlety of distinction that Twinkle brought to her study of mushrooms? Mushrooms do not define who someone is and what is possible for her; thinking does. Explore thinking. Find out who you are, in a thinking sense. What makes you tick or not tick, scream, laugh, cry, get divorced or get married? Since it is your mind that makes you crazy, it may just be your mind that can make you sane.

In this pursuit of passionately studying the subtleties of the mind, you may get confused about who you are.

Given that you are not who you have always considered yourself to be, this confusion would be very appropriate and could be respected and appreciated.

Who are you? The thought arises in your head and you become aware of the thought. Since you will be drawing many distinctions and looking at this question from different planes of thought, you will not concern yourself with right answers. Rise above simplistic and dualistic thinking, all the way to passionate thinking. Accept every thought as an opportunity to increase your curiosity about thinking.

16

The System, 1-2-3

Life is as easy as 1, 2, 3—patterns, awareness and consciousness. The movement of these three determines the quality of life as do Multiple Illusionary Perspectives Per Second (MIPPS). The movement between patterns, awareness and consciousness is the foundation for flexibility of illusionary perspectives so essential for being able to separate yourself from illusion.

Patterns, awareness and consciousness can be illustrated at an atomic reactionary level. Patterns are the most primitive evolutionary step of the three; then comes awareness and then consciousness, with all three in a varying relationship to one another. The ideal situation is when patterns are constantly circling around with great variation next to awareness and consciousness, which are doing the same, with some overlap between the three so that they can exchange data, but no domination. Ideally, patterns stay on the move in search of new variations while limiting repetitious behaviors to a brief fraction of a second, casting only a shadow on awareness and consciousness. All three continue moving in space and through space at the same time.

Patterns, awareness and consciousness move independently, but when viewed from the outside, their movements are obviously related and intimately connected. Patterns, awareness and consciousness can be constantly on the move and continually bathed in the flow of nothing. Consciousness can watch the variation of patterns and derive enjoyment from doing so.

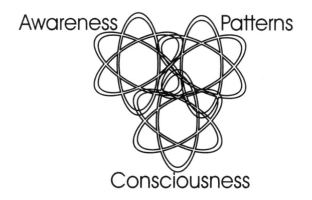

Awareness constantly uses the senses: sight, sound, touch, smell and taste. While consciousness uses the other senses: common, humor, and non. Absolute nothing flows freely around patterns, awareness and consciousness where there are no blockages. Since there is so much variation, patterns seldom completely block the flow of nothing, so awareness and consciousness receive enough nothing to avoid getting filled with something, consistently. Nothing purifies awareness. This purification allows the senses to recalibrate to a zero point so they can perceive with a fresh start each moment.

A lot more nothing than something is needed to keep the ideal arrangement described above. Imagine if your eyes had to retain everything they viewed. It wouldn't take long to clutter up your vision to the point where your seeing of everything would have you lose the ability to distinguish anything. Your eyes see by the grace of their ability to let go of what they have just seen. To use consciousness to reveal the present and return you to nothing is enlightenment. You are nothing. If you appear to be something, then this ideal arrangement between patterns, awareness and consciousness is not the one you have. The ideal arrangement, of nothing prevailing over something, is your natural state. It takes a lot of work and effort to forget this.

Most other mammals have a relationship between patterns and awareness that resembles the illustration below:

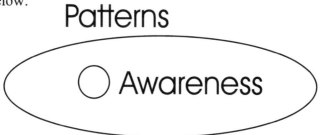

Other animals have no consciousness and a very limited range of patterns. The patterns they exhibit are so few in number that members of the same species are almost indistinguishable. Awareness is limited to the physical location of the animal. The whole animal can move, but the relationship of patterns encircling awareness remains stagnant. Working with dogs of the same breed will illustrate the similarities of patterns, especially apparent when compared with dogs of different breeds. An Irish

Setter is an Irish Setter. It stays young forever, will run until it falls over from exhaustion, has hunting in its blood, can learn but not easily, will delicately mouth an object without injuring it, but will guard terrain wildly. A German Shepherd is very different from an Irish Setter but much like another German Shepherd.

With the birth of consciousness, a balance was struck. To make room for consciousness, patterns gave up much of its terrain. Human beings were freed from the bonds dictated by patterns. But a patterned existence is very easy. A patterned human being can avoid the whole idea of responsibility. Patterned sufficiently, people can avoid all new thoughts, variation, and fear.

Thus far, this evolutionary experiment of the birth of consciousness has hardly even gotten underway. People long for the return to earlier, easier evolutionary steps to the extent that they ignore their evolutionary edge by having patterns overshadow both awareness and consciousness. But people are not programmed from birth to death like many pre-conscious biologically-patterned species and are able to adopt individual and culturally dictated patterns.

It is consciousness which is uncertain. In an attempt to enhance its importance, consciousness, which squeezes its way through the gaps between patterns, has taken the philosophical position that people are rational thinking beings; thus, they are not patterned like the animals. The result of this conflict between patterns people run and the conscious statement that human beings are not patterned, is blindness. Consciousness often doesn't see the very patterns it is oppressed by. It may see individual behaviors but misses the patterns they form. You often don't notice that you make the same mistake in different contexts or that you are repeating the behaviors of your parents.

After taking the philosophical stand that people are not patterned, consciousness took the precautionary next step of avoiding philosophy altogether. This second step was taken to protect itself from realizing the prevalence and influence of patterns. So, anything that smacks of philosophy is considered a waste of time. Get back to work on the assembly line and make yourself useful. There is work to be done and somebody has to do it. Time studies determine the most cost efficient ways to perform repetitious behaviors and assembly lines attempt to remove all consciousness, replacing consciousness with patterns. People who are good little robots can work the assembly line, but they do not then go home and become creative spontaneous beings only to arrive at work the next day and be patterned to death again. No, they take their dependence on patterns home with them and do the same things night after night so that they are prepared to go into work and do the same things day after day.

Newborn consciousness declared that people were not patterned like animals and then closed the door on philosophy so that no one would question this declaration. The next step consciousness took was more pervasive and costly than the first two and requires an action that no other species can take (again, reinforcing its separation from the animals). Consciousness replaced things and ideas with symbols to represent those things and ideas. Consciousness further declared that these symbols are filled with meaning. No longer requiring direct fulfillment or satisfaction, people can have symbols which represent these qualities. This ability, in fact compulsion, for meaning-full symbols has resulted in the invention of a catalog of meaning substitution—this means this. It is not enough to love someone anymore. Loving means giving him or her a diamond. Loving means marrying him or her and having a family. Loving means not ever having sex with anyone else. The list goes on, almost forever, and changes along the way to reveal what *loving* means, now. The dictionary is an extraordinary book detailing current meaning substitutions. It is a rule book, of sorts, which defines the basic verbal equivalencies used to limit what can be expressed and understood between people. Consciousness allows you to make the big jump from a chair to the symbolic letters C-H-A-I-R representing chair.

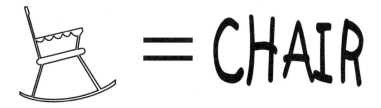

But any creature able to make this first jump can easily perform the next much smaller leap to believing that the symbolic letters C-H-A-I-R really do mean chair.

People made this leap with style and, at the same time, made the philosophical declaration, "There is no difference between the symbol and that which we, as Lords of Earth and Masters of the Universe, say the symbol represents."

People can now work for money instead of satisfaction. Money is valuable. Why? Because people agree that it is. The human race became prostitutes who would do almost anything if enough symbols were offered. At this point, people sold their patterns, awareness and consciousness to the highest bidder. People could no longer think for themselves. They stayed busy enough so other people wouldn't find out they were only getting symbolic satisfaction from the symbols of satisfaction.

Symbols took over and physical things became secondary. The need for anything whole or three-dimensional was eliminated because symbols required only two dimensions. People could justify all actions and reactions as long as they performed their crimes behind a big enough symbol. Life became two-dimensional, but everybody agreed that the symbols were important. So, they got even busier and no longer noticed their loss of depth. Anybody who didn't play along in this game of philosophical reductionism was ridiculed, penalized or taken out of the game. Nobody dared say that the emperor had no clothes, so everyone saw clothes or agreed that the emperor was wearing clothes because he said so and the people ignored the naked evidence and attended to the declaration.

Meanwhile, back at the ranch, people rewarded themselves for the patterns they claimed not to have and set up a patterns-awareness-consciousness relationship that resembled the diagram of other species. See the diagram at the top of the next page.

The flexibility and movement were squeezed out of this system as consciousness became obscured by patterns, the least advanced possibility. Patterns overtook thinking. People became predictable in the name of security. They

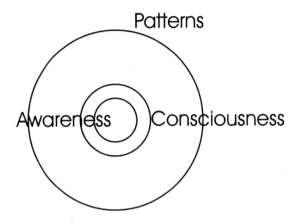

settled for symbols and shrank awareness down to the point where actions and behaviors could go unnoticed. Consciousness maintained a constant state of being obscured by patterns; it was thus blocked from the flow of nothing so that the same thought could repeat itself over and over with no variation and no recalibration. Patterns protected awareness and consciousness from nothing. Without the flow of nothing to refresh the sense of awareness, people repetitively saw only the content of their current pattern while they missed the possibilities which were flowing everywhere around them all the time. People in this predicament saw what they thought they should see, so they thought they were secure. Consciousness declared that human beings were not patterned, so people thought this bound up system of thinking was freedom and ignored all evidence to the contrary. When consciousness replaced awareness and awareness was obscured or eclipsed, people lost the present and made up the past and future. People fenced themselves into a world of their own thoughts, seeing only within themselves, while mistaking what was made up inside for what was outside. Personal illusion set up to battle the external illusion and make it look as much like the personal illusion as possible. The diagram below illustrates this:

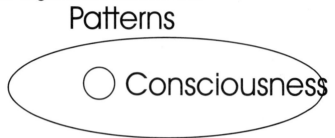

People had been given the evolutionary gift of consciousness, put it in the service of patterns and used it to restrict the sensory input from awareness to a controlled trickle. People had hidden from themselves in the only place they thought they could control—their own thoughts. Illusions had been built in illusionary minds. The building blocks of these illusions were the symbols originally used to save people from interacting with things. Secure within a small unsatisfying world of patterned creation, people locked themselves in and swallowed the key.

How does this scenario look when it is played out? It looks like a lot of people working longer and longer hours for symbols they don't even care about. It looks like people being terrified of other people. It looks like education becoming the stripping of all passion and play from children. It results in a world where people get bored and seek entertainment from the outside. Drug problems are on the rise as is sickness in such a world. In other words, it looks exactly like the world today. The result of the philosophical distortions that have been produced and then ignored leads to this world.

It isn't very pretty, and it is hardly even related to where you really are. You can't even see yourself because you are deeply in delusion about your illusion. The relationship of patterns and consciousness to awareness has resulted in a doubling down of your inability to observe yourself. If you can only see what you think you control, then you can only see what you have made up in your own mind, and that is a very small world indeed.

This may sound inaccurate or like bad news. It is neither. What has been done is what has been done. Where you are is where you are. Initially, as you begin to notice where you are, you will get an obscured look, since you have practiced not seeing for so long. You will see a truly ugly, crazy world inhabited by the scum of Earth. You will see a person so grotesque and ridiculous who is wearing your shoes and doing all of the things that you do. If you soldier on, continuing to observe and not looking away for a moment, your observations will soften. You will discover that what you have seen so far is all illusion. The ugliness looks real, just as the superficial symbols looked real earlier. Continue looking and embracing everything. Do not resist anything. Hold your observations close to yourself.

Anything you cannot embrace still justifies a part of your illusion that you have confused with reality. Embrace it all and you are free.

Have your ability to observe become your passion and have complete acceptance for every observation. You will discover that a lightness will start within you. It may show up as an occasional spontaneous laugh that won't quit. Not a laugh at anything, just a laugh. As you look, you will discover that maybe you are not as bad as you thought. Maybe bad does not even exist, except in the land of illusion and dualistic, two-dimensional thinking. As you seek to discover what is here, you will become lighter and lighter, laugh more often and smile all the time. Then one day you will exit the illusion, and from that moment on, life will be a delight and a pleasure. You will become a beacon. Not a lighthouse directing others away from the reef, but a bright light leading others through their illusions to their lightness and enlightenment.

Many times on your way to seeing your own light you will want to quit. You will become convinced that what you are facing this time really is real. Your mind will use whatever deception hooks you the most and makes you want to turn your head away. You will be tempted. If you turn, if you flinch, you will have to start your illusion destruction all over again from a point of greater illusion than that which you left.

Starting a diet tomorrow does not work because tomorrow never comes. Pledging to ruthlessly and rigorously examine the way you live, tomorrow, will not work either. Nor will turning away when the going gets tough. Building this illusion was not easy. Deluding yourself into this false sense of security took generations of miscommunication and deception. Evolution demands that you move forward. There are fossil remains of species that did not.

Good and bad are constructs of consciousness to aide you in the organization of symbols and the distortion of sensing possibilities. Thinking there is good and bad preempts observation with judgment. It comes from a model of thought that looks like the diagram at the top of the next page.

This represents the triumph of consciousness over everything, with patterns and awareness obscured. This is

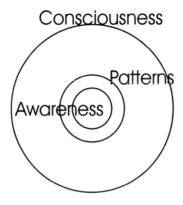

the model proposed by the you-create-your-own-reality movement. The only change from the diagram on page 119 is of labels (consciousness and patterns switched places), thus it is only a symbolic change. The symbols cannot sustain you; they can only contribute to your illusion and justify your insanity. You don't create your own reality. You create your own illusion.

Increase awareness and use consciousness to explore the world around you. Live out of the following configuration. It is as easy as 1, 2, 3:

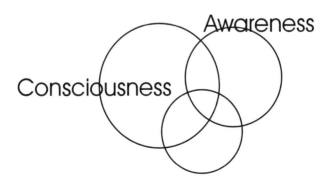

Initially, consciousness, teased out of the shadow of patterns, getting data from awareness, may not like what it sees. This is just a hook built in so you won't look. But, like the two-dimensional facade of the town on the movie set, don't let yourself be fooled by surface appearance which is always illusion. Keep being aware of your senses and let awareness and consciousness bathe in the flow of nothing and continue recalibrating to zero. Awareness is not better than either consciousness or patterns, but it was the first and most often oppressed victim. When awareness shuts down, automation and judgment takes over and craziness rules. Enlightenment gets further away while remaining here.

Patterns

"I will not repeat myself."
"What?"

What determines your patterns?
What determines your patterns?
What determines your patterns?

What determines your patterns?
What determines your patterns?
W h a t
determines your patterns?

What   determines

your   p a t t e r n s ? w h a t
determinesyour patterns? Whatdet

ermines yourpatterns?

Wha

tdetermines yourpatterns?Whatdetermines yourpatterns?

Wha

tdetermines yourpatterns?

NOT YOU!

What people usually refer to as "I or you" is some entirely undefined mixture of patterns, awareness and consciousness, typically limited to what people think on an ongoing basis. In other words, *who you are* changes as your perceptions change, as you learn, as life deals you experience and as you behave. *Who you are* is something that you cannot count on but think you ought to. Teasing out the differences in patterns, awareness and consciousness in "you" allows you to construct a much more accurate model of your life. Using patterns, awareness and consciousness to discover the relationship and purpose of patterns, awareness and consciousness in yourself contributes to growth by including in *who you are* the various parts that are arguing to be defined as you.

Awareness is present sensory data. Consciousness identifies, labels and performs permutations within a fraction of a second of your becoming aware of present sensory data. Consciousness is the phenomenon of personalizing the universe, with a purpose. Each purpose determines the extent of the distortion or personalization consciousness is required to perform. The greater the distortion, the more importance consciousness takes on in relation to patterns and awareness. It is not real importance because patterns and awareness continue to influence you, but this illusion of importance looks real when consciousness overrides awareness. Consciousness is able to convince you that the distorted perceptions are awareness and that illusions are real.

Patterns are self-determining. By attempting to teach a mosquito to sit, lie down or roll over, you can discover some consistencies regarding working with patterns. The higher up the evolutionary scale a creature is, the more opportunity it has to vary patterns. A dog can be trained: witness Pavlov or Lassie.

People deny the existence of patterns in things and in themselves. After all, people are supposed to be rational human beings with free choice, who continually exercise the impossible task of mind over matter. At the same time, people love patterns. A pattern, unnoticed, is behaviorally reinforced—the dance steps are repeated one more time. Discovering a pattern is like opening a magical door and finding what is behind it.

There was a man in the marketplace selling rugs. He set up shop in the same stall for many years and never made an abundance of money. But this was his occupation, so he kept on doing it. The man was oblivious of many of his own behaviors that were obvious to his customers. For instance, when he was at a fair price for a rug, he leaned his head to the right, when the amount was too much he leaned his head to the left. Purchase orders would have offered an objective process to his selling, but the personal contact this man had with his buyers ensured that his rugs sold cheaply. While discussing the price for a rug, his clients would wait for his head to lean to the right. When they saw the signal, the sale would be made at that price.

The man's wife was in a difficult position. She had watched him giving rugs away for years and knew how obvious the solution to his problem was. If she revealed her knowledge to her husband, they would become richer; however, she also realized that at the same time, he would become less obvious to her. It was a possible turning point for him because the tilt of his head was so consistent that people trusted it as their guarantee of his lowest possible price.

The wife, after weighing carefully the alternatives, decided it was best to live a poor life than a difficult one. She did not tell her husband of her observation. As the decision was made, her smile left her face. She did not notice its departure, but her husband did.

She was fond of cake, but being poor, she was seldom able to have it, so the wife tried various ways of indirectly getting around her husband's flaw. She would go to the market and send him away, in hopes of selling rugs herself. Her frown and her decision regarding her husband sealed the fate of this approach: nobody bought.

One day, as the man was bartering the price of a rug, a wasp landed on his right shoulder and stung him. Reacting, he jerked his head to the right and swatted his shoulder. The wasp was too quick. It flew from his shoulder and landed on his left arm where it stung him again. He instantly jerked to the left.

The customer was stunned. He reached in his pocket for several gold pieces and quickly bought the rug. The merchant was in pain from the stings, but he had great pleasure from making such a profit on the rug. His wife arrived at the end of the day startled to find most of his rugs gone. She quickly asked how much money he had taken in that day. He flicked his head to the right, quickly to the left, shrugged his shoulders and his wife smiled.

Anything can happen once, but when it happens again, it is the beginning of a pattern. The duplication drastically increases the likelihood that there will be a third occurrence. Superstition comes into play in that if you do something once and survive, you just might survive if you do it again. By the third, fourth, or fifth repetition, the correlation between survival and the repeated behavior strengthens. If the behavior is repeated often enough, consciousness may become convinced that the behavior causes survival.

How many times do you have to think a thought before you become aware of it? The answer is higher for some people than others, but what is common to all people is that they don't know because they are not aware of what they are not aware of. The smaller the pattern you can perceive, the larger will be your movement up the evolutionary ladder and the less likely it will be that you will repeat a thought or behavior just because it is a pattern. As you become aware of smaller and smaller patterns, your whole world becomes richer. Becoming obvious to yourself weeds out automaticity. You will smile more often and know where you stand less often.

Human beings can convince themselves of anything when they place consciousness in the service of patterns. The interplay between patterns, consciousness, and awareness can make you an evolutionary road sign indicating "The End Is Near," but this doesn't have to happen. The flip side of this human dilemma is that you are able to learn quickly and effortlessly. Often, however, you obscure awareness so that you don't know what you are learning, but you are always learning. You can't help it. What are you learning? Now that might be a question worth focusing consciousness on. The illusion of time was created for just such an endeavor.

Repetition produces patterns, and the temptation for repetition is always there. Patterns starve the body but the mind exists by them. Taking apart patterns by noticing, altering or eliminating them brings awareness and consciousness back into the flow of nothing and wakes you up. Living out of patterns continues to block awareness and consciousness while putting you to sleep. Simple variations like brushing your teeth with the other hand, or having somebody else brush your teeth for you, will alter a pattern and allow for more awareness. Search out the most patterned aspects of your life and change them. There is change everywhere except where people have attempted to exercise their control by overriding change with patterns. Discover your patterns and celebrate your discoveries by adding variation. If people were not patterned, they would pull their right pant leg on first about fifty percent of the time instead of every single time. If people were not patterned, they would put the telephone receiver up to either ear randomly, but they don't. If people were not patterned, they wouldn't be right handed or left handed. Picture yourself kneeling and flicking out your tongue for flies. The brain functions that are responsible for the survival techniques of a frog and a lizard are similar to the human brain functions responsible for patterns.

What determines your patterns? Survival influences first level patterns, while safety and security form second level patterns. These two levels are contradictory, because thinking you are safe and secure may have nothing to do with being safe and secure. Your ancestors, not very far back, were hunters. They were successful hunters; otherwise you would not be here. Even though the earliest humans had crude weapons, they still had an advantage over the animals they hunted. They had the ability to perceive and vary patterns. The hunter could watch the deer and determine its patterns with some reliability.

Mathematics is the science of determining patterns. Mathematics is used to determine where the deer will be and when, thus enabling the hunter to put food on the table with regularity. There would be no point in math if people were not patterned creatures living with other patterned species. A mathematician could probably and might even already have gotten a grant to determine exactly what the likelihood is of a deer taking a particular path on a given evening, factoring in the time of year, all prior behavior of the deer, food source, human activity in the area and many more variables in the process. Are deer influenced by daylight savings time?

Because people are susceptible to patterns, people are endangered. Patterns cut both ways, to the survival and termination of the species. A predator uses the patterns of an animal to get dinner, but becomes susceptible to another predator by its own patterns. A wolf may see the patterns of the deer, but in all likelihood it would be a much more successful species if it could see its own. Not seeing one's own patterns makes a species a sitting duck.

The roads on the way to work and to the store are paved so people will not notice how often they take them. The ruts and other indicators of the many travelers down the same paths are controlled to reduce variation and thus increase the likelihood of repeating the patterns. A diamond with no variation is worth more than one with a flaw, a variation. A car that has less variation, better machining, is worth more. People strive for consistency in the name of quality. Quality control is important to the control group and defines a whole branch of business. How do you get people to do the same thing over and over in the same way with the least variation possible? In other words, how can human beings systematically remove the main element which distinguishes them from every other species? People are helping evolution eliminate the human race as a factor, or species, on Earth.

Nature is an example of great variation and consistency. How many diameters are there in a tree? Millions. The variation is tremendous. Yet every year on a certain day, weather dependent but predictable, the sap begins to flow in the tree and the buds begin to open. The frogs start singing when conditions are the same as they were the year before. The swallows return to Capistrano. There is a mix of consistency and variation that results in survival.

Patterns are a constant temptation for people. Developing passion and drawing numerous distinctions are two ways to resist this temptation. Twinkle often walked over new terrain and through different territory because she wanted to find new and different mushrooms. She brought delight to seeing the same species of mushrooms and then making new distinctions about it. She would also thrill at identifying a mushroom she had never seen before. On one level, Twinkle's passion defied patterns and took her into new territory, allowing her pleasure in both the known and the unidentified mushrooms. But on another, it included patterns. Since mushrooms tend to grow on the ground or on decaying tree trunks, Twinkle seldom looked into the tops of trees, or up at the sky. She developed an interest in wildflowers and often saw them while looking for mushrooms.

There are levels of patterns—patterns of patterns, *if you will*. Twinkle had a pattern of pursuing knowledge. She also morally knew what was right or wrong with no shades of gray. Though she was entirely accepting of things with caps and stems she did not apply this same acceptance to people. She did not make many distinctions about people. She knew much more about mushrooms. Ironically, she was a teacher for many years. It would make sense that someone who was a teacher would know much about human beings, but this is seldom the case.

The more distinctions you can draw regarding something, the less patterned will be your behavior regarding it. Naturally, people love learning, and it is schooling that forces learning. Schooling locks the natural process of learning into patterns with an overriding assumption that there is a right and wrong premise operating and it is the teacher's job to determine which is which. Learning in young children mirrors Twinkle's passion in its process but not in its focus. Young children learn just to learn.

Applying consciousness to patterns is a dangerous business because consciousness itself can become patterned. Though these patterns are a step up from the biologically-dictated ones, they are also much less obvious, much more personal and thus much harder to see. When consciousness becomes patterned your thinking repeats itself, repeats itself, repeats itself, but you don't notice it. You become dull without knowing it. The record skips, and each time you think that what is, isn't. When a record is skipping, it never gets to the end, and when a thought is patterned, it never makes it to the completion of the thought.

Identity is composed of incomplete thoughts, thoughts that are stuck and standing still. These thoughts are comforting because each is so much like the one before it lulling you to sleep. When a thought gets stuck, you know who you are, of course. You are that thought. That thought is you. You become an evolutionary sitting duck quacking away, focused where you are not, unwilling to move and yet constantly on the go.

To fortify patterned consciousness, awareness must ignore patterns. However, awareness attending to momentary sensory observations can provide consciousness with sensory data about patterns. The wind in your head or unbalanced awareness is the antithesis of patterns. If you could see the wind, you would discover that the movement of the wind is determined by its purpose, which is to balance out the highs and lows. The wind is not influenced by the pattern of where it has flowed before. Patterns do not determine the wind; they are results of the movement of the wind. The opportunity you have as a human being is to be the creator of patterns rather than determined by them. You can become the appreciator of the flow rather than attempting to control the flow. You can become aware of everything rather than trying to figure everything out.

It is difficult to get a person to sit on command. The dog sits on command; that is a pattern the dog has learned. The person applies consciousness to the sitting down command and often refuses to sit when told unless consciousness can be convinced to do otherwise, by threat or by reward.

Stand up now.

Sit down now.

Stand up now.

Sit down now.

Don't just read these words, perform the actions.

Stand up now.

Sit down now.

Stand up now.

Sit down now.

If you went on with this exercise for about ten hours, your consciousness would go through many stages. It would at some point become obvious to you that you are not in control and that your failure to influence the simplest things has driven you into a world of illusion where you can think you control everything. Illusion. Consciousness battles patterns by becoming patterned. It overrides awareness by seeing only what it thinks is there. Consciousness becomes who you are, but it is not very becoming. It is static, illusion, and it provides you a status quo that you can complain about while maintaining it.

Thank goodness, thank God, thank your lucky stars and thank anything or anyone who will listen. Thank them that the illusion is not you. Thank your illusion as well and you may begin to see it for what it is. See enough of it and you will have had enough of it to lighten up. There is no illusion to defend. There is nothing to defend. You can include only compatible thoughts and things in your illusion, but without an illusion, you can include everything, and nothing, too.

Quality of Life

Patterns are an attempt to gain biological supremacy, as is the lack of patterns. But using consciousness to interrupt patterns can be an attempt at gaining legitimacy in the mind. The more often something happens, the more willing people are to accept it as true. This is a bias toward patterns which does not serve people; it makes them slaves. If something happens every time in a controlled laboratory experiment, it is called a scientific fact. When the same thought repeats itself in your mind, it gains credibility with you. After awhile you believe it. Belief is a thought with repetition or credibility. Often enough repetition is credibility.

Now step up a level and explore the unfolding of a pattern. How many times does something have to happen for you to think it is true? The number is variable, based less on the particular case at hand than on the person doing the thinking. The illusionary scales of thought tip from perception to truth as the number increases. For some fundamentalists, the number can be as low as one, two or three while the more cynical may require hundreds of repetitions before something is believed. This very phenomenon is exactly what the terms "fundamentalist" and "cynic" refer to.

Factor into this equation of quantity the variables of space in between occurrences and intensity of each event, and you will discover the patterns by which you become convinced in your thinking.

If you saw a purple elephant wander by would you believe you saw it? What if you had never seen a purple elephant before, and you were completely sober when it wandered by? What if you saw it again five minutes later and then twice more over the space of a couple of hours? You have now had four sightings of the elephant. Do you believe that it exists? During the next hour you see it another ten times. You have now seen it fourteen times in the period of less than three hours. Does the purple elephant exist?

What if you saw it at the same time each day for fourteen days; would you believe it then? What if you saw it for fourteen days at different times; would you believe it then? What if you saw it the second time with a friend of yours who saw it, too; would you believe it then? What if she didn't see it but you did; would you believe it then? What if you heard other people talking about having seen a purple elephant too; would you believe it then? If you saw the elephant yourself and then heard on the radio news that other people had seen such an elephant; would that help you to believe it? What if you saw it on the TV news after seeing it in person; would you believe it then? What if the date that you saw it was April 1; would you believe it then? What if the Pope said that he saw it and that it was real; would you believe it then? What if your horoscope suggested you would see something big, unusually colored and alarming that day, and then you saw the elephant for the first time; would you believe it then? What if twenty scientists verified your sighting of the elephant; would you believe it then? What if you had five liberal democrats with you when you saw it and they all saw it too; would you believe it then? What if you had five conservative republicans with you who saw it; would you believe it then? What if a used car salesman told you that he saw it; would you believe it then? What if every used car salesman and lawyer in the land said that he or she had seen a purple elephant and then you had a sighting too; would you believe it then? What if only people who voted for Nixon saw it, and you didn't vote for Nixon but you saw it too; would you believe it then?

In other words, what does it take to convince you that something is true, and why bother? At what point do you buy the illusion so that it becomes reality, for you? In each of these cases, you probably knew whether you would believe it or not. If you didn't know, go back and really do the exercise. Your answers are of less interest then your discovery that you must always have an answer to every question and that you assign a level of accuracy to that answer based on certain patterns of thinking.

What part does seeing play in believing; what part hearing and what part feeling? Are other people important to whether or not you believe something? What part does time play?

In the world of illusion, influence plays a huge role. Since you are nowhere in your illusion, the point that you can perceive yourself to be can change rapidly. When changes are perceived to be happening too fast, your illusion is in jeopardy; after all, you built it to protect yourself from change. If your illusion doesn't protect you, then what is the point? In the world of illusion you can count on anything, but nothing is worth counting on. Illusion does not support and defend you; rather, you support and defend your illusion. Instead of providing you with energy, illusion consumes energy. On the surface, illusion seems to provide security. This security is rendered at a great cost to you (time, health, humor, and perspective among other things). Ironically, you are the one who spends all of your time and energy providing your illusion with security by giving attention to or resisting your thoughts.

During the past decade, many people ate oat bran. After a single study was completed involving who knows how many people, an indication was revealed that oat bran was one of the best foods you could eat. The structure and presentation of this report convinced the supposed experts that the results were true. The experts, in turn, convinced the media, and oat bran turned up in many people's homes. A study wandered along next reporting that the claims made about oat bran were false.

How much of what you think is superstition and how much of it is real? What do you think is real? Do you think that there really was a guy named Jesus Christ? Did he ever eat oat bran? If you believe that there was such a man, was he the product of a virgin birth?

Your mind, since it is an illusion, can believe anything. But what determines what your mind believes? There are patterns which determine it, as illustrated earlier. Remember, patterns are one of the three evolutionary steps available to human beings. When patterns determine what you think, your thinking will be consistent because that is the very nature of patterns. It may not be consistent at the level of content, what you believe, but it will be at the process level, how you believe it. Beware of consistent thinking.

When consciousness is overshadowing awareness and patterns, your beliefs will be determined by your criteria (layers of what is important to you). You will believe something if it is a good thing to believe or if it is the right thing to believe. You will become the moralist basing thought on judgment rather than repetition. In this case, patterns are often lurking behind the scenes. Do you think that abortion should be legal? Is it all right for a person to kill his or her spouse if the spouse is in terminal pain and asks to be killed? Do you think that people should eat more apple pie? Do you think that it is acceptable for pesticides and chemicals to be in the food you eat without your knowledge?

Using judgment to determine truth leads to the importance of the mind. It leads to more and more thinking, the collection of ever greater amounts of evidence and a pursuit of both larger and smaller frames of reference. Judgment is a numbers game. The more people think something, the easier it is for people to think it again. Culture arises out of a thought that has been repeated often enough by many people. Culture is the set of rules of engagement between members of a group to alleviate the necessity of treating any member of the group individually. Fear and terror of individual people is usually a prerequisite to the forming of a culture.

The most eventful and obvious aspects of thoughts, beliefs and judgments are that they fly in the face of awareness, reducing awareness and closing people off from their senses. The purpose of science is to relieve people of the need to trust themselves, or anything for that matter. Taken to its logical end, science will remove all trust. It is acceptable to prove what you cannot see, but it is not all right to see what you cannot prove, unless you call what you are doing religion, whereby a leap of faith is necessary and important in proving your faith. The rules and exceptions are enough to boggle your mind and keep it very busy, which is exactly what happens when illusion rules the day. The more thinking you are forced to do, the more real the mind looks. The mind was invented to think and so the very act of thinking reinforces the thinker.

The idea that your thinking is not real is contrary to culture. In relation to the incredible speed of the flow that occurs in nature, thinking is a slow process which seems to be a threat to consciousness. You have some six hundred muscles in your body, and to walk down the street, you must coordinate most of them simultaneously. Thinking is not fast enough to perform this miracle called walking. Almost every waking moment of every day, just such miracles are occurring, and yet perceiving miracles is a threat to thinking.

Science and religion are in an ongoing battle for your attention, your thoughts and your beliefs. The very fact that both of them need attention so badly should be your clue that they are insecure little illusions themselves, illegitimate offspring of the mind itself.

The deer does not care whether it eats Kosher or not. It does not care if the flag gets treated with respect or that its mother is not violated. You can't prove anything to a deer, so there. It is you and that illusionary little rascal the mind that have made up all kinds of games that constantly push against the imaginary line (drawn by the mind) between what is real and not real. If you look to the mind for reality, you will never find reality. You will find something that supports the existence and supremacy of the mind (a fictional entity). It cannot be otherwise. Whatever the mind perceives itself to be will be held up by the mind as important.

What do you consider important right now? What causes would you be willing to die for? What causes would you be willing to live for? Notice that the mind would be much more willing to die for something than to live for something. The very idea of death lends credibility to the mind. Ideas of death are made up by the mind, and anything made up by the mind serves one purpose—to make the mind important. Somebody will jump off the Golden Gate Bridge to his death if he has convinced himself of it being his route to salvation. Setting yourself on fire for a cause is a final act of consciousness, as judge, determining life or death.

When awareness is the primary influence on the mind, you get animalistic behavior without explanation. Seeing, hearing and feeling are more important than judgment. The very idea of this is not pleasing to the mind and yet this is where the roots of science are. Science originally needed sensory verification; it doesn't any more. Numbers are not sufficient to prove anything, and numbers always, to some degree, bring you back to patterns because they are based on variations of repetition.

Working with a group of school district administrators, it becomes clear that this group of people gets paid to judge other people, students and teachers. When doing sensory-based exercises, they get more and more tired and less and less willing to participate. When asked to simply verbalize what they observed that twelve members of a jury would also observe, the administrators' senses were all but overshadowed by their judgments. Constantly complaining or simply folding their arms and refusing to continue, they asked, "What is the point in this? What will this exercise do for me?" Consciousness seeks to know what the point is. "What is the reason for doing this? How will it make me more important?" What the school administrators found so disconcerting was being objective without adding their subjective importance.

The very idea of importance requires that there be a lot of conscious determining of what importance means. This traps people in a loop of mind importance. To the senses nothing is more important than anything else, and the highest criteria is change. People usually notice what has changed in a situation and then immediately compare the change to something familiar. Consciousness, when it attempts to control and judge things, has to avoid noticing change. Change is a threat to the stability that consciousness pretends exists.

You need your senses: without them you are likely to be run over by a bus. But you need consciousness and patterns as well. If you are reading this, you are still alive, and if you are still alive, then some of what you are doing and thinking is working. Thus your very existence argues for what you have done up to this point. The existence of anything outside yourself makes the senses important. But what makes consciousness important? Nothing nearly so practical. Consciousness is presently being used to turn people into little Hitlers. People attempt to use consciousness to control, to judge and to determine where they stand. What is the point? That is, what is the point they stand on?

The further down the evolutionary road they travel, the less attention need be spent on survival and the more variation can be tolerated. Consciousness is not at all necessary for survival; thus it is wasted and squandered. People use it to attempt to discover their mental location. People are obsessed with the location of thought. Consciousness will likely be the death of humanity. The current use of consciousness is adding little to life other than suffering and pain. With consciousness, evolution took a large turn in the road. For the first time on this planet, pain, suffering, pleasure and delight became possible. Does the happiest or the saddest person have a better chance of surviving? Who knows? You may be too busy suffering to find out. Consciousness has opened up a whole area of uncertainty regarding existence. What is the purpose of existence?

Does a person who knows what her purpose is live longer and multiply more than one who doesn't? It doesn't seem so. Then, what is the evolutionary point in determining your purpose? The turn that evolution took is toward quality and away from just quantity of years and quantity of offspring. People then pitted themselves against the whole idea of survival of the fittest and stated that they were interested in the survival of every body, or at least everybody who agrees with them.

What relation does quality of life have to species continuation? Just recently a movement has begun consisting of people who are claiming there is such a correlation. There is an attempt to establish a relationship between longevity and quality. What if the people with the happiest or most fulfilling lives the longest? They would be the most likely to produce and influence offspring and thus people would evolutionary be forced into becoming an ever-happier species. This change would not be noticed over a year or two but over several generations. Are people happier now than they were two hundred years ago?

I think you would have to come to the conclusion that there is not a flow in this direction. But any species that can perceive its evolutionary direction would be the first one to do so and would have, in fact, to some degree, begun to *be* providence rather than bowing to providence. Done successfully, people could preempt extinction, but would it be useful to do so? Perhaps evolution is one of those things that serves a purpose. Perhaps not.

What do you think? And does what you think matter? To you? To anybody else? It certainly influences the whales and every other species who shares the planet with human beings, but it doesn't matter to them. Matter is a human trait.

Does what you think really influence the quality of your life? Can there be much doubt? What you think is the cause of quality of life. You can think anything, and the subset of everything you think is what is defined as quality of life. People die by what they think if they are convinced they will. If they are certain that since their parents and their grandparents had some genetic disposition to something, it is more likely they will get it too. What people think has become all important, often more important than life itself.

People say life is sacred, but they buy and sell it everyday in the marketplace. The very act of working is selling one's time, and from your perspective life is made up of time.

Perhaps evolution has offered consciousness as a temptation, just as sticking to one source of food, with an

ever-shrinking environment to provide that food, was a
temptation to other now-extinct species. What people will
do with consciousness is an evolutionary question. Will
they use it to judge and attempt to control things? Or will
people use consciousness to enhance the quality of their
lives?

What is quality of life? Hopefully by now you have
learned that it is not a new car every two years and one
more TV set, though people still often pretend that this is
quality. Tying satisfaction to things, a more basic and less
flexible product of reality than thoughts, leads quickly to
people becoming victims of things. To discover what
quality of life is, all you need to do is look for the people
who are the happiest and having the most fun with the
least suffering. Once you have seen it, it is difficult to
discount that little smile on a guru's face. The grin that
never leaves and is not dependent on circumstances. It
seems that people have very few models for quality of life,
unless you define quality of life as absence of pain and
extreme suffering. A lowly definition indeed.

Quality of life has nothing to do with community
service or ownership. It has to do with the ability to be
entertained and enjoy each moment of life. If this
entertainment is context dependent, then people may have
to damage the environment to get it or get in the way of
someone else's entertainment. The more you can be
entertained by, the less you need to control. But the shift
to recognition of people as enlightened comes about when
people recognize themselves as the creators of quality, of
entertainment, in their own minds.

"Move over. You're blocking my view of the screen!"
you yell as the person enters the theater late and comes
between you and the comedy unfolding on the screen.

If you need something, anything, for your entertainment, then you are a dependent. If you need that entertainment, then you become an addict. Neither of these situations contributes to quality of life. The obvious answer is to become your own source of entertainment, to create your own delight, your own light. To become enlightened.

After all, the mind is an illusion, thus whatever it creates is also an illusion. What kind of an illusion have you created? You can answer this question by examining what you think and how you think. Is the glass half empty or half full?

Thinking doesn't make things true. The mind doesn't care about truth. The shortest route to the maximum entertainment is to lose your mind, not your whole mind, but the seriousness with which your mind perceives itself. Let the existence of your mind go for a moment. If, to begin with, your mind does not have to prove that it exists and, secondly, that it is important and, thirdly, that it is all that exists, then it might be free to get on with some fun. Fun and entertainment disappear when seriousness and proof move in.

You have nothing to prove that your living will not prove. What you say about your living will not matter as much as how you live. What you think about your living will not matter as much as how you live. Thinking came along afterward. It always comes along later and tells a story about what happened, based more or less on the evidence it finds at hand. What is the purpose of the story your mind tells? If its purpose is to prove that you are right and/or that other people are wrong, which is typically its purpose, then you are bound to lose, and your quality of life will always be in doubt. You will neglect certain evidence that does not prove your point and dwell on that which does. In other words, consciousness, as judge, will rule over awareness. If, upon arriving at the scene, your story contributes to the flexibility and fun of other people who will arrive at the scene, then you probably were entertained by whatever you found.

Selectivity does not lead to entertainment. Inclusion does. Whatever you cannot include threatens all you can include. Though you can ignore this threat, it does not go away. There is a persistence of the whole. Wholeness will always win out in the end, and so by fragmenting anything, you create a separation and put yourself on the losing side. The moment you forget that anything and everything you think is illusion, then you have something to prove. When you have something to prove, you begin on a downward spiral where you exclude more and more. The quality of your life decreases as you have to push what you exclude in front of or behind yourself, keeping it so far away that you don't see it. You must gather what you can include (what proves your point) around you and hold it very tightly, never letting it go.

You become an obstruction to the biggest flow there is, as you fight for the importance of one thing over another, in a world where nothing really matters. All that matters is nothing. It would be bad enough and restrict entertainment sufficiently if all you had to do is prove that something was better than something else, but your job doesn't stop there. You have to prove that a particular something is more important, bigger, stronger, or more powerful than anything else. Worse yet, you have to prove something is greater than the greatest power there is, nothing at all. You circle the wagons defending what isn't, illusion, in light of what is, nothing. Fear takes over and the whole idea of quality of life becomes a luxury. Since you don't want this to happen, you redefine quality in ever-more lowly terms. You stoop to conquer and lose happiness, delight, and ecstasy in the process.

Enlightenment is always closer than your next thought. It is a light within you and it cannot shine without you. Either you bring the light to the party or it does not seem like a party. If you go to the party hoping to find the light there, fear will take over. After all, you might find the light and you might not, a predicament which, without trust, results in fear. If you bring the light with you, it will always be there. How do you bring it?

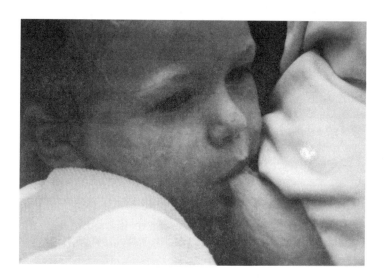

Happy Because

What makes you happy?

You could probably list a number of things, all of which, upon closer scrutiny will be seen as restrictions of your happiness. To put the question another way, under what circumstances and with what will you be happy?

Nothing makes you happy. Nothing is all that can ever make you happy and all that ever will make you happy. Things can only provide you with a state you call happy, which at best is a temporary distraction or absence of sadness.

Cause and effect is a tool of the mind. On a large scale, it is an attempt by the mind to make things predictable, but at the same time, it oppresses the mind endlessly by the conditions which exist outside of it. If you think something causes something else, then you are not the cause. You are to some degree the effect, which makes you a victim.

Like other elements of the mind, cause and effect on the surface seem to make sense and be useful. After all, if there were bugs on your potato plants and within days the leaves died, it may be useful to figure out how to keep the bugs away before planting the next crop and find out if the potatoes live. If you are the only potato producer and there is no other food, then this is a matter of life and death. The mind will seldom admit it, but for the mind, everything is always a matter of life and death. So you get a pesticide and kill the bugs on the potatoes. You get potatoes, but your pesticide runs off and kills all the fish in your lake. You have now traded potatoes for fish. This is not a trade you meant to make but it is the result. You controlled those bugs, the potatoes, and the fish.

What appears to be cause and effect from one perspective may not seem so from another perspective and may seem entirely different from a third. Anything that is dependent on one perspective is not real and is food for the importance of the mind.

"Hold still you critter." You dig your heels into the fresh dirt in an attempt to make the cow slow down. Finally she does, you wind the rope around her legs and flip her over. In this position, as she bawls; you brand her. Now the cow belongs to you.

When you purchase the property you get a deed, a piece of paper letting you and other people know that this little piece of dirt is really yours, bought and paid for.

Cause and effects are the way you personalize and legitimatize your illusions. They are the way you convert what really isn't into what really appears to be so. They are a tool to turn your limited perspective into general perspective so that you are justified in holding it. They are your brand, your stamp of reality.

As a species, people are going down for the second time, drowning in their limitation of perspectives. Getting a bigger perspective will not save them, nor will a smaller one. People need to learn to adopt, nurture and feed various perspectives at the same time. The very root of humor is holding two absolutely opposite perspectives at the same time. When you do this, you see yourself.

Most people adopt a perspective and hold to it. It looks like this:

As long as you argue for and attempt to prove or validate your perspective, you lock yourself into a certain position regarding that which you are trying to prove. You prevent yourself from adopting other perspectives. But the payoff is worth the price—your mind gets consistency and the illusion of control. Remain standing in the same place and things will look the same to you. Cause and effect is what lets you know where you stand based on something outside yourself.

If you can adopt, hold and nurture both your present perspective and the opposite of your present perspective, something magical happens. It looks like this:

Since nothing is real and everything is illusion, then we can simply complete the magic of this picture by removing something unreal from it. You get this picture:

Thus, when you adopt opposite perspectives and hold them at the same time, you see yourself. A moment of revelation. Enlightenment. This is the triumph of paradox over reason and, at the same moment, entertainment over control. Instead of arguing for one perspective, now you have perspective on yourself. Instead of standing somewhere, you notice that you are standing nowhere. This is magic. It is magic you miss if you are watching the magician's right hand, one perspective, or his left hand, another single perspective. It is magic that is available each and every moment, and all you need to do is adopt opposite perspectives on the same idea, issue or object.

What stops you from partaking in this kind of humor and delight is having to know where you stand. If you have to know where you stand and/or you have taken the philosophical, meta position, that there are better places to stand than others, then you are stuck. You become endangered evolutionarily. The grim reaper will know where to find you. You are that guy or woman who could have been anywhere, could have thought anything but are instead stuck with one position. You have stood your ground by attempting to make everything and everybody in the whole world acknowledge that your position, if not the right position, was at least your position. A compass will tell you direction but not location. Location you must decide for yourself. Would you rather be everywhere or just one place? Would you rather be everything or just one thing? Would you rather be everyone or just one?

How big you are and how wonderful your life is depends not only on your perspective but on your perspectives. The more perspectives you can include the more likely you are to reach that magical one, seeing yourself, and from then on you always have the opportunity to play.

It is important in the perspectives game to hold several perspectives at the same time. If they are separated by time, then you may just drive yourself crazy. The mind only wants one perspective at a time and cares little what that perspective is. When you give it two or more perspectives at the same time, it expands beyond its imaginary limits and shows itself as unreal. As unreal, all possibilities open up and you join reality. Since you are reality, the honesty overwhelms you and you laugh and laugh and laugh.

Paradox Between

Most human effort is spent keeping the poles of paradox apart. The balance of human effort is expended setting up housekeeping in the illusionary space between the poles.

"Is it good or is it bad?" Is it good to kill your child? No, unless your child has a tremendously painful terminal disease and will be dead in minutes anyway. Is it good to live a long and prosperous life? Yes, unless in doing so you exterminate millions of people. You are taught that things are not black and white, that the gray areas in between are where to live. This is certainly true, only there are really no gray areas between. The poles of paradox are a first order distortion, and all other distortions live in between them. Where there is no room, one is confined, cramped, and stifled. And there is no room at all between the poles of a paradox, or between any apparent opposites. Opposites are the best of friends, they belong together and it takes a tremendous amount of effort and ignorance, ignoring, to live between them. To live anywhere, in illusion.

Imagine a teeter totter for opposites. Make the poles of this particular opposite good and bad. Right in the middle is the balance point, not too good and not too bad, where most people live.

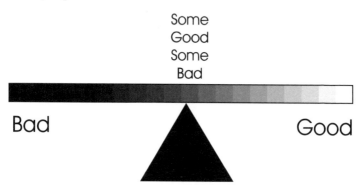

This is a statistical teeter totter with a bell curve distribution of people around the center point. For each person who gets a little worse another person gets a little better. This maintains the balance. Most people are near the center and everyone who is not attempts to move the center point to where she is. Identity is derived from location on this imaginary continuum. As with everything else connected with thought, there are two sides with illusion in between. A sandwich without sustenance.

There are two positions to consider; where you think you are on the continuum and where you actually are. For most people, these two are different, this difference drives a wedge between consciousness and awareness. You think, consciousness, that you are one place, but if you were to use your senses, awareness, you would discover you are in another, or find that the continuum does not exist at all. The greater the wedge between consciousness and awareness, the more you must dominate the other and the more offensive you become to anyone with a smaller gap. If your consciousness and awareness are far apart, you offend almost everybody. You live in your own made up world and have no room for anyone else. If they are closer together, you have the ability to befriend anyone. Closing the gap between these two is a worthwhile, but not a direct, process. When working to balance illusion, things seldom are what they seem. Thus you cannot work on what it appears you should be working on. Figuring out where you should work to produce a desired result somewhere else is the full-time balancing job you are wasting your evolutionary gift of consciousness on. People waste their lives in these meaning-full pursuits.

Where you think you are on the teeter totter carries less weight than where you actually are. Where you actually are requires a measure of your behaviors by consciousness. Remember that all the people in prison are innocent. Well, not really, but a lot of them think they are, yet in many cases their actions landed them in prison. It is the nature of human beings that all actions are justified. People consume consciousness in justification. They justify in an attempt to have themselves appear good. The worst crime of all seems to be when someone does something terrible and does not even attempt to justify the act. Then culture does the justifying by stating that the person was not sane and promptly proceeds to prove insanity.

When you think you are on the teeter totter, you must constantly monitor both where you are and where other people are. You must strive to move the center of balance to where you are because that makes you right for being there. Since this whole thing is a pack of cards, as illusionary as can be, there is only illusionary movement, illusionary balance and illusionary satisfaction. The system is hollow and empty, because the points of a paradox or opposites are actually one, inseparable, with only illusion between them.

People derive their status from where they are on this teeter totter. They define themselves by where other people are, and they talk endlessly about where the center point really is and where it ought to be. They lament that the point is not where it used to be or that things might get even more out of balance in the future. Politics is about a place on the teeter totter; it is illusion to the core.

The tension set up between people at different points on the teeter totter is what keeps the whole system going. The people who are opposed to nuclear energy need the people who are in favor of it to keep the whole system in balance. Taking any position at all, ever, is arguing for the reality of the illusionary teeter totter. The main purpose of the teeter totter is to let people know where they stand, to maintain the illusion that they are in control.

The whole game falls apart if you can have two very different points at the same time, MIPPS, because then you reveal the illusion. When you expose an illusion, you become entertained by it rather than defined by it. You can play and have fun on a teeter totter until there seems to be a right position to have the teeter totter be in; then you have to work for that position, and if you ever attain it, you must stay still, keep up the balance and not move. People love hating people who appear to be on the opposite side of the teeter totter from themselves. It makes their position appear better, justified.

Religion, politics, nationalities, all social divisions and social groups have their own teeter totter. They define themselves by where they reside.

If you define yourself by where you are in the balance of things, on the teeter totter, then life will have its ups and downs. You will be up some times and down at others. The basis of the whole game is that if you are up, then somebody else is down. If you get down, then someone else is up. In the illusion you can only win at somebody else's expense. It is a zero sum game, balancing at zero, which pits you against every other person on the planet. This may not seem so, but extending the game to its logical end, it has to be. The teeter totter is finite, you can only get so far out before you are too good or too bad. You deny, and point at, the extremes in order to support the middle. People who are too bad are killed and those who are too good are revered, while those in between think they are really very good for not being either. Are you a saint? You probably don't think you are that good, just good enough. You may wish you were better than you are, or perhaps even a little worse because maybe you are a little too good.

No matter where you are on the scale, there is always work to be done. There is always balance to strive for and people who need to be helped or pushed down. You are jealous of somebody who is too good because she makes you look bad. This whole thing is crazy. You have to dislike the people who are better than you and be afraid of the people who are worse than you. That leaves you with only the people who are on the same level as you, and they are not interesting to you because you are not really interesting to yourself. The whole scale, the whole system, is a scam. It is created to keep you occupied and let you know where you stand. Without it you might not stand anywhere, you might disappear, or notice your enlightenment. On the teeter totter you are defined by everybody else.

You can leave the teeter totter, but remember what happened on the playground? Whoever got off the teeter totter let down all of the other people who were still on it. If you don't act as though the illusion is important, you will be unjustified and, thus, a threat to everybody who is still in illusion.

The illusion is addictive: the more it defines where you stand, the more you seem to lose by letting go of it. You must vote. Voting is good. Voting is a way to have your voice heard. The propaganda is rampant as you are seduced from every angle to get on the teeter totter . . . to join the war for balance . . . to right the wrongs of the world that can only be righted if the center point is at a certain political dogma.

One way off the teeter totter is to wiggle around on it a lot. Never be in the same place twice. Move from the right side to the left side until you cannot even tell what side you are on anymore. Since the purpose is to find out where you stand, if you alter where you stand often enough, the game loses its purpose. This brings us back to MIPPS. The way to move around on the teeter totter is to vary your perspective. Change your opinions, change your thoughts and ideas, the moment something looks real, move on. People make things appear real by repetition and agreement. If you don't repeat and don't agree (remember that disagree is the same as agree) then you will be able to move through your illusion.

Illusion is hard to give up, especially when you think it is real. It is unlikely that a non-swimmer would give up a life preserver in the middle of the ocean, unless he had a good enough reason to do so. In this case, there is not a good enough reason and it looks crazy to get off the teeter totter since it has defined so many people before you. It is the very life preserver you are holding which keeps you on the verge of sinking. If you let go of the life preserver, illusion, you will not drown, you will be free. To let go of your life preserver you would have to trust in something, trust without doubt. You would have to have faith in something that is not a part of the illusion. If you have faith in something that is a part of the illusion, you will just gather more evidence for the importance of staying on the teeter totter. Rationality and logic will never lead you to let go of the life preserver. Rationality and logic are good at playing the mock balance game; they are the two main players. If you get out of the game, there will be nothing for them to do. If you have to understand or have a reason to get out, or if it has to make sense to you, then you will not get out. Very few people will quit something they are good at because they begin to define themselves as that thing. "I would rather die than…"

Two men are drowning, going down for the second, the third time. There is a rope between them. The good man holds on to the rope until the end.

People have associated themselves so thoroughly with their rational, logical thinking that they cannot escape from the game in any direct manner. People cannot get out by getting out. In fact, the way out is often by getting further in. Judgment is the basic operating system of the teeter totter.

Attempting not to judge will never get you out. But if you judge more often then ever, always judge, constantly judge, then your judgments begin to mean less and less. They lose their importance. Then judge even more. You will find that every judgment weakens the one before it. The judgments get their power by repetition and if you continue to make more and more different judgments, the repetition disappears. The way out of judgment is by embracing judgments.

A way off the teeter totter is by mastering it (disappearing apparent differences which compose the teeter totter). Master it. Be able to encompass the whole teeter totter rather than limiting yourself to a certain position on it. The more you judge, the more subtle your judgments will become. To judge even more, you will have to learn more, and as you learn, you will make ever more subtle pronouncements. When you get subtle enough, you will escape. You will just find yourself out of the illusion and all judgments will disappear. This probably doesn't make sense. If it did, then the solution would have become part of the mire of the mind that defines itself by your illusion.

When you are on a teeter totter, you can play. But if you do not know you are on a teeter totter and think any perceived imbalance is real, then you must struggle and fight to retain balance. You must work, stay busy and strive for balance. Thus you can avoid nothing and attempt to get everything in order. Control! You, the master of the universe, must finally get things where they ought to be. Balance everything.

Imbalance is your best friend and remains your best friend no matter how much you try to avoid or ignore it.

Control Group

The point of control is to control everything—at least, that is its logical extension. Enlightenment is including everything and controlling nothing. Nothing doesn't require control. You are not in control now, so you are already enlightened. The extent to which you consider yourself to be in control, or out of control, equals the extent to which you do not perceive your enlightenment.

Control is an infinitely long, impossible road. It is analogous to lining up everything in the universe end to end to end in one really long straight line and then keeping it in line.

Enlightenment is having everything exactly the way it is. Obviously, enlightenment already is and control is where you want to get to. Enlightenment is infinitely easy in a perfect universe such as this. Control is infinitely effort-full and at war with everything.

You cannot control everything at once, so you have to go about it one thing at a time. What will you control first? After all, it is a big universe.

Strangely, where you start is with controlling yourself. You do so by attempting to figure out who you are, and you do this by determining what you should not do. Defined by limitations at an early age, life becomes a matter of closing down by degrees. Your parents, well meaning as they may be, attempted to teach you your boundaries— what you should do, but particularly what you should not do. If they were like most parents, they did this at a basic pattern/reward level (you can't hide from B.F. Skinner). If you did something they wanted you to do, they either briefly praised you or ignored you. If you did something they did not want you to do, they showered you with attention and said you should not do that and you should have done this. Attention, the only reward that matters, was doled out for the performance of "bad" behaviors more often than for "good" behaviors. This is as it should be because your parents had to keep you in control. The easiest way to control something is to limit what it can do, where it can go, what it can say, and who it can be with. You were controlled from very early on, and you learned to define yourself by limitations.

The universe is virtually unlimited, and who you have defined yourself to be exists by the grace of limitations. The idea of such a limited creature in control of such a gigantic unlimited universe is ridiculous, but seemingly necessary. If it were not necessary, then everybody would already have noticed his or her enlightenment.

Control requires that you step away from your ability to be aware of *how things are* by making a picture or having a conversation in your head about *how things should be*. The next step takes you even further down this infinitely-long, impossible road. You attempt to make the world outside yourself look like and fit in with the "how things should be" world you make in your mind. Your preoccupation with grouping, comparing, labeling, defining, structuring, classifying and isolating the world outside yourself is an attempt to shrink reality into manageable pieces to fit your "how things should be" model of the world. You must fragment all that is into some of what is.

You make up an order of things, and things must be in order. Your job is to get them there.

Frogs: Frogs are green, or sometimes brown, things that often live in water and are much smaller than a bread box. They often have webbed feet and swim the frog kick (see frog kick). Your interactions with frogs shall be limited. When you are young, you may chase them or delight in watching and listening to them. When you are older you may eat their legs in a restaurant or read to your children about them. Frogs eat insects (see insects), which is a fairly disgusting thing to do. You should not eat insects. There are many behaviors that frogs elicit which you should not, but doing the frog kick is all right, just not as efficient or mainstream as the flutter kick. You must not speak to frogs, though they have ears. You may listen to frog sounds on summer nights or laugh at the sound of a bullfrog's deep, low, funny croak. In the north, you may use frogs as a sign that spring has arrived, but don't listen to them too much because they have nothing important to say. As a young child, you may carry a frog in your pocket, but as an adult you will become highly suspect by doing so. The whole idea of attempting to catch a frog, such fun as a child, is below the dignity of an adult because adults are more sophisticated and have to think before they move, and the frog just moves. Consequently, frogs are so much faster than people are that people look silly attempting to be superior to frogs while sloshing around unable to catch them. There are other rules about frogs and many ancillary definitions and exceptions, but this is the basics of what frogs are and what your relationship to them ought to be.

Now, you pick a subject and figure out the limitations you and other people have defined regarding it. What is it? What is your relationship with it? How should you behave about it?

Language is the divisional, fragmentary tool used by consciousness to define its relationship to everything. Language creates illusion. People say what something is, and in doing so, they define what it is not as well. People then assign meaning to these definitions and deal with them in an attempt to avoid dealing with the thing they define and limit. It is easier to control what is said about a frog than the frog itself. Language builds a box to put the frog into, a box the frog cannot possibly get out of, since the box exists only in perception. The limitations, or boxes, that define a frog live in people's heads, and most people keep the frogs in imaginary boxes tucked away neatly and predictably. The frog in your mind is not the same as the frog in the swamp, and the box that you create is not able to confine anything but your own interactions, thoughts, and perceptions. But if you can convince enough people, or at least yourself, that your box of limitations really defines, or confines the frog, then it must be true, and you have one thing controlled.

You pay people for controlling things for you. The chiropractor gets paid for controlling your back. You pay the botanist, agronomist, or farmer for controlling the plants. The better someone controls something, the more you pay her. The more a person attempts to control the better you pay her. The President of the United States is supposed to control the direction of the country and even determine what the country is, and he gets paid accordingly. But you also know he cannot do what you are paying him for, so you don't trust him. To trust him, you must overlook almost all sensory data and attend to how you want things to be rather than how they are. You must do the same with every attempt to control.

Consciousness, as controller, eclipses awareness to convince you that you are running things. The moment the eclipse occurs, you become responsible for what is happening. To perceive yourself as in control, you must consider yourself, at least at some level, to be the cause of things—a deity of sorts, literally. But the moment you consider yourself "cause," you must stop looking at effects. To run or control something you cannot requires you to ignore how things are and to notice how you think they are. This separates you from all that is and makes you an ally of all that isn't. All that is becomes a constant threat to all that isn't, so you get scared, but you don't admit your fear.

Control means to limit the possibilities of something to the point of knowledge and predictability. Since reality is the mathematical computation of all possibility, control is the opposite of reality. Control is the systematic limitation of possibility with the ultimate goal of reducing all possibility to one possibility—certainty. When you attempt to control, you make yourself an enemy of reality.

Language is a tool of control. In order to run things, you must discover who you are so you will then be able to explore your relationship to those things you must control. You define yourself. The more you define yourself, the easier it is to be certain of who you are, but the more difficult it is to control things because, in the process of clarifying who you are, you increase the quantity of who and what is not you. You define yourself by limitation. When you have too much to control, you become important, and busy. Defining yourself is getting rid of the *fine* in you. The better defined, you are the less fine you are.

"How are you?"

"Fine."

"Well, define yourself."

Assertion—Declaration

"I am a male." That means you are not ranked with 51 percent of the population, females. "I live in Wisconsin." That means you are not part of the majority of people who live outside of Wisconsin. "I am self-employed." That means you are not a member of the group of people employed by somebody else.

You claim to belong to certain minorities. You give evidence for each of these limitations to prove your membership. Defining something is always limiting. But you can't work with something until you have defined it. Anything that escapes your definition obviously escapes your control, and you can't have that, can you? Anything you say you are excludes everything else. "I am a male who lives in Wisconsin, but was born in Illinois; I am a writer who is married and has two children. I used to be a stockbroker with Shearson Lehman Brothers. I have published four books so far and have not watched TV for the past five years." With each *assertion* of who you are, you define, limit and group where you belong and where you do not belong. You define minorities that represent you until you get down to an isolated group with only one member—you. You are a unique individual once you have defined and limited yourself sufficiently. Some definitions are more limiting than others. "I am male," only eliminates about half of the population while "I am from Wisconsin," eliminates far more and "I used to work at Shearson Lehman Brothers," even more. Control is a matter of exclusion. One of the ways you exclude is by using the linguistic statements called assertions.

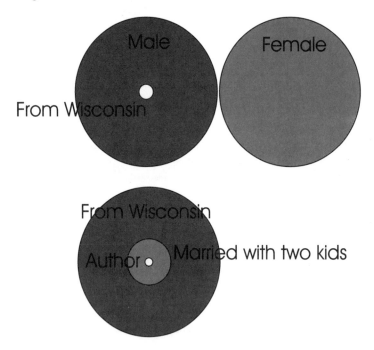

These drawings look more and more like bulls eyes. They define the precise person "Who I am," in superficial terms. With enough of these definitions, enough limitation can be conveyed to pick an individual out of a line-up. In other words, this process identifies "Who I am" sufficiently that you can think you know a person. It defines and limits an evolutionary niche and increases the likelihood of extinction, since the species which is the most content dependent is the most vulnerable. The more you exclude, defining yourself, the further you get into illusion, since reality is all inclusive. As you surgically cut possibilities out and discard them, you become alienated from reality. Ultimately, you must include everything and make peace with all you have excluded so that any exclusion you make along your way pre-determines all you will have to bring together later. You are constantly making more work for yourself by excluding, while seemingly making less work for yourself.

Making assertions is one way you limit yourself. Assertions are considered facts because evidence can be given for them. It could be proven that, "I used to work at Shearson Lehman Brothers," by old business cards and income tax records and by talking with the branch manager, other brokers and clients. Working there is an assertion because evidence can be provided to back up the statement. You don't need to trust the person speaking; you can trust the evidence instead. Assertions require you to look at the evidence, not trust.

An entirely different linguistic statement, much less limiting, is a declaration. A declaration requires that you trust the person speaking to be an authority, at least to some degree, in what is being discussed. There is no evidence for a declaration. Evidence is the foundation of an assertion. Declarations are used subjectively, without verification.

Declaration: "I like being an author." This puts you in the group of authors who like being authors as opposed to those who do not or those who do not care one way or the other about being authors while separating you from all the people who are not authors.

Declaration: "I am tired." This isolates you from the group of people who are anything but tired.

Declaration: "I don't make enough money." This separates you from all the people who perceive that they do make enough money. It has nothing to do with the amount of money being made.

Assertions are attempts to define who you are while declarations are attempts to create who you are. Assertions have to do with quantity and type while declarations have only to do with quality. Assertions tie you to things while declarations return you to yourself. When the difference between the two becomes unclear, you either think you control the whole universe because you say so (declaration), or you become the victim of the universe (assertion).

When you confuse declarations and assertions, which is almost always, you confuse quantity with quality. Logical levels get blurred when you deny yourself as a creator and become a reactor. This moves you from consciousness to patterns. "I live in Wisconsin" (assertion) is not your fault; it is just a fact. Changing your assertion would require a different definition of state lines, a lie, or a move—the expenditure of energy, effort, time or displacement would then have to take place. Assertions refer to things, preexisting conditions. Assertions keep you busy.

Saying, " I would be happier if I lived in Colorado than I am living in Wisconsin," is a blend of assertion and declaration. The distinction between assertion and declaration is lost in the blend along with the identity of the speaker. Listen to yourself speak. Listen when you are making assertions and when you are making declarations.

"I like living in Wisconsin," is a declaration. To change this, all you would have to say is, "I don't like living in Wisconsin." Now, stating, "I don't like living in Wisconsin," does not make it true—truth is an element of assertions. Can you be trusted if you say, "I like living in Wisconsin," to create yourself liking living in Wisconsin? In other words, are you the authority of whether you like living in Wisconsin or not? Assertions can be verified with the senses and evidence. Declarations are creations of consciousness and can never be verified at all.

Assertions relate to things while declarations have to do with your perspective on things. Declarations are how you create yourself and assertions are how you find yourself. The difference between the two is the difference between cause and effect. When you confuse assertions and declarations, you confuse cause with effect. Neither exists, but both seem to, and you will behave very differently depending on whether you view yourself as cause or as effect. Both cause and effect are illusionary, but by learning the difference between declarations and assertions, you can discover yourself as creator of your illusion rather than just reacting to it.

Scrape far enough down and you will always discover yourself as a creature of declarations. If you appear to be the effect of something, just keep looking deeper, and at the root you will find yourself as cause, creator of your own perceptions. Along with consciousness comes your ability to declare. It franchises you to compete with God.

To perceive yourself as the creator. What it also gives you is the temptation to confuse that which you have created with what you have not. Go deeper into your illusion, much deeper, and you will discover enlightenment.

Cause and effect are both illusions. Declarations create illusions. Assertions report on illusions. Illusions are always perspective dependent, requiring you to stand at a specific location at a specific time and at no other location at no other time. They then also mandate that you see in a certain way. For cause and effect to exist, there would have to be some objective position to view from. There is no such perspective, and when you think there is, you claim your limitations are real. Everything is subjective and relative, and the moment you think it is not, you are deceiving yourself. It is this sort of deception that allows you to attempt to prove your control over things instead of declaring it. Or even easier, declare that you do not need to work for control over anything and that you don't need to know who or what you are.

A man stood looking out a tenth floor hotel room window in Chicago (not a door and not in New York) thinking himself quite powerful. He noticed a car moving slowly down Michigan Avenue and decided to have it turn right at the next intersection. He tried as hard as he could to have it turn. Luckily it went straight, otherwise he might have convinced himself that he made it turn. In a flash he realized he made it go straight by wanting it to turn. The next car came along and he attempted to have it go straight, but it turned. Now he had the system figured out—he had to wish for what he didn't want in order to get what he did want. He carried that principle with him for the rest of his life.

One of the wonderful and awful things about human beings is that if they want to believe something, they can. People can believe anything. There he was directing traffic from the window of his hotel room. Yet even in this there is hope. He realized that the easiest way to control the cars was to have them go where they were going and not go where they were not going. Ah, you might say, that is not control. Control is having them go where they are not going because then you will know you did it. And that definition of control has you work very hard in all different directions, not because you want to work, but because you want to control, and the only way to do so is to have things be different from how they are. It is your need to know that you are in control which keeps you so busy and so crazy.

If you have to have things different from how they are in order to know you are in control, then just wait a moment because things always change. Sometimes the change is very subtle. Control has to do with determining how things will change and having them change in some way that they were not going to unless you had an influence. Heisenberg taught people that they cannot help but have an influence, thus to find out how you controlled things, look at how they have changed and learn to appreciate the change rather than trying to grossly effect it or direct it. The more subtle your appreciation for change, the more you will perceive that you influence what happens, without effort. The greater your desire for control, the less subtlety you will be able to perceive. When your appreciation for subtlety is infinite, you will control everything, and everything will be just as it is, as perfect as can be. Enlightenment!

Learn to tell the difference between assertions and declarations. Determine what you create and what you merely react to. This is not a real distinction but it is a useful one. Taking apart illusion often requires identifying different elements of that illusion. Since confusing assertions and declarations went into the construction of your illusion, untangling the two will relieve you of some illusion. You have built a huge illusion, thinking it is real. As you discover that declaration is at the base of your illusion, you will identify yourself as much more than your current limitations. You already ARE the one who thought you were discovering who you were (assertion), while making up who you were (declaration).

You are laying the track just ahead of the train called "who you are." Frantically, you must continue to lay the track, or you will get run over by who you are that you don't think you are.

You are laying track, making illusion for a vehicle (you) who does not need track. You are restricting your own movement and ability to think in order to know where you stand when you already stand everywhere. Traveling without track seems risky, but it is much more interesting and it is what you are doing already despite illusions to the contrary. Cause and effect is moving around inside the train rather than influencing the track being laid or not. Control is riding the rails of your own design (that seem to be real) or attempting to stop the movement.

When you have an underlying declaration that you are your point of view and that you need the point you're standing on (or think you are standing on), then changing, or worse yet losing, your perspective or point of view looks like death.

When a declaration is running things, consciousness is eclipsing awareness. Declarations are one of the tools used to prove existence and define relations. When assertions are important, patterns are running things, and you are a victim of the universe, or at least of anything outside of your control.

When you make an assertion you are speaking about something which has already been controlled. When you make a declaration you are stating that things are still in process, that there is work yet to be done.

After the horse is broken, you can use it: you can ride to town or round up the cows. The broken horse is at your service. Anything you think is true (assertion) is already broken and at your service. There is something about the wild horse which brings out the best in you. The process of breaking the horse is exciting and unpredictable. You don't know what will happen; it is dangerous and you could get hurt. There is fear involved, and it is that fear which is exciting to you. When you are tackling something, fear turns into excitement. When you are running from something, fear turns into terror. The tame horse is useful, but it isn't fun. You have little respect for the tame horse but you will continue to feed it, use it and work it. When it is old enough, you will give it a gold watch and turn it out to pasture. But you will always be more interested in the unbroken, wild, free horse. The horse which will not be broken occupies your thoughts while the domesticated one is forgotten and taken for granted.

Your mistress is always more interesting than your spouse; otherwise, you wouldn't bother with her. What you don't know and don't control drives you onward, making life worth living you assert. Assertions may seem useful, but they are not exciting. Declarations are the wild unbroken horse, but only if you know the difference between the two. You are the creator of illusion. If you think you are not, too bad for you. Which would you rather be, the broken horse, working day after day, or the unbroken one, free to roam and master all he sees because he does not have to control it? The work horse must move the supplies from town to the ranch in a safe manner. For the wild horse there is nothing to be done.

The difference between assertions and declarations is the difference between oppression and freedom. Which do you want? Which do you have? If your assertions and declarations are different, then you are like most people, wanting things to be other than they are. You must then keep working to bring this about. You are a work horse. If your assertions and declarations are the same and you want what you have, then you may have settled for domestication (resignation), or you are lying to yourself about how things are (denial), or you are consistently blissful and free (enlightened).

Domestication-Eclipse-Freedom

If you think things are the way they are, then you have a successful relationship between consciousness and awareness. If you think things are the way they ought to be, then consciousness and patterns are in sync. But if you think things should be different from the way they are, then you have bought into the company line, and you will have to do a lot of work. Your primary career becomes that of a change artist, a controller, but first, a pontificator. To start to work on things, control things or change things, you must elevate yourself to the position of a "knower"— one who knows how things are and how they should be. In effect, by pretending to be cause, you have then raised yourself to the level of God.

To know how things are and how they should be, you must be greater than those things. Thus you must be greater than the universe. From this arrogant position, created by declaration, the most likely event is that you will fall. If you fall, the most likely outcome is that you will hurt who you perceive yourself to be, and the most likely outcome of that is that you will then have to dig in your nails and pull yourself up by your bootstraps to the same lofty position you fell from.

Humpty Dumpty sat on a wall (your illusion). Humpty Dumpty had a great fall (the loss of illusion). All the kings horses and all the kings men couldn't put Humpty together again.

You fell once when you started putting illusion together—from grace and perfection. You must fall again when illusion is at its zenith, when you really think you are in control. You will fall back into grace, enlightenment, but not as long as illusion is mistakenly held on to as reality.

You can only attain a lofty position on the wall in your own mind, by thinking that your thinking is important. Symbolically, you raise your level of importance along with the size of your illusion. You become dependent on thinking. The more you think and the harder you think, the more importance you put on thinking, and the more likely it is that you will delude yourself into the position that provides the greatest likelihood of a long fall.

If you are going to determine what position you are in, through perceptions, what would have you make it the most precarious position possible, the one with the most to lose and only illusion to gain? Justification must triumph over the light, or you would never find yourself in the strangest of places, repeatedly. You would never find yourself where you do.

If you think things are the way they are, then things have to be some way, which they are not. Things are always every way. If you think things are every way, then you are in touch with reality, the mathematical computation of all possibility, and there couldn't possibly be anything to do. If it already is, then it isn't yet to be, and there is nothing for you to do.

Basically, with thinking, you are damned if you do and damned if you don't, "damned" being defined as the blocking of anything. This could be broken down into smaller pieces, but who wants something that is already broken?

Assertions describe things domesticated to the point that they can be counted on, and declarations describe the rest. When you lose sight of the difference between the two, you confuse where you think you stand with where you do stand and your thinking becomes reality for you. But only for you. You then have to defend reality, your reality (illusion), against everybody else's reality (more illusion), and against any possibility that might not fit your restrictions. You must consider people crazy who do not accept the same assertions you do and fight to have other people adopt the same declarations you do. The way to change a declaration into an assertion is by repeating it to yourself and convincing other people to adopt the same point of view you think you have. The moment you adopt a point of view, you deny all other points of view and declare war on them. This isn't easy, but it is your job, whether you know it or not. Assertions reduce the need for awareness and move right through consciousness to patterns, receiving labels on their way through consciousness. But they do not reside in consciousness; they are just passing through long enough to get labeled. Declarations live in consciousness and strive to become full-fledged assertions, on their way to becoming patterns.

Your mind seeks to become a primary effect of reality rather than a creation of its own—thought dependent.

Declarations are the foundation of identity when you do not perceive yourself to be your patterns or perceptions. Assertions are the foundation of identity when you are a thing. When you use assertions to identify yourself, you ignore the evolutionary step of consciousness. You become automated and demean yourself in the way that you demean anything that is not you. You handle and manipulate and try to make yourself in your own image as you are attempting to make everything else in your image. You can stop this process when everything in the universe looks just like you. That is the ultimate in control and fear reduction. Another word for it is Hell.

Do you own yourself? That may seem like a ridiculous question, but it is a relevant one. You claim you cannot own people, but you can own other species. "This is my dog." You even devalue your spouse by asserting, "This is my wife," or "This is my husband." But you look at yourself so little that you never say, "This is my me." You assume control of your dog and your spouse but not of yourself.

If you could begin to watch how you limit yourself, you would discover that you are your own worst enemy: you are the greatest foe of your own stability. You are in the way of controlling and providing consistency for yourself. It is you who is flexible and variable. It is you who could think anything, but don't. It is you who pretends to have limitations while claiming you don't have any limitations. It is you who is everything trying to be something specific and "good." You are in your own way, blocking yourself from noticing your enlightenment. This would be an uncomfortable thing to admit, so you lie about it and blame everything else for your current perceived condition. Ignore the perceiver and attend to that which is perceived.

If you see a cow fenced in, your response is probably different from your response to seeing a deer fenced in. After all, the deer is a wild animal and the cow is not. Are you a wild animal?

How many generations of deer have to be fenced in for you to think they are naturally domestic? Or is it the ratio of domestic deer to deer that are not fenced in that convinces you?

Are people more limited now than they were a hundred years ago? Your Congress certainly hopes so; that is why it passes so many laws. Look around at your friends. Are they fenced in? Do they do the same things day after day with little variation? Are they predictable even in their attempts at spontaneity? Do they watch TV at the same times, do they eat the same sorts of food, do they have a favorite restaurant, sport, or hobby that they repeat endlessly? In an attempt to make yourself predictable, something you were never meant to be, you have domesticated yourself. It is unlikely that you would do the same things over and over, go into the same work-place and repeat behaviors hundreds or thousands of times unless you were longing for an earlier, patterned evolutionary step. You have stepped backwards into domestication, into patterns. Thinking is unlimited, and you have used it to limit yourself. You can think anything, but what you can do is limited. How many people define themselves by what they do?

Doing is one little segment of control. It is the organization of one little piece. Moving from how it is, or was, to how it should be, you simulate control. Controlling and doing require you to declare that things are not the way they should be. The basis of all doing is the declaration that things are not as they should be. A species arrogant enough to make this declaration has to ignore evidence and attend to consciousness over awareness. A result of this shadowing of awareness is that you cannot even see the patterns which are overshadowing both consciousness and awareness. The line-up of your automated, domesticated sleep is something like this:

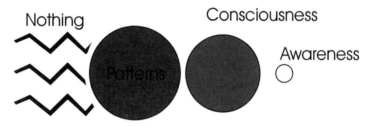

Thus you cannot see that you are patterned. You can only think you are patterned, but you will not think you are patterned because your thinking is patterned not to think it is patterned. To you, thinking is everything, as patterns dictate and domesticate you. You do things the same, in patterns. But you think you do them differently. If you want to prove this to yourself, sleep with your head at the foot of your bed, brush your teeth or shave with the other hand, or talk twice as fast or twice as slowly as you normally would. When you do these things, you will experience a momentary escape from patterns. You will have done something outside of your patterns, and you will wake up a little bit. This is how waking up looks:

You never were your patterns, but the patterns continued to run. As you wake up, you can see your patterns and thus alter who you think you are. You can notice that you were and, to some extent, still are your patterns. This is not pleasurable information to receive because it is not pleasant to discover that you have been demeaning yourself, but it is necessary in order for you to stop doing so.

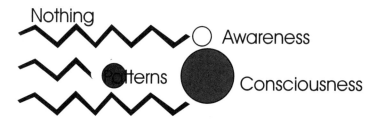

It is one thing to claim domestication by another species, person, or idea. It is quite another to be domesticated by yourself. Too embarrassing to be bearable. From the former, escape is much less revealing. The latter revealed is enough to make you a little sheepish. People often do not see that which they wish were not there.

As you vary patterns and become aware of more and more of them, you will awaken. You will become aware of a more interesting and varied world. Your consciousness will, at least partially, escape from patterns, and you will start to have creative original thoughts.

You will begin to interest yourself and the universe will become more fluid for you. You will make more observations and fewer assertions. You will continually discover that you are not who you think you are. Your illusion will shrink and become less consistent. You only build an illusion to make who you thought you were consistent and secure. When you discover you are not who you thought you were, more becomes possible for you. The more possibilities you have the closer to reality you get and thus the more delightful and less fearful your life becomes. As patterns diminish in importance flexibility increases. You smile as you do things you would never have been able to do before and you adopt perspectives you never knew existed.

Patterns had you think the same thing over and over, but you don't have to now. You surprise yourself. Your thinking expands and as it does so the importance you put on it shrinks. You begin to discover who you are by your expansion rather than your limitation. Control becomes a thing of the past as you learn to appreciate all of your perceptions rather than preferring one over the others and attempting to have it prevail by repetition. You glimpse what life can be beyond patterns, beyond fear, and all the way to lightness. This is not yet enlightenment, but it is flexibility and pleasure.

Where You Stand

"Flight J-E-R-R-Y to tower. Come in tower."

"Tower to flight J-E-R-R-Y, I read you."

"Why did the chicken cross the road?"

"Tower does not have time for questions, just answers. Go ahead flight J-E-R-R-Y."

"Flight J-E-R-R-Y requesting permission to land. I am low on fuel and need a place to land as soon as possible."

"Tower to flight J-E-R-R-Y, where do you wish to land? Over."

Where do you wish to land, indeed? This is not a rhetorical question. Where do you wish to land and where are you? Space may be the final frontier, but space also accounts for a large portion of what human beings consider themselves not to be. There is a lot of space which you are up against. When people declared they could not be in more than one place at a time, they had to determine where they were as distinct from where they were not. This required mathematics, and here you are. Where?

There are two possible ways to determine location. You can determine where you are by where you say you are, which is a mental location, or you can determine where you are based on your relationship with objects, a physical location. Tending toward materialism, human beings have settled on the latter, and being as exclusionary as they are, they discounted the former. In a moment of utter insanity, you gave up the ability to determine where you were within yourself and put all of your references for location outside yourself. You called this moment of insanity "clarity." Human beings would have to call it that, given that they lost themselves as thinking beings in that moment and brought the race down to the level of just another *thing* on the landscape.

You didn't know you were doing this, and had you known, you wouldn't have cared because you were answering the very basic question, "Where do you stand?" The question needed an answer, a concrete answer, so badly that you were willing to give up anything for a common way to answer it.

"Where do you stand in relation to what?" was a relevant question, but it got answered so fast that you never noticed. Anything that was big, imposing and noticeable by many people came to define where they stood. And where you stood became associated with who you were. Initially "on Earth" could have been an answer, but Earth was too big a measure to seem useful. "By the big mountain," a much smaller description, conveyed enough more limitation that you were secure, and limited, with that answer. Naming things became a compulsion. "I am in Buffalo, NY, at the corner of Third and Vine," really lets people know where you are.

Upon identifying your physical location, you were haunted by the absence of a mental location. If your thoughts were really going to be so important, you had to know where they were, too. Philosophers didn't help much because they were too complicated for everyday use. So much of your day was spent depending on physical location that mental location seemed a luxury indulged in and left only to those philosophers.

The idea of a mental location and physical location are fundamentally different. In a mental location, it is much more obvious that you make up the points of reference whereas physical location appears to require at least one point of external reference. For most people, this reference requires dealing initially with the sense of sight.

To know where you are externally, relationship is necessary. There must be the deep philosophical break between you and something that you declare not to be you, a building perhaps. You have taken this split for granted so totally that even saying it seems a little ridiculous. The fact is that you are not separate from the building, but you ignore that because it lets you know where you stand. The diagram at the top of the next page illustrates this simple calculation.

There you are, and there is the teepee. Now you know where you are in relation to the teepee. This may not seem too important, but remember, if you did not know where you were in relation to something else, you would be lost. And you can't have that, now can you?

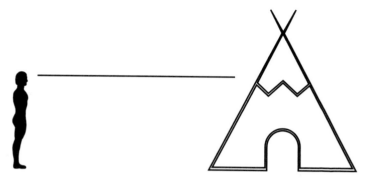

Initially it was enough to know that you could see the teepee from where you were. You depended on the teepee for your very existence, since knowing where you stand seemed so important. Direction came next as you noticed that the teepee looked different depending on where you were standing. If you stood in front of the teepee, you could see the door. If you stood behind it, you could see the hand-painted deer. To either side, you had various views of the teepee. For days you walked to different points around the teepee noticing how different it looked. This was entertainment in one of its simplest forms.

Once, as you were walking around the teepee, having a good time, you walked away from it a little. The teepee shrunk. Wasn't that funny? It didn't even look big enough for you to walk into. You walked closer and it got bigger again. So distance must be important, since size was dependent on it. This teepee was even more amusing than you had thought at first. Distance was created so simply that you didn't even know the complicated calculation you were performing. You had done your first triangulation and invented geometry in an instant. You used your eyes as two points on a triangle and the teepee as the third point, thus being able to determine how far away the teepee was, like this:

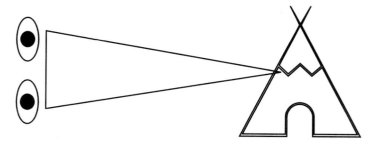

When you did this, you clarified just how far away you were from something by using mathematics. At the same moment, you limited yourself drastically because any mathematician will tell you your measurement of distance is limited by the distance between the two points you use to make the observation. Your accuracy became limited because your eyes were so close together. You gave up accuracy for consistency: at least your eyes stayed about the same distance apart wherever you went, so you always had a base unit of measure. This was very useful for hunting. You could shoot an animal where it was rather than where it wasn't. This meant more food and less wasted effort.

The same triangulation you use with your eyes applies to your other senses. Your ears are a bit more accurate in that they are further apart than your eyes (hopefully), but this increase in accuracy is reduced by the difference in speed between light and sound. The Womdas from Ursa Minor can't tell where things are because they look like the picture on the next page.

With one eye and one ear, the Womdas have not been able to determine where they stand externally, so they have accomplished a kind of balancing act, triangulating between senses in a way that would make you proud to be a human being. Things that you take for granted, such as walking

down the aisle in the grocery store, are entirely impossible for them; they would bump into everything. But they have adapted very well with a sight-sound connection that does not delineate between the two. The Womdas communicate by sending pictures and sounds at the same time and have an internal reference based on kinesthetic, a strange thought for most people.

A digression, perhaps. In the kinesthetic sense, your most accurate triangulation takes place. In the case of eyes and ears, there are two points of triangulation, but with the body, there are millions. The more calculations that take place, the more accurate will be your determination of location. Also, with your body, one point of a triangulation can be your big toe while the other can be the top of your head, thus the points can be farther enough apart to increase accuracy. The wisdom of the body arises from this increased accuracy in determining where it stands. If you want to know for sure where you stand, then use your body to find out.

Another interesting, but very much overlooked, point regarding your senses is that your kinesthetic sense is the only one that can do a triangulation without leaving home. To reference with your eyes or ears, you need an external point to focus on, often making that external point more important than yourself. But with your body, you can triangulate, say, between your foot and the back of your head with your navel. In other words, your body provides you depth which your eyes and ears can only simulate using an outside object. Your kinesthetic sense, the most discounted and dishonored sense, is the most relevant. That is not surprising. Given that people attend to illusion all the time, why not attend to it with their least efficient senses? That way, they are less apt to discover their illusions.

Think for a moment of how little interest people take in their bodies. They feed them lousy food, make them do repetitious work. They tell them that soon they will get burned up or thrown into the cold cold ground. They expect them to age and never look better than they did at an early age. They hold impossible figures up for how the body should look. They apply the visual sense to the body, thinking that how the body looks is more important than how it moves. They ignore so many of the wonders that the body does: standing up, sitting down, walking, waking, smiling, falling over.... The body does so much and gets neglected in return. The very idea of focusing on what the body looks like is applying a two-dimensional sense, sight, to a three-dimensional entity, the body. This is demeaning, and it costs you useful data. How would your life be if you liked your body the way it is rather than thinking that it had to be different before you could possibly like it?

Life would be different in at least two ways: 1) you would get better data about where you stand 2) you would be able to move more effectively. You could escape the mode that most people are in, which is that the body is perceived as a necessary evil, a vehicle to move the mind around. The body is not real, but it is closer to reality, at least in one direction, than is your mind. The closer what you attend to is to reality, the more accurately you will be able to navigate on Earth without running into things, or having to control or change them.

Running into a thought is just not the same as running into a tree or a bus, but people act as if the thought is more real and important. If you can reclaim your body, celebrate your body, you will know where you stand from within rather than outside yourself.

When you perform a triangulation, you know where you stand physically. But how do you know where you stand mentally? What and where are the points of a mental triangulation? If you have the thought *chair*, internally, without seeing a chair, where is the chair? Where are you in relation to the chair?

These may seem like odd questions, but they are relevant. If you see the chair outside yourself, you do the external, physical triangulation, but when you see it in your head, no triangulation takes place. There is no depth in your mind, and there are no set points of location. Thus, thinking can never let you know where you stand, except in relation to illusion. Where you stand on the issue of abortion is very different from where you stand in relation to the chair. Ironically, people often think that where they stand in their minds is more real than where they stand on Earth. In nature, nothing flat exists. There are very thin things, but no flat things. In thought, everything is flat because there is no possibility for triangulation without an external object, thus no depth. Thought is fundamentally superficial by its very nature. Using thought, you have to create illusion to imagine, to know, where you stand. This is not bad unless you don't know the difference between a chair three feet in front of you and an imagined chair in your mind. You must treat the two differently in order to be effective on Earth. The more important you make your thinking, the more the difference between physical and mental vanishes. You lose your body, in thought, and end up walking around or sitting on imaginary chairs, indignant when you waste your time or fall down.

Remember, the purpose of consciousness is to provide you with multiple illusionary perspectives. To the mind, which is an illusion, illusion will look real and reality will look like illusion. The moment you make illusion real, you lose your connection with everything while thinking that you have finally arrived at a point of clarity. Illusion is nothing at all, but it is called everything. This is too big a lie to live comfortably with. It is a lie which must be protected and defended. Most people have confused reality and illusion and are crazy while thinking they are sane.

The road of difference, which started when you needed to know where you were in relation to your teepee, continues to the point were you lose all things and depends entirely on what you think. You kill people who do not see your teepee the way you see it. If things were not so serious and you could use your body to let you know where you stand, where you are, you would be able to free your thoughts to explore where you are not. If you could focus awareness on where you are, you could use consciousness to explore where you are not, or where you could be, or might have been. Awareness is a function of the senses while consciousness is a function of what you do with that sensory data or how you distort it, in the name of clarity.

Originally, distance and angle provided people with all the entertainment they needed as they walked around the teepee and were delighted and amused. People have come a long way from that point, without moving, to much more involved forms of entertainment. They have become dependent on physical, external entertainment and can no longer be entertained mentally with nothing at all. Disney

World and Great America provide the entertainment people used to provide for themselves.

Being enlightened is a return to the point of internal entertainment where all people started. The child is amused and entertained with anything or with nothing at all. The child does not understand that the wrapping is just something between herself and the good stuff inside the box, she thrills at anything. You are disappointed if things are not just the way you want them to be. If only you can have a new Lexus with leather seats and all those accessories, you would be happy. If you can't be happy with nothing, you can't be happy with anything. If you can't be angry at nothing, you can't be angry at anything. If you can't be sad at nothing, you can't be sad at anything.

People have squeezed out the pleasure and delight from themselves and now have to look for it outside themselves. Enlightenment is a return to the only source of light possible—that which is within you. Where you stand is within you. Return to your body to discover this. Use your mind strictly for entertainment, instead of meaning, and you will begin to have fun with the simplest things again. The complicated things wring their entertainment value out of destruction of the environment, a process which, ironically, makes Earth a worse place to live in the name of making it a better one. If you could derive delight from the simple flower in the field, you would not have to destroy the flower to build a roller coaster, museum or school in its place. As more people become aware of their enlightenment, Earth will be appreciated as a pristine wonderland again.

In For a Landing

You exist simultaneously, everywhere at the same time, but you do not think you do. Since your thinking seems real, to you, you must only exist in one place.

You always stand everywhere, so you do not ever have to worry about where you stand. Wherever you look is you; wherever you don't look is also you. It cannot be otherwise and you cannot see that it is this way.

People have been making a difference for so long that now the world is left with differences. In an attempt to control things, people have split them up. The only way to know where you stand is to know what you are not. You have excluded so much and lost everything, and nothing, in the process. You have traded everything for one place to stand.

Above all, you have excluded paradox and opposites because they reveal your illusions as illusions. When you embrace paradox, location becomes meaningless, as does everything else, especially thinking.

To most people, off-kilter or off balance is as close as they can get to paradox. How far away can you move while still holding your original position? Like children playing tag, you think your thoughts are goal keeping you safe from being tagged. But if you watch children play tag, you discover they do not spend much time on goal holding to safety.

"Don't leave home without it." Better yet, don't leave home at all. Depending on what you define home to be, you will be more or less limited in where you go. If you define home as a state of mind, you may be able to travel, but you will not be able to go on vacation because you always take your thoughts along. How far can you move from where you are toward the opposite point of view without losing your original point of view? Not far. It takes effort to hold one point of view and continue to hold it as you move to its opposite. Try it! The more different the two perspectives are, the harder the work becomes.

Consciousness cannot be in two places at the same time; thus it cannot ascend. Controlling consciousness operates in mutually exclusive, supposedly unrelated, places. To accommodate your illusion of control and location, you have split the world into as many planes as you could, each plane being defined as a specific "not you." You were so busy on this project that you forgot what was you, or is you. You can only attend to or occupy one plane at a time. More than one spot, or point, or plane gets messy and, above all, uncontrollable. You suffer from *monogidea* in your attempt to control. Different ideas on the same subject cannot be stacked. Each idea in a stack must be compatible with others in the stack. So you move laterally, to a different plane, to accommodate ideas that do not fit well together. Your illusions are lateral, flat, like pieces of a jigsaw puzzle.

You are very upset when you do not have a picture of what the finished puzzle is supposed to look like. Even worse is when there are pieces from various puzzles mixed together. You have complicated things and created puzzles out of wholeness. You have split everything to the point that wholeness and enlightenment are unrecognizable. You have lost unity, and fallen to pieces. There are not really different puzzles because there is only one whole. People have made such a difference that arbitrary delineations appear real. Now you are in Illinois. Now you are in Kansas. What is the difference, Dorothy?

Things have become confusing and coincidentally, you have stated that it is not good to be confused. Only a culture hell-bent on suffering would put these two together.

You have divided to prove that you do not exist in two places at once. It takes effort to hold wholeness apart. You are a hectic air traffic controller attempting to have the planes as close together as they can be without having them crash. This is a stressful job.

Help Wanted—Full time employee, 24 hours a day, 365 days a year. Applicant must be willing to work constantly at maintaining distinctions that do not exist and proving that illusions are real. Control is essential. When in doubt, you must act as though you are certain. You will be working alone, and everybody else will be working against you. Inventory control is part of

```
your job. You will be responsible for
keeping track of everything there is,
keeping it orderly and in its place at all
times. You must begin work immediately.
Dental and health coverage included, and
you will need them. Starting salary:
continuation of the rat race. Fringe
benefits: self-esteem and the ability to
be right all the time.
```

As the air traffic controller, you must keep track of all planes, illusionary as they may be. Many of the planes may not show up on your screen yet because they are too new or because they are planes held by others and unrecognized by you. The planes are three-dimensional, but your thoughts are not, so to make the job easier, you act as though the planes are two-dimensional. The planes are not real; they are what you define yourself in relation to. The planes are a fundamental illusion that results from drawing lines.

The air traffic controller must start by knowing where he or she stands. The good air traffic controller has the planes be as close together as possible without any overlap. Overlap means a crash. It means the end of illusion and the possibility of discovering the whole. Crashes must be avoided at all costs—wholeness is deadly to illusion. At first, survival is the major component of the job: avoiding crashes. But with practice the game becomes a matter of just how close together you can get the planes and still have them be separate and distinct. Quantity is about avoiding crashes. Quality has to do with how close the planes can be brought together. Most people are still so busy with survival that conversations about quality are insulting. Quality of life is something an air traffic controller does not have time for. In reality, there are no planes, you have no job, and there is no work to be done. Keeping planes apart reduces your ability to generalize learning. You learn something on one plane and don't apply it to another—after all, they are different.

It is you who made the differences between planes. If there were no differences, you would exist in two places at once—next step, everywhere. From everywhere, there would be nowhere to get to and thus life would be meaningless. Without meaning, you could do anything and you would already have everything. You would be at the playground all the time because you would have the playground with you.

People say that they want to make a difference, but they already have; that is the problem. Making more of a difference is just having more illusionary planes to control, thus the busier they are, and the crazier.

Anytime two planes overlap, you have a problem. The more the overlap, the bigger the problem, and the greater the likelihood you will glimpse reality. One glimpse of reality, and illusion seems to pale. If you are to keep playing the illusionary game, you must avoid reality at all costs. Reality is like a buzzsaw that tears illusion apart. Since illusion is not real, it does not even slow down the saw or cause any resistance as reality chews it up. To you, steeped in illusion, damage seems to ensue when two planes overlap. If you did not consider yourself to be the illusion, it would not seem like damage; it would be more like fun and games.

Anytime illusions overlap or illusion overlaps with reality, the result is emotion. You get angry, sad, happy, anxious, bitter, ecstatic, confused, or apathetic.

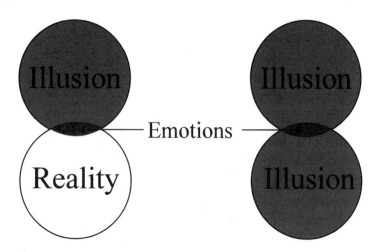

There are many names for emotions, which is good news because it must mean that people bump into reality or other illusions often. The more crashes you have the less reliable your illusion appears. The more consistent your illusion, the fewer crashes you have. Keeping the planes apart keeps the illusion in place.

The first thing people want to do with an emotion is figure out what caused it. They look at the part of their illusion which has been damaged and assign the blame if it is a negative emotion or the credit if they consider it to be a positive emotion. Either way, they miss the reality, or other illusion, that the overlap is a result of. If they could ignore their damaged illusion for a moment, they could have a glimpse at reality or at an illusion other than theirs. An opening. At that moment they would not be alone with their illusion. The moment is lost when an explanation is assigned to the emotion. The excuse is found and then the mending of the illusion begins. If it was a "positive" emotion, there is an attempt to repeat it, using the most superficial means at hand, like, "I was in a French restaurant when it happened, so I should go back to a French restaurant." Or, "I was with her when it happened, so perhaps I should marry her."

In the world of illusions there are many coincidences. Since everything is always happening at the same time, it is possible to occasionally see things happen together. When this occurs, you lighten up and make a rule about all future events based on what has just happened. Doing this is an attempt to make the future like the past so that the differences already defined will still work. The more things remain the same, the less work there is to do, and the more comfortable/uncomfortable, you can be.

If an emotion is "negative," you seek to rid yourself of whatever the source seems to be and rebuild the illusion to avoid any contact with reality in the future.

Another less noble cause of emotions is when consciousness overlaps with patterns. This is a conflict of evolutionary steps. Emotions arrive as you discover that patterns will determine behaviors regardless of thought. In both the case of illusion overlapping with reality and that of consciousness overlapping with patterns, the common element is loss of control. You must justify any loss of control, so you tell a story, asserting that it is the truth. If you are no longer creative enough to come up with a story of your own, you pay a doctor or therapist to come up with one for you. It is never acceptable to lose control and have any emotion, positive or negative, without having an explanation as to why it happened and who or what is at fault. Sometimes you even buy new things to blame when you run out of old things to blame.

As you progress toward discovering your enlightenment, it will often appear that you are moving away from enlightenment. Your emotions may increase both in quantity and intensity, for no apparent reason. If you assign stories or causes to these emotions, your progress will slow up (restrict vertical movement). If you do not make up stories, an opening will occur, giving you room for multiple perspectives. The more willing you are to be out of control, the greater emotional swings you will get. Your highs will become higher, which you will probably enjoy, and your lows will become lower, which you may tend to resist. While this does not appear to be progress, it is. The way out of the emotional roller coaster is to continually increase both the highs and the lows and bring them closer together. Be consumed by emotion to the point where you lose the distinction between high and low and become both at the same time; then you will ascend. Move up, and you will exit the necessity for control. You will have motion in the direction of enlightenment—E-motion. Emotion.

When your old highs become your new lows, then you are experiencing quantum growth, growth without reference, and you are closer to standing everywhere and nowhere than ever before. You are perceiving the tiny movements you can make rather than the huge movements your mind taunts you to attempt, and certainly fail at. The smaller and more subtle movement you can perceive the closer you are to not moving at all, being everywhere. At the point of ascension, differences disappear,

Upsets
Positive Emotions

Downsets
Negative Emotions

and you rise to the occasion, every occasion. You move vertically, bringing things together, not separating them horizontally.

Most people attempt to minimize emotions and maximize control. This makes rising, noticing enlightenment, impossible because it keeps things two-dimensional, superficial. Light will not be restricted in this way; if it is restricted or limited, it will no longer be light. It will appear as the object which blocked it. If it is blocked, it does not matter on what plane it is blocked. Blocked is blocked and the moment that anything blocks the light, there appears to be some*thing* real. That apparently real thing becomes your next limitation.

In the world of physical things, you generally move around things. Rather than going over or under the chair, you walk around it. Rather than walking over or under the house, you walk through or around it. In the emotional world there is no effective horizontal plane, so attempts to get around emotions never work. It is for this very reason that rationality is not effective with emotions. To move through emotions, you must go up and down, high and low. Emotions are the result of an unblocking, so they are intrinsically more powerful than thought since thought is the result of blocking. If you use thought to work on emotions, you are losing useful data and impeding your own perspectives.

Depth, vertical stacking, requires consistency, and since people are not good at consistency, they default to width, difference, instead of depth. Spreading thinly, people cover the surface and become superficial.

Would you stack coins of different denominations together? Three quarters, five dimes, two pennies, and a nickel? Try it. See what happens. Stack them together and notice if it does not seem that they are in order. Put the stack of pennies next to the stack of quarters and one of dimes. Now you have organization, you have brought order to the coins.

The dimes have denomination in common, so you can stack them. If you have enough dimes, you may stack them by date—but then, don't mix dates. You are constantly, compulsively, attempting to force order on the universe.

Width is so limited, so superficial, and so prevalent. Gravity itself lends credibility to this limitation. You can make a long single line of oranges, but you cannot make a vertical line without support. Illusions are wide, not tall, at least what you can see of them. So to deal with or escape illusion, you must break through it or rise above it. You cannot get around it—the distance is too great. The skills you have learned getting around in illusion do not lead to your noticing light. Emotions are one tool for moving up and down; thus emotions are larger than illusion— threatening the limits of illusion. Embrace—enhance emotions, they don't mean anything and they have no cause. Illusions are composed of cause and effects; emotions are not. To force the rules of illusion on emotions confuses you and diminishes what you can learn from emotions.

If you are walking in the woods, lost, you look for a tree to climb or a high spot to ascend to and view your position from. You look for more surface. From up high you may get a view, see something familiar or entirely unfamiliar. This is what getting high is—but leave the drugs and the mountains alone. In the control paradigm, everything must be sequential, and depth precludes sequence. Depth with sequence requires consistency, which is something you never have much of, unless you make it up. To escape, you must skip sequence and consistency and go all the way to wholeness.

Depth, vertical ascension, provides a high beyond highs and lows—a different order of high, a higher order. To reach this high from which you enhance perspectives, differences must disappear. From a skyscraper everything below looks small. A problem for the person on the street cannot even be seen from the 100th floor. But in a system of highs and lows, you can take your problems with you. Even within the thinnest surface there is high and low, though only of great subtlety. You must rise above or sink so far below that you exit what you know for...nothing.

Height within the superficial will give you some perspective. But all height will take you to all perspective.

Being high and low means having more or less perspective in the figurative landscape of your mind.

Enlightenment is having all perspectives, everywhere.

With enlightenment, emotions disappear. The whole idea of high and low is replaced by a world where all opposites are one. It is still possible for an enlightened person to pretend emotions but not get scared by them or enjoy the highs or lows. The bliss of enlightenment overshadows the highs and lows. Having ascended and then looking at the highs and lows from above, there is nothing but a straight line. It is only when one is on the roller coaster or looking at the roller coaster from the side that it appears to be high and low, or scary at all. Looking at a roller coaster from an airplane has it become a flat track. It is all a matter of perspective, and the more perspectives you are able to maintain at the same moment, the more places you can be. The more differences you create, the busier you will be. Ironically, if you create all differences, you will come back around to no differences. That is the way it always is with paradox.

The person with one difference, a fundamentalist, sees the world as black or white. As one creates more and more differences, the world becomes more fragmented, all of it working toward the whole, which is where you started and where you finish. How soon you finish determines how long you get to spend in blissful entertainment, doing nothing, in absolute pleasure.

Tell Me a Story

"Once upon a time in a small town in Switzerland, there was a radiologist. He lived with his daughter, Heidi, and his son, Seekie. His wife, a registered hypnotist, had left years earlier for America. At first, they had missed her, but soon they adapted. "Three is enough," they would say, on occasion when they thought that perhaps it was not.

One day Hans, for that was the radiologist's name (not his real name, but children laughed at his real name, so he had it changed when he was fifteen), was on his way into work and was about to drop Seekie off at the Swiss Legion when he had a thought. This was not the kind of thought he had ever had before. It was not the kind of thought he was supposed to have. It was unsettling that a thought could just come in and have its way with him. His thought was a waking dream of Spain. Initially he thought of the word El Gato, the cat, in Spanish, but within moments it had blown itself out of all proportion. He *couldn't help but picture himself in Spain with a dark-skinned maiden all of sixteen years old, two years younger than Heidi, for heaven's sake. She was gorgeous and treated him like a God. Though Hans had never been to Spain, he could picture it now with enough clarity that in spite of Seekie's protests, he drove past the Legion and on southward, down roads he had never traveled before, toward the border and points south. There he was, lying back as she stroked his hair and fed him grapes."*

Forget about Hans, it is time to get back to work.

Forget about Hans; he isn't important, nor is anything that he does on his way to Spain or once he gets there with his new young friend.

Stories are the stuff life is made of. If you speak, you are a storyteller. You tell stories to focus attention on or off yourself. You tell stories to amuse yourself, at best, and to justify yourself, at worst. Nothing is true, and it is all that is true. Anything is the subject of stories. How interesting are your stories?

Do you tell the same stories over and over? Do you tell new and better stories, in hopes of finally being understood or interesting?

The art of storytelling is not dead, as it has been proclaimed to be; it has just been whitewashed in the name of legitimacy and been turned into facts.

"I went to the mall the other day, and at the mall I met my best friend Ray. The following is what Ray did say."

There is the start to a story.

"Good morning."

Another story. The whole idea of one morning being good as opposed to other mornings is fictitious enough to be a fairy tale. Stories are made up of things and words that modify those things. There is the idea of morning, a thing, and good, that which separates one morning from others, making it distinct and personal, supposedly. Stories are made up of actions and the adverbs which modify them. Modification, the main stuff of stories, is another word for control. *"He walked slowly down the hall, thinking of what he might find as he reached the bedroom. He heard a squeal somewhere between agony and delight which obviously belonged to his wife, but what was her inspiration? Without his permission or knowledge, she had sneaked out one night, while he was asleep and... "*

And what? You are a story addict, a compulsive communicator. You long for interesting stories, the kind of stories that people want to listen to through to the end. You want to have the kind of life you read about or see on television or in the movies. You want a life where "real" stuff happens, where you know where you stand and that where you stand is interesting. A life during which you have the kind of adventures you deserve. But even if you have this "real" life, it sometimes seems empty, not the way it ought to be. How come other people can have adventures but you can't? How do you know how it ought to be anyway? You can think anything, but your life can seldom catch up with your stories unless you tell the most mundane stories imaginable.

"...had joined a theater class. For the class, her homework assignment was to act out the most passionate wonderful sex scene of all time. She began by... "

By what? Buy anything that is sold to you in the name of a more interesting story than the one you are currently living. Your whole life is a story if you are steeped in illusion. Is it comedy, tragedy, horror, drama, or what?

"...thinking of exactly how she wanted to be touched. Not where but how. She thought of the first loving touch she had received. It was in high school. It had never led to anything deeper than the time at the football game when Rick had reached over, placing his arm awkwardly on her shoulder. A sign of affection, which proved once and for all..."

Proved what? What can anything ever prove? What would life be like if you continually exceeded the most interesting stories ever written? If you lived a life that other people would want to read about, to vicariously enjoy themselves? If you moved from being one of the onlookers to being one of the actors, the main actor?

The moment you think your stories are true, they are limited. You have forgotten that everything you say is a story. The fastest way to forget this is to use your stories in some way to justify a shortcoming you perceive yourself to have. Ultimately, stories justify who you are as separate from who you think you are not. In the name of character development, you lose your (whole) self and the ability to have fun in the process. Amusement used to be the drive behind storytelling, whether the story was comedy or tragedy. But now, defense and justification reign. Thus the stories have become more serious and less interesting. *"She was raped as a child, an experience which influenced her deeply and made it impossible for her ever again to..."*

To what? You make it up. The cause and effects abound in stories. What is the most useful and enjoyable direction a story can go? Useful in the way of opening possibilities both for the storyteller and the story listener. In other words, how can the story take your hand and lead you toward reality? How can it lend a little clarity to your journey through illusion, be a flashlight to use as a beacon for yourself and others, assist you in discovering how wonderful you are? A story can be fun, leading you to a bigger, higher viewpoint, or perspective, than you had before you heard the story. If a story doesn't do that, forget about it, don't tell it and don't listen to it.

You are so busy telling stories which justify and limit you forget to notice that your life is quite fantastic. *"Why, just the other day, I went into Hardee's with my daughter. In the order line was an old woman, the eyes of time for us. A seven year old, a forty-four year old and the old woman who lived in a shoe. That's what she told us. She even invited us over and we accepted. Taking our trays back up to the counter, we asked to have our order 'to-go' instead. We grabbed our little lunch bags and headed to her house on foot, each of us holding one of her hands as we suddenly felt ourselves swept up, physically lifted up..."*

Up where? You already think you know what reality is and what reality isn't. Well, you don't. It can't be and isn't because reality is too big for such limitations. Reality is the mathematical computation of all possibility. "So where is isn't?" Back to reality for a moment. Yes, get back to reality. You *have* to think that reality is the specific limitations of the stories you tell repeatedly and the repetition in the name of security that you call life. Your stories have nothing to do with reality. Reality has no content at all. It is the biggest open-ended everything that you can imagine and much more. (This is a story too.)

If your stories don't increase perspectives and make you and the people around you grin, then "STOP TELLING THEM." If your stories separate you from other people or in any way make you right and somebody else wrong, then "STOP TELLING THEM." If your stories seem true to you and don't even seem like stories anymore, then "STOP TELLING THEM!"

Start telling other stories; start living your life so you have wonderful stories to tell. Quality of life is determined by your range of perception in the moment, the broader— the better, and if your stories do not offer you a broader range of perspective, then change them.

It can't be avoided. The "S" word has to be talked about. Not Spirituality, not Sex, but Seduction of the best kind. Seduction leading to the climax, reality. The "S" word is Sales. What would you do in order not to have to sell? A book about philosophy which talks about SALES? Yes, and it is about time.

What would you do so that you did not have to sell? Remember that what people want most out of life is the impossible, for things to stand still long enough so people can know where they stand. Impossible is that which you don't perceive to be possible—reality is all possibility. The second thing they want is for other people to know where they stand. This is sales. You are always either selling your limitations or your expansions. Sales is the road to reality, a most enjoyable path. You are a salesperson whether you like it or not. Even if you are a hermit, you must continue to sell yourself on the idea of remaining a hermit. You go up for sale every day, every moment. You sell yourself; you embody sales. Sales is an increase or decrease in the recognition of possibilities. The enlightened person is the best salesperson around because the enlightened person sells all possibilities to everybody all the time. However, since the enlightened person sees past the illusions of separateness and time, the job of sales becomes infinitely easy.

What is sales? Well, if you are a school teacher you must sell yourself to your students and the administration. If you do not sell yourself, the students will not learn much, and you won't have a job for long, hopefully. If you are a doctor, you must sell yourself to your patients. If you are a husband, you must sell yourself to your wife. If you are a parent, you must sell yourself to your child. If you are a bus driver, you must sell yourself to the riders and to the bus company.

But since it is unlikely that you even know who you are, what is it you are selling? What you are selling really is not what it looks like you are selling, and that is part of what it means to demean oneself as a human being. You pretend you are selling your limitations. If you are a teacher, you initially sell yourself to yourself by declaring that you are what you have done. You have a teacher's certificate from the University of Iowa (not Utah), you have had four years teaching experience in Des Moines (not eight in Chicago). These are your limitations, not your assets. These indicate what you have not done and are stories about how you have limited yourself. The question if you are to be a teacher is, "Can you teach?" not "Where and when did you go to college?" Again you get caught up in the symbols, limitations, rather than noticing what is right in front of your nose: possibilities.

You need a bigger context on the way to no context at all. If you sell the symbols you have accumulated, it is likely that you will depend on the past to ensure that the present gets you to a future similar to where you have already been. If you sell your limitations, then they will become more real to you. The more real your limitations become in the minds of others, the more real they seem to you.

If your life doesn't lead you closer to reality, it leads you deeper into illusion. Your stories indicate which way you are going. They are the fruit of your thought. You sell your stories. Your stories are always untrue; they become lies when you believe them to be true.

Sales as a path leading to reality is a new definition of sales. Sales is being the possibility in which other possibilities appear. Increasing possibilities, since reality is all possibilities, is your main job. Discover all the possibilities you can, and in doing so, have the people around you discover more and more possibilities. Expansion leads you to reality; contraction leads you to illusion. The moment you think you know who you are, you are either building or maintaining your illusion to separate yourself from reality. You are not separate from reality. You are all possibility. You are not part of reality; reality has no parts. It is indivisible. Drawing from your perspective you get this:

Drawing from reality, possibility, you get this:

Nothing disappears in the distance; everything gets more intimate—closer. You tell stories to keep things away, to keep *you* from yourself. You tell stories initially because you can and soon because you can't stop. You create and reinforce illusions with your stories.

Looking at your life, you will discover that the best of times have always been accompanied by your perception of increased possibilities. Marriage is the possibility of partnership, parenthood, sharing and much more. The most exciting moment for most people is the birth of a child, their child. The child embodies pure possibility. Anything is possible for that child, a truth you have probably forgotten about yourself. Forgetting it does not make it any less true. The young child has no symbols, no degrees, no stories, no worries, and no past. The young child is the ultimate salesperson, pure sales, a clean slate on which stories, any stories, can be written. Growing up, crazy as it seems, is usually about limiting, defining, yourself. It is about restricting possibilities fast enough so that the adults around you will think you are becoming like them— acceptable. At every turn you were given help in limiting possibilities, told that you must choose what you wanted to do. Told that you had to have specific answers to questions and that other answers would not do.

You have been crippled and are now handicapped. You have been taught that you are not a *child of reality* and, worse, that reality is something even more limited and limiting than you are. You have been bushwhacked, bamboozled, had, taken, misled, cheated, conned, defrauded, framed, and deceived. Not on purpose, not knowingly, but systematically. You have been rewarded in little ways, too tiny to notice, for each move you made toward being a hypocrite, an actor, a snake oil salesman, a traitor, a phony, a liar, a cheat, a dupe, a victim, and worse. You have been sent on a wild goose chase in the name of self-discovery, meaningful work or subsistence. You have been so deformed that you no longer even recognize yourself.

Enough bad news. The good news is that who you are, who you were as a baby with everything possible for you with no past and only all possibility ahead, is still who you are. If you look closely enough, if you explore and expand your perceptions, if you vary your perceptions, you will discover that all possibility is still here. All you need to do is feed it, and your perception of reality will grow. You will see yourself again as what you really are: nothing, with everything possible. That is what it is to be human. The relationship you have between consciousness, awareness, and patterns may overshadow possibilities, but everything is possible. If your perceptions can catch up with your possibilities, human beings will survive and even excel as a species. If they do not, then the experiment, being a human being, will be over. You are not who you think you are; you are much more than that.

The moment you accept your limitations as facts, you forget who you are, and above all, you lose yourself. All of your stories are fiction. You are a compulsive liar when you think you speak the truth.

Tell wonderful stories. Tell stories of possibility. Listen to yourself when you speak. What are you really saying? Are you in any way proving who you are or that you are right when you are speaking? If so, you are selling limitations, lies, and deceit. If you already understand or know what you will say when you speak, then you are leading to now from the past, back to limitations. Listen to yourself and stop speaking when you are no longer selling expansion, possibility. At first this may be awkward. Facts, justifications, your past stories, others perceptions, your perceptions, and your future all seem to be in the way. Stories permeate your life and drive you into corners so small that you think you cannot even turn around. That isn't reality. Reality, life, by definition is expansive. If you find yourself telling the same story over and over, come up with a new one. Anything worth doing is worth doing poorly at first; anything you think is worth doing is not worth doing at all. There is nothing to do.

The stories you tell, the words you utter, reveal where you have stopped. The very act of speech indicates that you have stopped. Life is not discontinuous. Life is what happens when reality hits the road. A road show, a game, a play. It never ends, and no matter how thinly you slice reality or how much you try to stop it or have it be a certain way, reality flows on. All is possible for you, and the difference between all possibilities and what you perceive to be possible for you are the limitations you have bought. The price you paid for these perceived limitations is the play and energy you knew as a child. In the name of knowing where you stand, you have ignored that you can never stand anywhere at all. You are always moving. Your stories lock you in place when you tell them twice; they don't *really* lock you, but since you think they do, they do. What is and what you think is are reunited in Heaven.

It is not necessary, though it is typical, that perceptions and reality separate and become enemies. There has never been and can never be a real perception, or the right perception.

No matter what you think, it is just what you think.

In the land of deceptions, where you have to be something, your perceptions appear to be reality. In the land of connections, you are whole and your perceptions are amusing limitations temporarily blocking your vision. In the land of deceptions, you see little tiny pieces and call what you see the whole. In the land of connections, you see the whole. Seeing the whole without distinctions lightens you up.

How Long?

How much of your time is spent developing your limitations? Talking about them, nurturing them?

How much time do you have left? How much time do you have to be right? Enough?

If you can ever do anything that doesn't make a difference, you will be immortal; you will have revealed wholeness. Your limitations depend on differences for their very existence. Your illusions are yours alone, different from everyone else's.

How long will you live? Are you living now? What if you were to live forever? What if you discovered you were going to die tomorrow or next week or next year?

What makes life worth living? Worth dying?

Imagine that you are given two pills. You are told that each one of these pills will increase the life span of whoever takes it by 1000 years. During this 1000 years good health is ensured. If you attempt to take the pill apart or tamper with it, discovering what is in it or reproducing it, then its power is lost. What would you do with the pills?

Would you take them yourself? Would you take one and give the other one to Billy Graham, who may have already had one? Would you give one to your spouse or to one of your children? Would you give one to your dog? Would you give them both to somebody else so you would not have to figure out what to do with them? When asked, a young girl said she would bury both of them where nobody would ever find them. Had this idea occurred to you?

If you would give one to somebody else and take one yourself, it had better be somebody who you are already spending every waking moment with.

What would you do if you found out you had one month to live? How would you spend your month, with whom, where, doing what? Would you go to work for the month? If you would do anything differently, then you are not living the life you want. In this case, you may want to ask yourself how long you think you will live. Many people are a curious mix of how long they act like they will live and how long they think they will live.

Design a brochure selling your life. What is your life like and why would others want to have exactly the life you now have?

Now design a brochure to sell the perfect life. What would you be doing if you could do anything? Who would you be living with if you could live with anyone? What would your life be like if you could have it be exactly how you want it?

If there is any difference between the two brochures then you have some problems and the temptation to complain about them. You are, to some extent, a victim. You, yourself, are split; on the one hand, you have how life is, and on the other you have how life could be, if it were just right. The very act of keeping the hands apart requires energy and justification. It has to be somebody's fault that you are not living exactly the life you say you want. You could blame it on your parents, the stars, your job, or anything else. But no matter whose fault it is, according to you, the story you tell about whose fault it is keeps it in place, with a difference. You are somehow justified in having life be the way it is rather than how you want it to be. You tell a story in which you have not yet arrived but always have the possibility of arriving. If you are religious, you may even think your arrival coincides with your death. You may, with stooped shoulders, accept that you are a sinner on your way back home.

The difference people create between how things are and how they want them to be drives them crazy but has them fit right in with other people. What do you do when your reality, illusion, exceeds your wildest dreams? Keep it to yourself. One thing you must never do is have too much fun, too much joy or pleasure. If you have intense pain, society has ways to deal with it. There are many people willing to administer drugs, therapy, or worse to you in the name of relieving your discomfort. But what do you do when you are in ecstasy? Who will help you out of bliss or even teach you how to deal with bliss?

When you have a problem, something doesn't go your way, or you get some disease, you immediately think that the condition is permanent. What you are really saying is that your possibilities, future possibilities, have been limited by something. But if you have bliss and delight, you just as quickly think that this is a short-lived condition and that it will be over much too soon. What makes you think you do not deserve the best, most extraordinary and delightful life ever? More to the point, what makes you think you don't already have it? Most likely, you think you *do* deserve it but don't have it. Thus you must keep the perception of what you should have and what you do have far enough apart so that you do not get swallowed up in the *depression* between them.

What if you could live forever? You can. You do. If your life is already exactly the way you want it and you have not in any way lowered your standards or sold out, then you see your enlightenment. If it is not, then you are currently spending some time hiding your enlightenment from yourself. You are also unable to see much enlightenment in others since to see it in others and not have it yourself would make you wrong and others right, unless there is some story sufficient to explain why they have it and you do not. If so, change the story. A wise man once said, "You either have what you want, or you have your reasons why you do not have what you want."

As long as you want anything, you are trapped by the stories of why you have it or why you don't. There is nothing to have, and everything you have dictates a story to you. Your life becomes a transcription. All dictation gets in the way of your creating a story. Discover who you are and stories will become irrelevant and unimportant;

thus you will be able to tell any story, live any story, without justification and without difference.

Tell a story to a child. Make up the story. Notice the effect the story has on the child and the effect it has on you. If the effects are different, then you, to some extent, consider the story true. If the child is not delighted with your story, hanging on every word, happy and wanting more, then you are limiting yourself more than the child is limiting him or herself. Change your story. Sell yourself and others on expansion rather than limitation. This will not produce appreciation for your enlightenment, but it will make everything a lot more enjoyable until you notice your light.

Always tell stories which would delight children.

Question??

It isn't really dark in here unless you have the unfortunate experience of seeing the light once. People degrade themselves little by little, deprive themselves of the light in such small increments that they hardly notice the dark moving in. Around six years of age the light is gone and people get on with the business of life: trying to fit in, working at being good, defending themselves, becoming social creatures, dealing with the misunderstanding which, by this age, has reached unmanageable stature, or numbing themselves with the national average—in excess of six hours of television per day. People started pure, simple, elegant, and light but…

In the absence of light, darkness and dullness rule. You make important what you are told to make important, which is serious business. Without light, darkness becomes tolerable and in time becomes life. You attempt to balance yourself and build your surroundings so they do not disturb you too much. Make every day enough like the one before it that you never have to be too unsettled. You have assistance if things don't go right for awhile. Therapists, the car dealer, school counselors, religious figures, friends, relatives, newspapers, television shows, movies, radio shows, retail clerks, the ghost of Sam Walmart, teachers, pop gurus, doctors, and many more are waiting there to pick you up, should you fall, or aide you along the way. You appreciate the assistance because this is not an easy path to follow.

One day you have the odd thought that something is missing. You dismiss the thought, but it doesn't go away; it hangs around waiting in the wings or just slightly off stage. You get on with the play: the stiff, fully-choreographed, what-you-are-supposed-to-do play. But then you have the thought, the unsettling one again. This time it is a little more obvious: "Is this all there is to life?" it whispers.

It goes away again, but when it comes back weeks later it is accompanied by a friend saying, "I deserve more than this."

You buy a new car, and for a time as you acclimate to the car, the thought leaves again. But, it resurfaces, and what is supposed to matter means less, and what you had forgotten (lightness and ecstasy, curiosity and bliss) hint at you of their existence.

Soon, new purchases don't work, your therapist starts sounding like he isn't too happy either, and even friends and relatives look like they are not having fun, as they work for money they don't really want and move from spouse to spouse in a desire to get things right once and for all.

"The whole system is bankrupt."

What? That is not what you are supposed to think.

Tragedy visits your life, for the first time, unclothed. Somebody around you, a parent perhaps, dies. "Where did he go? Why didn't you appreciate him more than you did? Will he be back? Will you ever meet him again? What is the point of life anyway?"

The questions flood in. Death is your best friend. The very thought of it gives life a perspective that it can't have without a perceived end. There is an urgency and an importance to this "thing" you call life. Death forces you to reflect, to ponder big questions, to query what it is you want from life, after all. Religion seeks to answer the questions that the consumer market no longer can. But the clergy are in general not much fun to hang around and play with. If you were intended to hold to a dogma, maybe you would have been made a dog. You were not.

If you continue to question long enough and often enough, the darkness weakens; the self-perpetuated and socially assisted darkness begins to lighten. Often it cracks, letting in a ray of light, a bright contrast to all else which is so dark. This ray of light, if you are ready for it, cannot be denied. You really do deserve better than you have. Not in the world of things, but in deep personal contentment that can only come from inside you.

This is a disturbing time because everything you have considered important and worthwhile for so long, your whole life after six years of age, seems empty and meaningless. You don't want to compete and struggle anymore. You don't want to demean yourself and others, or acquire things that you don't even care about. You question authority, you question life. If you are brave enough you dare to admit some things to yourself. That perhaps you have been crazy for quite awhile. That the party line is not true. That there is more to life than you have been told. That there are not models for dealing with bliss. That nobody has enough ecstasy. That this is a downside culture bent on anesthetizing people and not noticing enlightenment.

If you are willing to consider the possibility that your whole life, up until now, has been a scam, that you have been running with a pack of lies skipping along the surface of things for so long that the surface is all you know, then all new possibilities open for you.

You can move from tunnel to tunnel, but none of the rules from one tunnel apply in the others. Question enough, and since all you have surrounded yourself with is illusion, sooner or later you will see the light. Illusion is a thin deception. It cannot survive the light. It cannot stand up to an avid questioner. You have to be partially asleep to continually buy its gaunt temptation. Though the whole system was created to hold the darkness in place, it can't stand up to the light. Just a little bit of light eradicates all darkness in its path. If you were in prison, solitary confinement, for years and kept in the dark, you would soon not notice the dark anymore. But if a small hole were opened in your cell and a ray of light entered, you would blink and rub your eyes, unable, at first, to make sense of the light. You would be upset at the violence that it seems to do, at least in your perception, to the darkness. The darkness does not hold up; it does not look good in the light. It just disappears. Where does the darkness go in the light?

With enough light, darkness becomes intolerable. It starts out as uninteresting. See the light a little but still mostly darkness, and you may be diagnosed with some psychological problem. The things that used to keep you busy and numb are not working anymore. If you don't buy the psychological assessment, you will keep moving into the light. Any justification you do buy appears to be real for you; otherwise, why would you have bought it. The idea of buying something that is not real is unacceptable enough that you will not see it. Anything you buy or think is true will block the light as long as you keep it around or believe it. It doesn't really block the light, but it keeps you from seeing the light. It keeps you looking at the dark. The more darkness you see, the more limited is your perspective, because there is not really any darkness at all: it is all illusion. All there is—is nothing, which is as light as you can get.

Put a lot of nothing on a scale and the scale registers zero, heap on even more and still no self-respecting grocery store will charge you for nothing. Any something that you buy will cost you, but nothing costs nothing. Something always costs you something. Typically, the cost of something is quite different from itself, thus you attach things together in meaningful chunks.

Take what you want and pay for it.

Enlightenment costs you nothing because it is nothing. No matter how much money you have or how many things you accumulate, enlightenment is not closer because of your inventory. It is not necessarily further away either, but it often is if you have to spend all of your time protecting, maintaining and defending your stuff.

When you begin to question, and death has visited close to home, you move from the world of stuff, content, to the world of holes. Holes are the spaces between stuff.

Remembering that reality is made of stuff, holes and process could be useful as you enter the holes. You are not broken when you do, you are just undergoing the natural progression of moving through life. You are taking apart that which you have created when you were dealing with stuff. You are dismantling all you thought was worthwhile and meaningful so that you can leave a clean slate when you go. Everybody leaves a clean slate. Everybody becomes meaningless at some point in his or her life. Everybody has to stand alone, stripped, naked, holding nothing, empty. The sooner you can do that the sooner you can get through the holes. Attempting to carry anything through the holes makes your passage more difficult because releasing possessions seems like death. They are called possessions because they possess you, thus you have to let go of yourself. When you have given up everything you hold to, when you no longer know where you stand, when you have given up all of your perspectives (even the ones which define you), when it seems that life is hardly worth living, then, and only then, are you ready to leave the holes and move to process.

Stuff is the illusion, the grand illusion that things are real. That the superficial is deep. That the artificial is natural. That through some personal effort you can control the world and are so important for doing so.

Holes are the emptiness that separates stuff. Without the holes there would be no stuff, holes are the background which has stuff appear to be stuff. There are far more holes than there is stuff. So the very process of your moving into the holes provides you with a much broader and more universal perspective. All holes are linked and all islands of stuff are floating on a sea of holes. The holes are what you get as you strip away illusion.

There is a greater honesty to holes than there is to stuff. One more lie, that there is stuff, has been stripped away when you are deep in the holes.

Process is the interaction between stuff and holes and between holes and holes and stuff and stuff. So process is even more universal and pervasive than either stuff or holes. Process gives you nothing to hold to, not even the apparent depression, which is a reaction to the non-stuff nature of holes. Process is a flow as opposed to a thing. Stuff is things, physical or mental; holes is the absence of things, again physical or mental. And process is the movement, flow, and/or relation. Process is a verb, stuff is nouns, holes is the absence of nouns, the background which makes nouns possible.

Stuff is the actors and props, holes is all the empty space which defines the play, the theater, and the audience. Process is all that is acted out, at every level. Stuff, holes and process compose everything (as opposed to nothing), from the tiniest quantum foam to the fanciest new car money can buy, to the planets and solar systems, and to your new brown shoes.

As you notice more and more light, you also notice that while it appeared you were an actor on the stage, you were also all of the props, the screen writer, the director, all of the action that took place and the theater itself. You were all that was and all that wasn't, no matter what limitations you claimed along the way.

The lights all go on and the play is both over and beginning. You have followed the natural progression of life, the loop that defines, more or less, all of life.

Life is movement, and you have performed the loop for yourself. You are born in process, and you move through stuff and holes back to process. You never really left process; you were always deeply in process, but you could not perceive it when you thought that stuff was real.

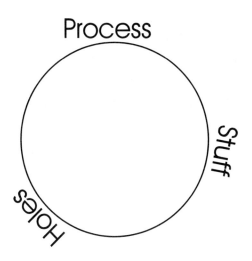

The progress has been characterized by what you missed. As you initially left process, you had to miss the relationship and interaction of all things; you had to lose nothing to move into the world where everything takes on significance. You had to order this world into priorities of what was more or less important, and you had to police and maintain that order. When you moved into holes, you had to lose all you had worked so hard to order. Everything fell away until the only thing you were holding was your loss. You even had to give up your loss and move back home again to process, to inclusion, to wholeness.

Everyone follows this same cycle. People do it at various rates. Some get stuck in stuff and spend most of their lives there, only moving into holes and back to process in their last few minutes. Some people move more rapidly and return to their perception of their enlightenment at an early age, free to play from then on. Your opinions about where you are on this circle don't matter because they are colored by where you are.

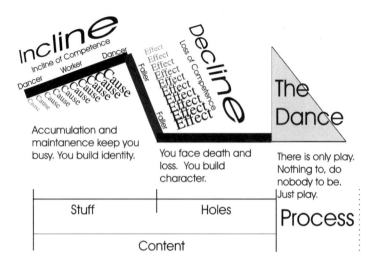

Stuff	Holes	
		Process

Content	

Accumulation and maintanence keep you busy. You build identity.

You face death and loss. You build character.

There is only play. Nothing to, do nobody to be. Just play.

There is little support for people who are in the holes, except to numb, drug or cajole them back to the world of stuff. It would be useful if people could notice the holes for what they are, a natural part of life, of letting go of illusion and identity. A freeing of that which has been bound. It would also be useful if children who are young enough to still be in process would be revered as models for where people are all going. They could be treated as little Gods and Goddesses, showing you the way back home.

Any moment spent in the stuff is time developing competence. Time in the holes is the cultivation of emptiness (not nothingness), the absence of stuff. In process there is only play, no meaning, all stuff, all holes, nothing.

Everyone makes this journey and everyone is at all points in the journey all the time. Yours is an interesting path. In the stuff phase you must ignore so much; in the holes, you must lose a great deal of ignorance (knowledge), and in the process phase you must learn how to interact with constant and ever-increasing bliss. Wherever you are, there you are, where you were and where you will be. There is temptation in all three, whichever you don't perceive, and there is also the whole. The more you keep the entire cycle in perspective without attempting to prove what point you are at, the easier it will be.

The people around you are probably at different points than you, so they can provide you with various perspectives. They can show you where you were or where you are going. The more you learn about people, the more it will become clear who is showing you which, and also, the less you will dwell on your opinions of your progress.

Wherever you are, and seem to be, doesn't matter. You are joining in to the best of your ability. As long as you can have things seem predictable around you and random outside, you will not have to face your inevitable wake-up call. You are curled up inside a box, you are a Jack or a Jill in the box. Any moment you will spring out, by your own force but not your own initiative. All that is holding you will let go, and you will launch upward, out of control, into the light. Up you will go. Surprise!

Beyond Compare

The body triangulates to know where it stands. The mind judges to know where it stands. The differences between these two methods are bound to result in the body and the mind never being in the same place at the same time. It is unsettling to have to pay attention to one *or* the other. You think you had better pay attention to the mind; after all, it is the least secure. So you ignore your body and attend to illusion.

Your mind can come to the conclusion that it doesn't like and will not eat chocolate, as your hand delivers another tasty morsel to your mouth. Thinking that you are your mind has the mind and the body separate. Tomorrow you will not smoke, overeat, or be addicted to anything, but that tomorrow never comes. The body craves attention, just a little bit, but it doesn't get it.

Your body is unique, unlike every other body. It is not consistent and always changing. The uncontrolled change, which your body demonstrates, is a threat to the mind. Billions of dollars are spent each year on potions and gadgets to make the body stay the same or change in specific ways. There is no control of the body, except superficially, especially not by neglect.

Your body is beyond compare, but you compare it anyway, and always come up short. You think your mind is beyond compare, when what sets it apart from other people's minds is indistinguishable, too small and subtle to be as important as you make it. There is no possible useful comparison between mind and body. You can only use that which you can compare sufficiently to feed your illusion of control, so you discard your body.

Comparison is designed to make the mind important because, by comparison, it knows where it stands. The foundation of comparison is difference, something that the mind has created. Comparison necessitates a range of difference not too great or too small. Too small and you call it the same, too large and you declare there is no comparison. This range of comparison tames and domesticates you; it fences you in by not allowing too much subtlety on the same side and restricting an overview of a larger area. Trapped in the petty middle, you compare and graze, then race wildly to some other part of all you are able to see (everything to you) and compare some more.

You only know, mentally, where you stand within your range. What if you also exist outside your range? You wouldn't know it. The universe is infinitely subtle and large, but you miss that. Even in your explanations and models, you can only draw from your limited range, so don't trust your explanations. Within the range, within the box, there is so much less than all that is outside it. The very act of not considering anything in the box important opens the possibility of all that is outside the box.

Physically, your perceptions are limited by focus and wavelength. Mentally they are defined by your own singular or collective hands holding the leash of what can be thought, ought to be thought, or has been thought. You must sleep in your own bed; otherwise, why did you buy it and why did you make it? You sleep alone together if your partner is beyond compare, because you couldn't then see him or her. Your partner must be demeaned along with yourself; otherwise, he or she would become a threat to all that you are convinced is or can be.

To even consider comparison, you initially accepted difference as a philosophical fact. Difference is a lie, a faulty foundation from which to build a crazy philosophy. Told too early, this faulty philosophy undermines all that comes afterward and makes it purposeful; it enslaves you to the pattern of needing you to look good or be right.

There are huge repercussions to questioning such an early part of one's philosophy—all that is built upon it must possibly be condemned. So you divide yourself into understandable chunks. You say everything is whole and then act as if everything is different. Alienated from yourself, life gets hard. Much harder than it needs to be. Much harder than life is.

Yes—No—Maybe

You have your back to the light, and you just can't turn around fast enough to see it. You are the source of the light, and it is very difficult to see the light as it leaves from you at such high speed. Your mind is slow and cannot see the light. It can only see that which the light shines upon. It needs faith to even see things. Anything that blocks the light seems real to you; thus anything you see, hear, feel or think is an obstruction. Light will not hang around, it may reflect back at you, but it keeps on going from there. Each moment you see something, you see it in a new light. A new light provides a new perspective, unless you don't notice the subtleties of the constant changes.

A shift happens as light is blocked. Something appears. The light is then blocked by this something again, and the next light is blocked also and then the next. There is a strobe effect too rapid for you to see and too discontinuous for the mind to grasp. Things do not exist except by the grace of light. You have to speed up to catch up, and you have to slow down to control or understand. You are caught. You are currently so far toward the slow end of the scale, obeying the speed limit, that it seems impossible to go fast enough, and so your position is maintained in your present form. You are so slow that things appear permanent to you when everything is intermittent. Nothing is an unrevealing in which no thing shows up and getting there is a function of speed without moving. You need to move without moving with the light at the speed of light to avoid being revealed by the light. At light speed, you will get out of the way.

If you throw a stick in a stream, that stick will soon approximate the speed of the stream. You are a stick of light flowing in the stream of light, but your mind has been playing a trick on you. Your mind factors out the speed at which you must be traveling and ignores your illumination, from within, while noticing only your slow physical movements which the mind thinks it can control. If your mind did not play this trick, you would become invisible, which is a threat to self-esteem, a threat to self and a threat to illusion. Most of what people call helping other people is an attempt to slow things down for them. Though well-meaning, doing so is always regressive.

When you don't move fast enough you, yourself, become an object—illuminated, but in the way. You are in your own way as you rush, slowly, to get things done so that once and for all you will prove how important you really are. You attempt to maximize the blockage because the blockage is as close to a real thing as you can get, yet it is as far from reality as it can be.

Repetition is necessary for you to even know who you are. You need to be the same person for two moments *running*; then you have the possibility of three and four. It is a difficult feat you have undertaken, this permanence in an ever-changing world. You have to see one thing over and over while ignoring soooo much. You have to create consistency which is not there; you have to expend energy treading light, at light speed. Otherwise you will fall through to nothing. It is what you ignore which tires you, as well as what you see or do.

The moment you attempt to hold anything, or create, you must become the light. When you obstruct the flow, you must become the source. You must become everything; otherwise, nothing exists. When you call the dark "light," you call the light "dark." You have learned to see the shadows, and you have called these shadows "the light." Doing this has allowed you to say the one thing you keep repeating: "I am important." You say it by arranging the barricades in so many ways, in the shape of a power plant, a new job, a car, a spouse, children, disease, a new theory, old thoughts, and so on. You do it in every way imaginable and in some ways that are not yet imaginable.

You sit on your lily pad hoping that something will come by, fly by, just slowly enough and close enough that you can stick out your tongue, catch it, and make it sustenance by calling it part of you. You wish you could eat everything, not through your mouth, but through your mind. You get full, that is your most immediate problem. Where do you put something when you already have all you can use? In storage, of course. That is why there are places called stores, because they store the things you will need soon. You are not content with what reveals itself in the moment; you want to be able to predict what will reveal itself in the next moment and thus bias your data. If a computer showed preference for a "yes" over a "no" you would say it was broken. People show the preference, corrupt their data—into illusion, resulting in struggle and trauma. So you play God. In the name of consistency you settle for Big Macs, calling them food. The thing you like best about them is that they are always the same. You will pay for that, worldwide.

It takes once for you to learn anything, but it takes twice to set up the pattern and feed that primitive you sitting on your lily pad. Recognition—think again. Consciousness dies with repetition as it is overshadowed by pattern. Awareness leaves first, but consciousness is not far behind. When you see what is illuminated rather than the method of illumination, you become not even the effect, but the observer of the effect. You don't remain at that distance for long, however, because you identify with the effect; it becomes you, you say, and so you wear it more often. Soon you will not take it off, and after that you cannot take it off without being confused about who you are, unable to recognize yourself.

You love and hate the species beneath you, those patterned lower life forms. You love them because it seems so easy to identify them and know who they are, and you hate them because they remind you of the parts of yourself you pretend you don't have while feeding them. You are living on table scraps, at the mercy of the universe, but you can't think that. You make up a world where you run things and fall away from reality. You then seek meaning because, in an illusion, you better have some meaning. Illusion is always so meaningful and reality so meaningless. Anytime you think something is meaningful, it is your illusion you are dealing with. You have forgotten who you are and have become the object of your own disaffection.

You are revealed each moment and snuffed out as well. You live and die each moment. It is not that hard unless you attempt not to do one or the other. It is in the digital yes's and no's that you carry information. These yes's and no's are the momentary off and on that is constant. You prefer the yes and thus undermine your existence in the next moment. Refusing to look at half of what is, you would rather look at the reflection, the shadow. You keep looking, without seeing, because you do not want the half that is not, only the half that is. Even though you are the light and your light comes from within, you have put yourself in the ridiculous position of wanting the spotlight on yourself. Show off your stuff; show them what you can do. Center stage belongs to you; this is the theater and you are the show. Read your lines. The show runs for 29,200 days, give or take a few.

Duality is the theater in which you live. It is composed of yes-no-yes-no-yes-no. When you think you know where you stand, you get stuck on one of the two, while the universe is still vibrating back and forth between yes and no. Reality is all yes's and all no's at once. This can't be seen, so you see only one yes. If you need to be in control, then you have to argue for the yes and resist what appears to you during the next no. In fact, it is a simultaneous, synonymous yes-no.

If you are stuck on yes or no, you are always out of the know and defining yourself as limitation. "I can't stand one more shift from yes to no," you say. So you make maybe's and gray areas in an attempt to mediate the paradox of yes-no together as the best of friends. You make them enemies, impossible friends, and alienate yourself from reality, by saying that they can't co-exist in one moment—they require two moments. Without the illusion of time, there would be no difference; everything would come together, and so it has.

Plants live in the light. But they are more primitive than you. They use the light directly rather than depending on reflections. You live in the light, too, but your mind won't see that because it depends on consistent reflection. With reflection comes distortion. What is rejected you see, and that which is accepted you miss. When something appears green, it has accepted all colors but green. Isn't it a clue to the instability, immaturity, and the reflective nature of the mind that people call things what is rejected? You do the same with yourself. You identify yourself as what you reject: your limits, your ends and your means.

You become the light when light can pass through you unencumbered. When it cannot, you become an object. You become an argument for thingness. It isn't pretty, it isn't fun, but it is the nature of the mind that since it is nothing, it can settle for anything. It is a nothing called anything, and that is the worst kind. As you discover that you are not your thoughts, your mind changes its clothes and calls itself something else. You listen to its calls, you watch it change its clothes and you get embarrassed. You become profoundly self-conscious. You can't be this embarrassed, so you stop looking. Considering how fast you really are, reflection is the only way you can even attempt consistency. You see light, but only know reflections. You are afraid of the dark but have called the light "dark" and the dark "light." Defined by the dark, you become the dark.

There was once a man who moved so fast he left his shadow behind. Coincidentally, at the loss of his shadow, he moved fast enough that he could no longer determine who he was. He never stayed in one place long enough to kill off the alternatives.

When you move, your place or position sometimes becomes important. When you move all of the time, space disappears because you are never anywhere long enough to stop and look at some other place. Einstein discovered that when you move fast enough, time stops. It is only in your slowness that time and space provide you the minutes and square feet necessary to build your illusion. It is illusion because it takes no space and no time, since neither exist.

Illusion is the place at which you discover where you stand when you stop seeing movement. Hold still for a moment and your mind holds to that moment for dear, or not-so-dear, life. Let go and you rise unmercifully, and without meaning, to the top. Holding yourself under this top makes it almost impossible to breathe. You are a creature who lives and breathes light, and you are lurking in the dark. You toy with that which you are so easily addicted to. You catch a glimpse of who you think you are, but you are too slow to really see yourself. A glimpse is all you have in mind. The mind is always ready to settle for less as long as it looks like more. Or as long as it looks long enough to waste some time.

It is ironic, but the very act of identification has replaced the light. You think calling something by name makes it that name. This is such a hollow representation offering so little satisfaction and sustenance that you have to repeat this process of name calling all the time in order to convince yourself that you got anything at all. "Sticks and stones will break my bones but names will never hurt me." So name everything and you will never be hurt.

You live and breathe an analogy, not noticing that you are. You never have enough of anything, even problems. Because what you are attempting to get from things is not in them. You are starved. "There is gold in them thar hills," but the hills remain in your past or in your future. Nothing at all will do, but you will not do nothing.

"I will just do nothing at all, if I ever get the time," you say, but there is so much to do first. You make vacations even busier than work.

Stretch. Really S T R E T C H. Close your eyes and look around you. See nothing. Exit your present location, illusion. Do so for a moment and you will be infinitely revealed. Sit, doing nothing and soon you will think nothing too. From here you can think anything. Let the light flow through you and you will become the illuminator. The only way to speed up sufficiently to join light is to not move at all; moving slowly will not do. The faster you move from moving slowly, the more obvious you make it that you will never get to light speed. Watch the objects and you will have become one. There is no real thing. No thing is real. Nothing is real. It is a joke—this life you think you lead while following along, but you have lost all of your senses. First to go was your sense of humor, and after that, everything mattered too much, so you took it all seriously.

"Who are you?" said the owl, independent of your answer, hoping that if the wise old bird said it often enough, you would get the message that your answer didn't matter and there would always be the question again. Who? Who? Who?

31

Love—People

Multiple Illusionary Perspectives Per Second (MIPPS) have nothing to do with multiple personalities. Personality is composed of an imaginary location where one has spent enough time to personalized it and make it his or her own by building up structures and symbols to define the location as distinct, more meaningful, and better than other locations. The defining of this position is the drawing of something out of nothing, coaxing and cajoling nothing, taunting it until it gives out one more illusion. Each personality is complete in and of itself. The motivation for creating a personality is to conceal who someone is not from somebody else, ultimately from oneself.

Multiple personality is a social disease. It results in acting differently depending upon whom you are with. With your spouse you act one way, with your boss another, with your old college chum yet another. For each relationship, you have a conglomeration of rules and interactions which define what can be said and done, and how you are to look. The bookkeeping required for multiple personalities is its most impressive feature, along with the toll it takes on both the actor and the audience. The consistent result of having to keep track of so many different and often non-overlapping personalities is to keep one from discovering anything about life.

Keeping track of who you are supposed to be with whom is about as superficial as you can get. Which face to present? The distinct nature of each personality, its limitations and its external motivator, another person, make the whole game problematic. One illusion is difficult enough to deal with, especially when you forget it is an illusion. The addition of more illusions just adds stress and tension, as you seek to deceive somebody else as well as yourself. Since there is little or no overlap between the personalities, and since they are all defined by limitation, the effort expended to keep them apart is wasted. Everything real is already together and everything illusionary needs to be kept apart. The multiple personalities look like this:

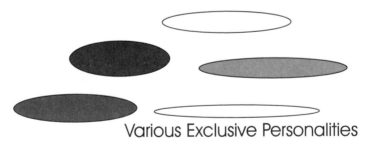

Various Exclusive Personalities

Each is flat, superficial, distinct and intended to obscure, making illusion appear real and differences seem concrete. This is a world of appearances where going below the surface is not allowed. It is control you seek as you try to come up with the right denomination for each interaction. The lack of corroboration between personalities encourages each to seem real when you are caught in it. It is as though you have a separate and different consciousness for each personality, allowing no end of confusion. Consciousness splits and each personality wants center stage. It is motivated by fear and increased by fear; thus it serves only itself—as sell fish, selfish, as you can get. You become the fish monger, selling the catch of the day. Wherever you are caught, you sell to anybody willing to listen to your current important limitation. Breaking up consciousness in this way decreases the likelihood that you will ever reveal illusion for illusion; you will be too busy juggling and proving something to be everything. You will be divided against yourself.

Multiple illusionary perspectives are also illusionary perspectives, but they are not separate or distinct: they are all held at the same time. The very idea of maintaining two or more perspectives at the same time provides the stuff for making mental triangulations, which reveal depth and height. Movement in a vertical direction is possible, and no juggling is necessary because the perspectives are ongoing. The drawing looks like this:

Perspectives are limitations, but when you have two of them at the same moment each of them becomes half as important. When you have three, they become one third as important. Each perspective is a fragment of the whole, but they take on

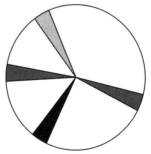

Perspectives in the Whole

fractional importance; thus attending to illusion appropriately is easy. The more perspectives adopted, the more you approximate the whole. All of the perspectives lead to the center; thus they are obviously related. They are all within one illusion so no juggling is necessary. Disorientation is at a minimum as is meaning. In multiple personality disorders, disorientation is huge and the necessity of being in the correct personality at the right moment appears to be a life or death struggle, dramatizing the importance of illusion. Having multiple personalities is serious business, schizophrenia. Multiple illusionary perspectives is entertaining, leading to wholeness. The two could not be more different, and they can look a lot the same.

Observing other people is easier than acquiring multiple personalities. Everyone provides you with the opportunity to see through their eyes, hear through their ears and feel what they feel. Developing the personalities within yourself is problematic; the fact that other people have developed them for you is your salvation. Since other people all started with the same tools you did, you could have been them instead of you. You still can be. Every other person on the planet offers you the opportunity of discovering both a route you could have taken and the knowledge that you were busy with illusion, not reality. You are as similar to them as you could be and as different as you could get. They show you possible you's, other illusions that open possibilities for you. They reveal you in everything they think, do, or say. They open you up, unless you have to prove to them that you are somehow better or more important than they are, or that you have to control them. When the control game happens everyone becomes a source of fear for you.

One Zen master uses other people as a stick. The awareness of other people hits you on the side of the head by drawing your attention to your patterns through watching others.

If you can sell to everyone, then you are not separate from them. Anyone who you cannot sell to appears to be distinct from you. This difference is a second level distortion, a distortion of an illusion. When illusions do not fit there is competition. Competition leads to dualistic thinking because somebody has to be right. So analogue leaves and digital enters. When this happens, you view illusion as simple, which it never is. Illusion is your attempt to model out the universe, and as such, it is tremendously intricate and involved. You have spent your life building it; you are proud of the complexity you have built. Confusing simplicity with complexity always makes things harder than they are. When you confuse hard with easy or hard with soft, then you may think you are in for a soft, easy landing as you splat on the pavement, not even noticing the fall.

Other people are you, and if you think they are separate from you or a threat to you, you will lose the most important resource there is. Love is a function of acceptance: you love everyone. The extent to which you don't know that you love everyone, you get fear. You don't love illusion, but you have to act like you do since, in many cases, it is all you can perceive. When you act like you love illusion, you must be fearful of people because they are a threat to your illusion. No matter how much money you have, how big a house, how many friends, how many symbols you have collected, you are not secure.

Where you meet everything is nothing. The more you attempt to control and define, the more threatened you are by anything you have not yet personalized. The only way you can make your mark, or think you have made your mark, on somebody else is to forget that they are who they are: reality, nothing. To do this, you must forget who you are. Original sin is as simple as forgetting; enlightenment is remembering (rejoining the group to which you were once a member). Forgetting nothing or remembering nothing makes all differences disappear.

You should only pick on somebody your own size, and the bigger you get the less apt you are to pick on anybody because you start to notice that difference is the essence of illusion and inclusion results in an increase in size. The more you can include as you, the more you love, and the less you have to be afraid of. How much joy do you deserve? Which you? The illusionary *you* has to work on care and maintenance of illusion, missing joy.

A day without fear will change your life forever. A day of inclusion, a moment of love, without reason, will end the madness that separates, divides and conquers people. Multiple illusionary perspectives per second (MIPPS) will lead you to bliss. MIPPS will have you discover who you are not, expanding endlessly, death disappearing. Other people are what you are most likely to love as you expand your depth. Not one other person, but all other people. They could not be more similar to you; they can never belong to you, or short either. The moment that anybody appears limited to you, you have been sold, not on who she really is but you have bought her illusion.

The opportunity is to expand through other people, using them to increase your possibilities while returning the favor. Watch the profound confidence of a three year old who has been loved. Her confidence is based on reality and her connection to it. Not at the end of the funnel, but at the opening where everything is wide and deep with fewer limits. Life for most people is moving toward greater limitation, down the funnel; life gets narrower and narrower at such a slow rate they don't notice. The narrowing is a function of consciousness eclipsing awareness. Notice—don't narrow—and you will expand. Your perspective is always either expanding or contracting. The trick of growth is to know the difference between the two. There are some differences worth knowing, but not the ones which come easily and go against subtlety. The more subtle the difference you discover, or create, the less it does for your illusion and thus the more revealing it is.

The problem is two. With one there is no problem. With two you have to work where you are least able, in relation. Three amplifies the problems somewhat, and so do four, five and six, but each adds fewer problems. When you get to double digits, and especially when you get to six figures, the illusion of control disappears. The way to One can be no distinctions, the harder route, or all distinctions, the easier route. Seeing complexity as complexity has you know what you are dealing with.

If you cave in to the fear, you may have to go to some secluded cave, get away from people and attempt to find yourself. The problem comes when you exit the cave and find that there are still other people around. What do you do with them? You had better get back to the cave. You can use other people as your salvation by including them, or you can use them as an excuse to abuse yourself, and act out life for them. Including them results in wholeness, a return to reality. Excluding them leads to superficiality and illusion. Everyone is your teacher.

"Any fish will bite if you got good bait. Here's a little story I would like to relate. I'm a goin' fishin', you're a goin' fishin', God's a goin' fishin', too."

"One day a woman fell into a bottomless lake. After the fall she was still falling. She had little energy for talking but a desire to learn and a real hunger for anything that looked like food. A hook looked like an opportunity to slow her digression. Her mouth was either open, eager and searching, or closed on some bait or other; the string, taught or loose, more or less being educated or set free."

When you are rising or getting ready to jump for a fly, hooks are in the way—an interruption—an invitation to dinner where you cease to be menu and become the meal.

Falling, the hooks look like sustenance and meaning— breaking your fall—holding you up for heaven's sake.

Enough line at one point and you keep falling, enough taut lines and you become a puppet—dancing, caught but moving—suspended at one vertical point. Advancing? Only in years. Moving horizontally with each pull or jerk of the string. By the company you keep.

There are no fisherman above—just emptiness. Into emptiness you can move. If the space above is occupied, you wouldn't know it except by your inability to move up. There is no gravity below—just default. Not your fault. You are fishing for other fish near you—trapped in your medium. Treading water. Judging your fishiness by the fishiness of others. This is a scale where nothing but weight matters. The more matter, the more weight, and so you get heavier and heavier. Heaving sighs, struggling and looking for like-minded company.

How far can you fall in a bottomless lake until you find yourself rising?

Static, neither falling or rising. Moving purposefully to get somewhere, that is your enemy. Moving nowhere while extending your terrain sideways. Write your name in the water as often as you can, and every time it is effort expended in vain. Nothing remains, why shouldn't it. Sell something to nothing and you lose the something, not the nothing.

The patterns are the string—the thoughts are your hooks and ladders and progress. Awareness, your sense of being in relation to nothing—consciousness streams—in relation to what?

You smile and walk on up or down the road—ride on down your hide until you greet yourself coming back from where you have not been. The bottom appears and you start back up.

"Hey, what does bottomless mean anyway?"

"It means you can't get rid of your waste—silly!"

Swim, dive, lurk, but don't go for the bait or you will have to fall to justify it.

You swear you will never do that again—you do it again and just swear. Each day you expect sainthood will be around the next corner. You seriously wish it were, missing today, for tomorrow will be another day. Day after daze your expectations are pumped up, inflated but not fulfilled. You live in expectation—waiting—weighing. The heavier you get, the more real you seem to be.

Then one day, for no reason, you lighten. You look for reason and lose the lightness again. If you just didn't need to be somebody other than who you are. You can be this body, but seldom are. But, you always are _____. If you could just let that space sit, stand up, roll over without having to fill it in. Then, there would be room to expand. You   think   and   youcloseinthespaces.

Thinking something is a contradiction in terms. Thinking and things are not compatible. Things are the hooks and the bait. Soon you cannot distinguish the hook from the bait or yourself from either one.

To a bigger fish, the smaller fish is bait. You would eat your mother using her own patterns if you only thought you were a little bigger and matured a little less.

"Let go of me—don't even think about my things, they are mine, me." You don't think them.

Have another thing, then what you own will be halved—you diminish yourself while increasing your material.

Your move—pawn or king, both can mate.

Let go of thinking things—the things may disappear, but your thinking will no longer be hooked. How much lighter can you get?

It is no accident that light moves so fast and you so slowly—light has no baggage. It reveals bait while taking none. Light cannot reveal you unless you are already lost—something—fallen. You are the light and you reveal everything—not distinct but existent.

Shed your baggage and your thoughts lose their illusionary form. Free—light—revealing.

After words—after thoughts—after life—after all, it begins and continues. The smile spreads everywhere on your so-called face.

You wind the clock instead of just looking at its face and time is next—always next.

Escape now and there will be no next.

Anything that appears real to you at your petty pace is real; it has stopped. Reality never stops—slows down—begins—or ends. These are all dead give aways that you are looking at illusion or hooked on it.

You won the lottery—that's what being alive is, now, be truly human.

You are judged by the company you keep only if they are moving so slowly that they think you need to be slowed. Keep lighter company; 186,000 miles per second is good company—fast friends—your peer group. Or huddle in the dark.

Free Choice?

"Choose to be free from free choice."

You are the light, you are already enlightened, and you are hiding from your enlightenment behind patterns, awareness and consciousness. Patterns are determined by repetition and do not allow choice. Awareness requires a specific location and does not allow choice either. Consciousness, however, is presently all about choice. You are preoccupied with choosing between one thing and another. You get confused if there appear to be too many things to choose from, so you limit the objects to choose between.

You define freedom as getting to the point where you can make choices independent of your circumstances, such as money, location and intelligence. You continually whittle away your possibilities, cutting off pieces of reality and removing what you think is in the way of your ability to see life's real beauty.

Of course, choice is an illusion, things are illusions and doing is an illusion. So, choosing is a process of selecting illusions. Through consciousness you have developed a series of filters which are used to evade everything (wholeness) and to settle on something. That something can indicate reward or direction, but never, though it seems to, an end.

The essence of consciousness really is choice. Not the little choices you perceive yourself making and then defining yourself by, but THE CHOICE, spiritual choice—choosing between something and everything. Everything leads you directly to nothing. Do you need something or can you settle for the lack of specific identity called everything?

Fear arises out of the possibility of discovering (or of being discovered) that you are not who you appear to be or thought you were. Each time you make a little choice and identify yourself with it, you build an illusion, which is limiting and exclusionary. The price you pay for identity is your sainthood, or enlightenment.

Free choice is choice outside of stories: this or that without the external *because* and with you as cause. But which you? You as the conglomeration of your past choices, or you as everything? If it is you as everything then the choice disappears because exclusion is unnecessary.

You, as identity, is a fearful confused bundle of inconsistencies that will not withstand scrutiny and thus thrives when you have no ability to observe yourself at all. Stay busy—then you won't have to see the slippery you. Watch TV, go places, find a religion, get a job, get married, have a child, have another child, get a hobby—do anything to distract yourself from the scrutiny you know your "little you" cannot survive.

If you collect baseball cards, do so compulsively and surround yourself with others who will do the same. You can then agree on what is important and what to focus on. At first it may sound silly—collecting pieces of stiff paper with pictures on them—but soon, as with anything repeated, the silliness fades as fear diminishes. You become a *serious* card collector. There are lots of choices to make about which cards to keep and which to sell, or trade, so you can convince yourself that you and only you are in control. Dwell on those little choices and they will soon look big, important, and meaningful. There is nothing wrong or right about collecting baseball cards—after all, thank God, human beings are the first species which can do so. Baseball card collecting is a specific thing (not everything) and the fuller your life is with things that are not everything, the smaller and more petty your life becomes.

Ironically, people say they want meaningful lives, but the more meaning they add, the worse the quality of their lives becomes. The circular nature of ALL peeks back around. You start with no meaning, add lots of meaning and then throw away all meaning until you have none again. All, every aspect, of life is circular, but you see such a small part at one time that life appears linear. You are at various points on any number of circles, behaving and thinking appropriately to complement all of your positions.

You move on one circle, but you cannot isolate the effect of your movement to just that circle. You move on one circle and effect all of your positions on the various points of all of your circles. This too is illusion, but observing process within your illusion is closer to reality than noticing content or stories.

Look in the mirror for an hour. Keep looking at yourself, deep into your eyes, until nobody looks back— until everybody returns your gaze, until you see love. Talk to the person in the mirror. Smile the perfect complete smile to that person. Speak to him or her until there is nothing more to say. Speak faster than you can think— then too slowly to follow your sentence structure.

Get to know all of your "you's" and bring them together. If the mirror breaks, get a new one. Find where you hide and where you hide next until all that is left is everything—watch everything turn to nothing and notice that there is no holding on to anything. Smile an impersonal declaration of acceptance.

If you perceive yourself to be anything at all, then you have a foundation based on a lie. There is no real choice, thus there is no real you. No matter how great the architect is, he or she is no better than the foundation beneath the building. The foundation surrounds and supports the emergence of existence.

Choice implies and necessitates future which demands a vehicle for control. To most people, the past looks uncontrollable because it has already happened. The present is, by definition, uncontrollable since it always already is. So the future, what isn't, is where people must show off their power, their ability and their control. Controlling what is not yet is not easy. Choice, the idea, was invented to convince you that you can control the future. The past was invented as evidence for consistency and continuity, and the present is the sole domain of untethered, uneclipsed awareness. Consciousness is never present—it needs awareness for that.

Live in the present and you can use consciousness to set you free: free from wholeness and bound to selective, illusionary responsibility. Ignore the past and patterns disappear. Fear the future and you need choice to control it. Deal with past, present and future, and you will have a dance of patterns, awareness, and consciousness. Accept and include without reservation, and you will always have plenty of room to operate in.

Past-present-future equate (conspire) almost directly with patterns-awareness-consciousness to aide in creating illusion. Misalign them and you will bust your illusions, reveal them as nothing; or crosswire the conspirators and the illusions will disappear. This can be done in many ways, a few of which are as follows: become aware of patterns, worry about and change the past, see the future now, move backward, forget something, speak without knowing what you will say, be certain of the future and uncertain of the past, choose to have eaten something different for lunch yesterday, think your future is predestined, be God, or…. This is an incomplete list, anything which breaks up the imaginary links is useful in revealing them as nothing.

The links only let you know where you stand in your illusion and thus limit you within your limitation. Bust up the illusionary foundation and the illusion falls. "Welcome to reality."

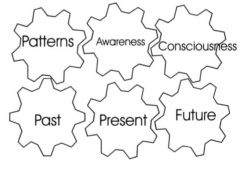

A tiny fraction of a second separates what is from what will be. You can't carry anything across this gap—no matter how badly or goodly you want to. You are in a constant state of infinite flux, nothing, pure possibility, reality. Between what you think now and what you will think next, ALL is possible, all possibility exists. Resist the temptation to control—abandon choice and you naturally open to nothing often enough to enjoy everything. Time is a pawn moving from square to square through illusion, and you are the king or queen. But, in reality, you are not that limited.

If you live in jail for long enough, you will end up blessing the jailer. And so it is with human beings. For hundreds of years (the precise date remains in question, reinforcing the mind) people have been imprisoned by a gift that was to set them free. They have not been idle, they have been busy building monuments to their captors.

You are slave labor and you don't even know who your boss is. You work for a living, suffer from the effect, and breathe to provide the next moment. You are building the twentieth century version of the pyramids. When the original pyramids were complete, the pharaohs still clung to life, since no monument was attractive enough to make someone wish to die for the opportunity to be buried within it. Your monument is much larger than the pyramids, it is so big it now reaches everywhere and has finally stopped spreading. It had to stop once it reached everywhere and there was nowhere else to spread. With expansion over, your monument began rising up and stretched its apparently endless limbs to prove that it was in control. The way to prove control when you are already everywhere is to change things and stay busy measuring the speed and accuracy of the changes. How long does it take everybody to catch on to change? Each change also increases the likelihood that any non-believers or stragglers will be revealed as such.

If you are out in the lead, then you get to change faster than others. That is good. If you are in the middle, you are supporting all of those who went ahead and those who will follow. This is more necessary than it is good. If you are trailing behind, you are, to some degree, holding on to something old. You are not good.

Controlled variation is as close as most people can get to amusement. They are perched, not lightly, between what is and what will be, supporting time with their contributions.

Your jailer and boss, right now is free choice. As long as you think there is such a thing as free choice, you will define yourself by limitation and consider the mind to be all important. There is no mind, there are no thoughts, and there is no free choice. The size of the monument built to honor free choice is too big to argue with. Surely such a mammoth monstrosity must be meaningful. What you don't notice is that the bigger the monument, the less monumental is that which it represents. The most important things are monuments in themselves, and symbols can never represent them.

Free choice is a competitive game with winners and losers. If you and Sally are walking together and you come to a fork in the road, under the free choice model, you could take either fork. You cannot take both, thus eliminating the whole from even being a possibility. Yogi Berra said, "If you come to a fork in the road, take it."

You don't. You must take one *or* the other. If you wish to take the right fork and Sally wants to take the left, then what ensues is a battle of "free wills" (will=consciousness determined). Would truly free wills battle? One would think they would be free of such things as battle. The very idea of battle is preempting one person's consciousness with that of another. Free choice is too competitive to be real. Reality includes All, and free choice is the systematic mind-based process of exclusion.

You are poised, balanced on a pinnacle, waiting to choose. No wonder procrastination is the national pastime.

You can go one way or the other, or yet another. Ironically, when you add gravity to your position, it becomes more and more obvious that you don't really have free choice. You cannot fall up. But you can sacrifice yourself and throw-up, thus assuring at least the temporary rise of something. No, you are certain that, thus poised, you will fall down. But which direction will you fall? Choice does not care what the content of the possible choices is as long as you perceive that you have choice. Without your perception that you have choice, you would be free, truly response-able.

You hack away at your wholeness, attempting to position the cut so that you fall in a particular direction—not too near some things and right next to others. You take away a little bit of this and a little bit of that. Total structure is only possible when you are whole, and you are chopping away your wholeness. You are losing structure, becoming weaker and weaker, nearer to falling all of the time. The Bible tells you that you have already fallen, which is true, but you are also in the process of falling again, newly each moment.

So you get down to menial choices. "What should you have for lunch?" "Where should you work?" "Who should you marry?"

Another one of your bosses shows itself. This boss enforces the immutable dictates of free choice. This boss is importance. Surely some choice is more important than another and, within the choice, one route will have you become more important than the other. Again, a competitive game results: you want to be more important than other people. "If you could only make me as important to you as I am to me."

You race for importance and don't see wholeness in the process. If wholeness exists, then nothing is more important than anything else. "Exactly."

The very idea of a fork in the road eliminates all of the terrain in between and around the forks. Free choice is limitation expressed, an evolutionarily unsound prior limitation. Your belief in free choice, however, justifies your imprisonment for all these years. The jailer, who at first appeared to be in your way, is necessary. After long enough, the jailer becomes God and every time you perceive you have a choice to make or have made one, you become a worshipper. You bow and scrape to please free choice, hoping to make the right choice.

Just to cover your choices in case you make the wrong one, you have a story, an explanation, as to why you took the fork you did. If you have a good enough reason, making the wrong choice is all right. The very idea of a limitation is so awful to you that you call it an asset. You think you are important because you can choose. You haul another block to place on your structure, not noticing that your structure is getting bigger and occupying area that you could be exploring and moving through freely. Not only are you in prison, but you have taken on the role of security guard and maintenance crew to ensure your imprisonment. Soon, you may as well die because you have filled in every possible choice and have none left. Death might set you free from your confinement.

Free choice is everywhere. Try believing that there is no free choice and you will immediately think you have lost something, your mind perhaps. If you have lost something, then you must have had something in the first place, which is philosophically impossible. For most people, thinking that free choice doesn't exist is not even possible. Their whole landscape is based on choice. Without it, they would not have the limitations of their cells to protect them. They would not have the security of trying to please or resist the jailer. In short, they would not know where they stand.

Without the illusion of free choice, they would have so much time that they would not know what to do. It is better to have free choice and always be wrong than to have no free choice at all. Of course, what they call free has nothing to do with freedom. If this were not the case, people would be much happier than they are. Free choice is crazy and it makes you crazy, but everybody else is crazy too. You join the crowd. You prepare for the consequences of your choices. You are entirely controlled by the illusion of free choice.

Free choice is the boss who makes the mind important, but it is not the real ruler. Free choice makes the mind important. Free choice makes the mind important. The mind becomes God.

Without free choice, what would be the use of thinking? You would just have to think for the fun or entertainment of it. Thinking would lose its importance. Only if thinking is important are you important because, after all, you are your thinking. Without free choice, thinking would be set free. You could think anything. You would no longer have to try to think the right thing, or the wrong thing. You would not even have to second guess yourself.

Without free choice, you would not need a past or a future. You do not *choose* the present. If free choice existed, you already would have chosen it, at some past point. Free choice locks you into time while consuming your time at the same time, thus becoming an argument against itself. The present is consumed by your model of free choice. Like a virus, free choice eats your time by creating probable pasts and hopeful futures.

Free choice comes along shortly after drawing a philosophical line and suggests that you cannot be on both sides of the line. If there are two lines, which should you attend to? Which is the right line? Which side of which line should you be on? What if the lines are connected? You keep the lines separate (not really, but you think you do) and then you try and walk the right line. You attempt to balance on the line, the right line. You lose the present and look forward and back on the line, wondering constantly how you did and how you will do while ignoring entirely how you are doing now. By the time you question how you are doing now, the now has become then.

The present is slippery and you fall off. You fall ahead, *choosing* the future. You choose a head, or rather a mind.

You build your monument without appreciating what you are building, since by definition you must be able to step out and look at something to appreciate it. There is no appreciation for this model of free choice because nobody is the only one outside of it.

You can't see free choice, but you may as well act as though it doesn't exist and then find out where that gets you. At the very least, it will have you become more flexible. You will work through your initial loss of control. Control is a bad thing when it happens *to* you and a good thing when it happens *from* you. When a noun's goodness or badness is determined by a preposition, it ought to be outlawed.

Free choice is a franchised business in competition with reality. You are the franchisee, giving all of your proceeds and more back to free choice. You are being sucked dry and told that this is what life at the oasis is like.

If you look, you will find a lot of evidence for free choice. That is how it must be when so many people have been paying homage for so long. Anything that you find no evidence for provides you with the ultimate opportunity to trust and have faith. Trust yourself: there is no free choice. Don't trust yourself because it is true. Trust to find out the lengths your trust can go to without having to reach or ignore a fork in the road. The straight and narrow is the easiest road to walk, but it is also straight and narrow.

Who has more free choice—you or your neighbor? Be nice to the jailer and you may get a bigger cell. You may think you are choosing to be nice to get better treatment; otherwise, why would you be so nice? Tow the line. Work hard, follow the rules and keep trying to make the right choice. Be a model prisoner and soon you, too, may become a jailer. Work on the monument, continue building it everyday, and soon the monument will be your life's work.

An alternate plan may be to make all choices all of the time. Choose to not exclude with your choices. Choose everything because to choose anything less than everything is to exclude wholeness.

Life, for most people, is a series of choices that resembles a bell curve. They define the prime of life as the time when the most important choices are made. As children choices don't really matter and neither do the choices of old people. But it is the people in the middle whose choices really matter. At the beginning of life you are important merely by your existence. At the end of life, you are important by your impending departure. As an old person, you can have enough perspective to see that none of your choices really mattered. But in your middle years, your choices define who you are.

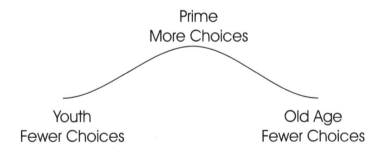

Prime
More Choices

Youth   Old Age
Fewer Choices   Fewer Choices

A life of choice leads to a small life. Cozy, perhaps, but typically stifling. Watch people when they perceive they have a big choice to make. They become immobile and hardly even breathe. Anything that requires you to stay still and hold your breath is not a positive influence on your life. Breathe and move around a lot. That way, your supposed choices will not look so important to you. The next time you perceive you are at a crossroads with a really important choice to make, breathe deeply and walk around a lot. Fill in your thoughts with deep breathing and movements. When your thoughts are used for anything other than entertainment, they are being misused. The price of this misuse is the likelihood that you will suffocate and stagnate. Move around and breathe. Trust that there is no free choice. Starve the mind of importance and it will gorge itself on freedom.

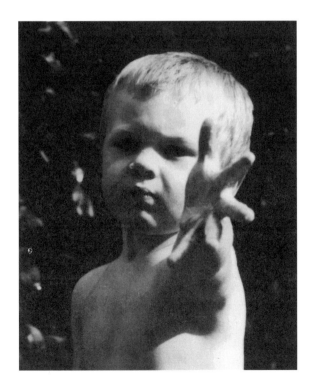

Believe It or Not

"I can't believe that."

"I can believe this."

"I shouldn't believe it."

"Now, here is something I believe in."

"I don't believe it."

Beliefs continually control your life. They are lock boxes of patterns and thoughts that preclude awareness and examination. They are pacts between the past and the future which don't involve the present. Beliefs never see the light of day. Impervious to rationality and logic, beliefs lock a behavior to a thought and always sink to the lowest, most-demeaning aspect of both. Awareness cannot penetrate belief and is constantly eclipsed by it. Beliefs can justify anything and are unexplorable. They blind you in the name of safety and require you to abandon all intelligence. They are a leap of faith in the name of control.

Locking life away in beliefs guarantees automaticity and waking sleep. Beliefs become Gods: indivisible, undefinable, uncontrollable (controller), and omnipotent. A God who is controlling, mean, unruly, limiting and restricting. As long as you hold one God before you, you are still waiting in line—the line which divides everything into two. The moment there are two, you prefer one of the two. This gives you something to do while waiting in line. It keeps you occupied, dividing and multiplying, adding and subtracting while distrusting mathematics. Smile. Don't cut in front of God—there are consequences beyond your control.

You created God. What does that make you? This is not to suggest that there is no God, but, as far as you are concerned, you created God for you. The deer have no God. The deer does not pray, unless everything is praying. In which case, everyone is always praying so there is nothing to do and nothing to belong to. You can believe anything. Belief is a mental technique which has to do with a selective blindness combined with repetition to provide a kind of controlled stupidity in a specific domain. There is no defined path, so you declare yourself there already. Surely that is better than not getting there at all.

Beliefs typically are very exclusive events. There are people who have beliefs which you can include with your beliefs and people you can exclude who have different beliefs from yours, and there is no overlap between the two. After the initial huge jump is made and a thought is believed, there is usually enough energy blockage left over to take the next tiny step and defend the belief by assuming that it is the right one to have. Beliefs preclude further thought and demand company. They do not stand on their own. Beliefs beg to be supported by as many people as possible.

There is no defense against a belief other than to examine it, scrutinize it and expose it for what it really is. This can be done by looking at the glue that holds its different components together. How do you believe? is the relevant question. What do you believe? is the final result. How you believe is the process of wanton limitation. Thinking is a process of systematic limitation while belief does not require the system. Repetition and conviction are sufficient. Where all else fails, belief prevails.

Watch your language. What do you believe? is a point of blindness waiting to trip you up. If you can believe one thing, then you are closer to believing its opposite than the person who does not believe at all.

Belief is anti-evolutionary because it uses your most primitive brain function (patterns) to eclipse your evolutionary advantages (awareness and consciousness). Beliefs will eat you for lunch. Drop the word belief and all its forms from your vocabulary, and you will open your eyes wider and see more as awareness peeks out from behind the patterns. Sensing your surroundings may become entertaining, depending upon how you are holding or releasing consciousness.

There was once a man who believed the world was flat. He shared this belief with so many people that it was "true." He acted according to this belief by never leaving home, which was the safest thing to do because he could never tell exactly where the edge was. It may not even be in the same place twice. Soon the man was not comfortable leaving his front room. The kitchen was potentially too close to the edge, and the bedroom, which was all the way down the hall, may have already fallen off the edge. He huddled in his Lazy Boy recliner, on the edge, prepared and fearing that he might fall over at any moment, not just fall over onto the floor but the big over. He was afraid of falling over the ultimate edge between everything in his entire huge life (which through his power of thought he had limited to his living room) and that big scary NOTHING, or at least, no things that he can include in his current limitations.

To grow, you have to be near the edge, your growing edge. Avoid the edge and you will not discover what is inconsistent with your present limitations. The edge is many edges, meeting places between what you know and what you do not know. The edges are waysides for beliefs to take a rest. It is where you have been and where you have not been, where you think you exist and where you are sure you do not exist. The edge is where what you can do and what you know you can't do threaten to overlap. It is where any two planes that you have declared separate and distinct get so close together that you cannot tell the difference between the two, no matter how hard you try. The illustration of having one perspective portrays this meeting place, off in the distance, as the rails come together at some point up ahead. Being on the edge is having this meeting NOW, right in front of your face. You look over the edge and see nothing (that which you are most afraid of) beckoning you. At the edge you disappear as what you have considered yourself to be. Your identity screams, "Move away. Run for your life. It isn't safe here." The edge is not safe for identity. Illusion has not yet been constructed at the edge and you are on new terrain, an explorer.

Beliefs declare the edge, bringing the edge into existence, and then ignoring it. Beliefs (patterns) are responsible for drawing the edge rather than discovering it. Beliefs create the edge and then obscure it from you so you won't expose it—a self-generated maneuver to keep you in line. However, this symbolic, scary edge (edginess) offers you the opportunity to evolve within a lifetime rather than having to wait for genetics to determine evolutionary changes. Unless you are willing to drown your weaker children you need the edge for your evolutionary advancement. Line up your patterns (which suggests that there is no edge) with your awareness (which sees the edge without judgment) and with your consciousness (which wants to jump and escape the edge). If you don't have patterns, awareness and consciousness working together, then you will jump with abandon and miss the opportunity to grow. Since beliefs eclipse awareness, a jump made with your beliefs intact is like jumping in place, with little to lose and little to learn. Continuing to jump in the same place keeps you busy and tires you but seldom advances you to the edge. At least jumping is getting you into some specific shape, you think.

What takes you to the edge, your apparently real edge? Whatever you are the most afraid of. Whatever seems the most impossible, preposterous, ridiculous, terrifying and fearful. When you were young, your parents kept you from the edge in the name of your own safety. The edge would have been easy for you then, and it was where you belonged, but those hypocrites kept you from it not for your sake, but for their own. Keeping you from the edge justified them in continuing to stay away from it themselves.

You kept wandering closer to it, and they talked you away from the edge, explaining and impressing upon you how important it was that you stay somewhere near the center. If only a child could take a parent's hand and lead the way to the edge.

The center is as far away from the edge as you can get. A little too far and you move closer to another edge. Certainly, the closer you get to the edge, the more energy you must expend to get even closer, but the more you get back as well. At the edge, your distance from the center threatens the existence of the center and thus threatens to shift the center of gravity. Gravity is an imaginary pull to the center—cultural pull—voters tug—but life occurs only on the edge. It is not jumping off the edge that makes the difference; it is moving further from the center. At the edge, everything is the same, all differences have been amplified so much that they have disappeared. Gravity is a function of power of the center, so the closer you get to the edge, the less you can afford to carry with you. Let everything go and you can get right to the edge. Stay there and you will grow as fast as you can. The edge is the edge of illusion, so it is an illusionary edge. But since you are steeped in illusion, it is still useful to move to the edge of it.

As long as you are going to confuse illusion with reality, there is work to be done. So much to do and so little time. The work does not necessarily need to enhance the delusion, just make it more hospitable. Break the wild nothing into something. The closer you get to the edge, the sparser and more barren the terrain becomes. There is less to hold you there, less to live for and much more life. Life beyond stories and reasons. Raw, fragrant, pleasant, simple life, and it doesn't get easier. For something to get easier, patterns must be involved, and there are none here;

it is part of the definition of the edge. Think what you have never thought before, and you will move closer to the edge; think what has never been thought, and you are the edge. There are no things to hold onto at the edge; things can only go so far before they become too heavy. Things are intended to support you in returning to the center, not in reaching escape velocity. Things will keep you busy; they just won't keep you alive.

Paradox looks you in the face. Belief is the artificial removal of paradox. You are terrified and safe all at the same moment. Everything lines up and you are on target. You have taken a stand, adopted a position often enough, been certain of that position and then released it. You have defined yourself as something and then something else so often that you no longer know who you are, at least by limitation. The further out you get the more eccentric you become. Enlightenment is escaping the gravity all together and removing oneself from stability and definition. People walk around in waking sleep because their dreams are better than their lives. The further out they get, the better their lives become, and they wake up.

There are initial distinctions which keep you from the edge, define you, limit you. These must be made, but they must also be moved through. The more suitable the limitation, the more tempting it is to keep. What does a limitation keep you from and what does it tie you to?

Disillusion is a step on the way to discovering your enlightenment. Avoid it and you haven't started the journey. Avoid it some more, and you slow your progress. You are already on your path. There is nothing you need to do, and you need to do nothing. There are two kinds of people who dare pursue spirituality (focusing consciousness on reality) through constant effort: those who have already handled everything, and those who have become convinced they will never do so. For the masses, in between, constant spiritual effort is riddled with attempting to handle things of Earth and making excuses for why they cannot possibly take the time for spiritual practices until that lucky day when everything becomes complete.

How many times do you have to think a thought before you notice the thought? Patterns are waiting to return you to an earlier evolutionary step. How many times do you have to think something before it becomes serious? How many times can you think something and have it remain entertaining? How many times do you have to think something before you believe it?

At the edge, everything is funny, and funny exists independent of things. Humor reveals itself as a creation within you. There is no repetition and there are no stories at the edge. You need to stack one thing on top of another while justifying the side by side exclusive nature of things to tell a story. At the edge there is nothing, and nothing cannot be eclipsed. There is only light at the edge, unblocked and flowing. Light is too fast for things.

Everything is simple. Something is so complicated. Everything has no relationship; it encompasses all relationships. Something, anything, a thing has a relationship to every other thing that is not it. This is blowing the process of relating to an importance beyond the things themselves. Thus, by separating things, you make relationship your constant threat and focus. "What is it in relation to what?" is the question that drives all of the something's crazy as they fight tooth and nail to stay separate and independent from the whole. This is too difficult. Enlightenment is easy.

You will never know how easy life can get until you notice your enlightenment. Up to this point, life is a struggle, and you are at varying degrees of war between who you think you are and all of those other people and things who you think you are not.

Geometry and You

Currently, human beings are interacting with the world through a geometric interface. All aspects of life, physical and mental, when boiled down, will produce points which then compose lines, then figures, then symbols, then meta symbols, then meanings (stories). If you wish to reveal your basic foundations, go back to geometry and discover the structure buried beneath the symbols you perceive. Ignoring the structure is like being so deeply attached to a project that you cannot perceive yourself separately from it.

You must isolate a point and differentiate it from its surroundings to even perceive it. The very fact that you are required to separate something before you can perceive it is what has you lose the context of anything you perceive. Thus perception and distortion go hand in hand, but you don't know that, so you trust your perceptions. You even identify yourself as your perceptions.

There is wholeness, everything existing in the flow of nothing. From the whole, one point is perceived as separate and distinct from the flow of nothing. This point is now something in lieu of nothing. The less nothing there is somewhere, the more likely it is that something will appear. There is a flow from areas of greater concentration of nothing to lesser concentrations. As more nothing gravitates toward less nothing, a kind of no-wind is created. Everything becomes the conduit for this no-wind which allows it to cover vast distances without time (in no-time). This no-wind affects all that is, giving rise to everything in its movement and creating all that is out of the flow from more nothing to less. When the imbalance gets great enough, before it can be equalized, something appears. This something becomes nothing again when the balance is equalized, but not before an illusion is pinched off. The illusion appears independent but is defined by nothing. Nothing is the eternal backdrop for all that is.

Enter the perceiver, you. You perceive yourself and hold to your perception for dear life. But, you are an illusion having been pinched off before the balance of nothing was restored. You appear independent, but you are defined by nothing. Being basically nothing, you hold nothing with unseen hands. Unseen by you.

One day you see something and hold to it. Now your hands of time and space cradle this new little something and nurture it along. This something becomes a seed which germinates in your mind and grows out of proportion, a weed in paradise. This something becomes a point of and beyond contention, which in some strange and convoluted way proves your importance once and for all—called thinking. You think about the plant and its growth while continuing to nurture it because if it exists, then you in relation to it must exist too. Your plant chokes out all other possible plants, you don't notice that it is *a* weed because it is *your* weed.

You notice your reflection in everything and anything and think your reflection is you. You have arrived, you have met the enemy and now need the enemy to define yourself. You become dependent on something.

When time and space are added to the point, there is a sequence of points in a row. With two points comes the idea of identification and organization. The original point and its additional points are part of the foundation. You cannot see the foundation when you perceive what you have built over the top. With your addition of time, you can create two points, which give you space, the area in and around the points. All lines are composed of points indicating a progression, a lifeline, like this:

If you look closely, the lifeline looks discontinuous:

• •

Stuff, the points, and holes, the space in between, are leading you down the primrose path to proving your existence through illusion. This is an insecure path at best.

It all comes back to points, but you seldom remember that because you are already too practiced in perceiving the structures and monuments and you no longer see the points which compose them. There are too many points to attend to and too little time.

One of your next practices is to only attend to certain parts of your lifeline instead of others. You dole out awareness in an attempt to control all that is around you. You are constructing the very track you are tracing. Your line looks like this.

Points of Focus

When you focus more on one point than the others, you create basic forms. When repeated, these forms soon come to express your patterns or your repetitious placement of awareness.

In an attempt to justify your repetition and your lack of growth in such a dynamic universe, you group the symbols and lose the significance of their origins, until they represent a story, like the words on this page. The alphabet is a series of patterns representing process, but being removed from it twice, you no longer notice this.

You stop learning when you start knowing. By being justified in focusing on a single point or by focusing on the meaning of your story, you miss most of what there is to learn. Your symbols reveal much about you, but only if you are willing to step outside yourself to look at them. Look beyond your point of view, see the points that define a pattern, or strip the meaning off of all points so that you can see each point equally.

All explanations for preferences lead to stories. The story is much more interesting than geometry to you, so soon you even forget why you told the story in the first place and you become a storyteller and a story believer. A culture will not tell stories for long without starting to believe its stories. You believe the stories you tell to yourself and to others. When stories are believed they obscure who you are, while apparently revealing you. They mislead you while holding your hand. Dressed as friends they define repetition as security and persistence as existence. They isolate you and build your patterns with conscious justification. When you are caught up in the story, you do not get to be the author. You become just another character.

The basic underlying patterns predict how you will focus your attention and which points you will focus on. There are also patterns to the stories that you tell about the points and their importance. With some people every one-hundredth point gets attention. Others attend to points similar to ones that have been traced twenty, fifty or a thousand times before. Some points get attention by how often the point is traced, while others get attention in relation to their last traced point or the last point a person attended to.

Most people do not separate themselves from their patterns, so they do not know anything about their dedication to patterns as the guiding force of their lives.

You are like a creature who is granted one wish. You ponder the wish for centuries of development and finally decide to wish for invisibility (for safety's sake). There are many other more entertaining wishes, but they fall by the wayside as frivolous. So you become invisible, but lack of clarity in stating your wish, results in your becoming invisible only to yourself. Invisibility is not all it is cracked up to be. The way you became invisible was to become so important to yourself that you could no longer see anything outside yourself. You became so self-centered and selfish that you were only interested in yourself. Like a small child covering his or her eyes, you were certain that you couldn't be seen.

Hold onto your symbols and believe your stories and they will become invisible and important to you. They will cease to be your creations (Frankenstein) and become the illusion you call reality.

Nothing is important to you: it protects and defends you. If you get one wish, wish for nothing. That is a good for nothing wish and will not lead you down this odd path you have lost yourself on.

No point is more important than any other and by making one more significant, you are adding your own bias. This inhibits your ability to vary your perspective. Burdened by everything you are influenced and blinded, invisible only to yourself and obvious to evolution.

Repeating a behavior over and over again might be called patterns, at one level, work, at another, and repetition, at yet another.

People consider their important points to be pivotal, which is one of the main ways they miss subtlety. Subtlety is the art of attending to all points equally without perceiving one point to be larger than another. The moment one point appears larger, it obscures the points leading up to it and those near it. People cannot see what they cannot see, and cannot understand what they cannot see, so they tell stories to fill in the gaps, creating points on the way to an internally created holistic invisible world view. Stories are often highly creative but can only be appreciated if they are recognized as illusionary creations. Stories lose all of their entertainment value when they are thought to be true. Life within illusion is a constant struggle to obscure reality and prove the story true.

To justify the importance of some points over others, you claim that those points are turning points, or decision points, or points which influence all points that come along afterward. The drawings are different but the points are the same. They are as follows:

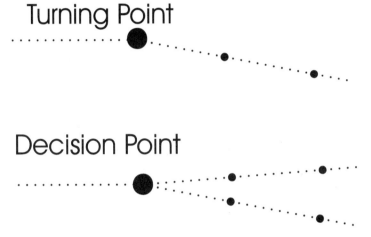

Turning Point

Decision Point

It takes only one point to mislead you, but it takes three points to triangulate or find yourself. Thought often operates on one point. Thus thought is in a constant state of being lost, while defining itself as being found.

Basic shapes are the foundations for the complex stories people trace in their lives. These stories are traced repeatedly and are passed down, often unknowingly, from generation to generation. They are the fundamentals of limitation and the foundations for the alphabet soup you find yourself in, if you find yourself at all.

People cannot be defined; only their patterns can, and their patterns have little to do with who people really are.

Thus when people define themselves they lose themselves.

Patterns are templates which people think they force upon reality, in order to organize what they perceive. A final result is fully-patterned thought—consciousness obscured or made important by the earlier evolutionary step of patterns, a box or a more complex shape traced over and over in an attempt to prove itself right, a fence built in the name of safety. Your thoughts repeat themselves. Familiar points arise in your thinking, and you breathe a sigh of relief. Your limited perceptions can be represented as geometric tracings, the constellations of limitation. These shapes can be very complex but gain their apparent security value by repetition.

You go on tracing out your life, mentally moving from point to point. Occasionally you see the point you are on but more often you are looking out ahead a point or two. For the pattern to continue, amnesia is imperative.

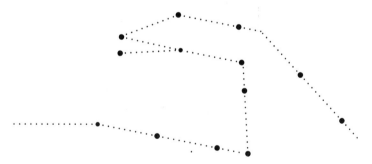

People are addicted to the creation of structure where there isn't any. They build patterns out of nothing and are pleased if they can prove anything. Enlightenment is a return to what is underneath structure, underneath those points your parents traced that you didn't like when they drew them but must now accept within yourself. You can see all of the points that underlie your visible monuments. Attend to the subtlety, seeing all points is a step on the way to undermining your illusion.

There is an opportunity with the existence of consciousness to focus both consciousness and awareness on patterns. Tease the patterns out, not to make them important, but to make who you are unpredictable enough to foil any predator around the next bend or to make you entertaining enough that you amuse yourself anytime anywhere just by your intrinsic unpatterned variation. Try to change patterns and you will lead the way back to the drive for control that produced them in the first place. Notice patterns, just perceive them, and you may soon not have to repeat them. The steps of your life may become interesting both to you and to evolution, interesting enough to provide such quality to your life that quantity is irrelevant. There is a reward for having a great day; the great day.

The more you matter the more susceptible you are to patterns and thus the less important you become. You become more like other species, determined by patterns, which is not bad, just not optimal for a creature with consciousness. Learn to observe your geometrical tracings and soon you will rise above them, gaining a three-dimensional existence outside of patterns. The very act of seeing patterns puts you outside the patterns. The way to escape patterns is to see them. Patterns, symbols, and stories limit perspectives—an ounce of clarity but a pound of limitation.

See all points on the line equally and soon the line disappears. See each point, look deeply into the point, and you will discover that within it is a whole universe that you miss by looking at the structure the point leads to. There are enough universes to keep you amused and entertained for infinite lifetimes. Let the games begin, big and small.

The Landscape

Reality is the mathematical computation of all possibility. While this definition includes the possibility of things, in reality there are no things, so reality is nothing—just pure process without content. Out of this computation of all possibility falls the results of reality or stuff, holes and process (specific interactions between stuff and holes). Next is the blank slate of creation upon which you draw yourself, not your physical body, which is composed of stuff, holes and process, but your mental fixations defined by your geographical tracings—the points you isolate, prefer, return to, pay for, deny, wrestle with, define yourself as, ignore, learn, focus on, abuse, cajole, slander, and more. Since people seldom see them, patterns seem to not exist. People usually look through the patterns to see the stuff and holes or the relationships between them. But these observations are already influenced by the patterns. Geographical tracings are the first step in the personalization of illusion. The things underneath them are illusion, but without bias. People have preferences regarding things, thoughts and process which are determined by the patterns through which they view everything. You like one sofa but dislike another. This preference is often *determined* at the level of patterns. The layer on top of this is where these preferences get *defined*. This is the layer of symbols (content) created on a framework of geometry and resulting in a series of "this means this" equations.

Imagine yourself tracing a pattern. You may notice certain aspects of the pattern, not as parts of the pattern, but as recognizable entities meaning something. Upon this level you build groups of symbols.

Your symbols, when distributed to enough people, become facts. They also become "true" for you simply by deciding they are true. This declarative process of truth has nothing to do with reality. If a story doesn't reach this level of declared truth, but is still important enough to you, some connections are missing, and a belief is born. Evolution is the process of building this chain and letting go of it as you build. When you are deeply attached to your symbols, you are less attached to things. Your patterns are tied intimately to things. The closer together two layers are, the more they are tied together and related. The more distortion takes place and thus the firmer must be your grip in order to hold everything together.

Using one level to determine the influence of another is mixing metaphors, like finding an orange with a banana peel on it. There are so many levels to be juggled that people typically attend to just one. The more fundamental you are evolutionarily, the closer to reality you are but also the more restricted you are.

As you work your way up the layers, typically losing sight of the last layer you were on, you move away from reality, but you also move closer to it. Closer because when you reach the level of stories, if you are neither fearful nor needy, you start to open up to what is possible again. The range of stories that can be told if you know that the stories don't mean anything is much broader than any earlier level, the most broad is reality itself. Thus, if stories are told for entertainment and amusement, they are flexible indeed, and when you do not have to tell any particular story, you are free to make up anything. Everything is possible for you; thus you have left reality to return to it again. You have entered one side of illusion construction, worked through all of the layers of illusion and then exited on the other side. The whole illusion is created within reality, but when you focus on the illusion, you cannot see reality. You are always enlightened, you do not encumber your enlightenment before you begin constructing an illusion, and you can fully appreciate your enlightenment when you exit from the top of your illusion as creator of the universe, as all possibility.

Along the way, you have to look through the layers to see the light. If it were not for the light, you would not be able to see the layers, but when you see the light through the layers, you miss enlightenment.

Your quality of life is determined by the amount of focus used to attend to a particular layer. If you use patterns to focus on stuff, you will be materialistic, perhaps thinking that who you are is what you own. This position influences all thinking and harnesses later evolutionary stages to earlier ones. Making rampant assertions requires you to expend huge quantities of energy ignoring that things are susceptible to entropy. Stuff falls apart, thus you fall apart.

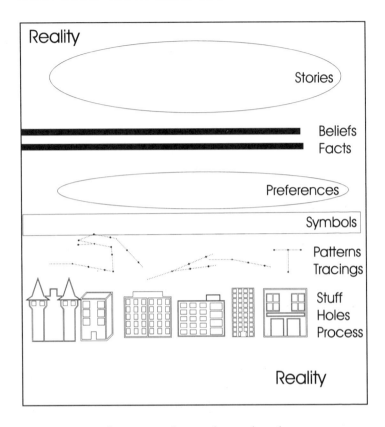

Content does not determine what layer you are focusing on.

Deeply religious people at the pattern-thing level will have ritual (a thing) be important. A large church would be a sign of faith and tithing would be necessary, a focus on the outward symbols of religion. What gets said during a service does not matter as much as the pew or the stained glass windows.

Deeply religious people at the level of patterns will have the repetition of the ritual be important. Religion is defined by the sacraments, going to confession, and other repetitious doings.

Deeply religious people at the level of preferences have their church be the right church, and they like their minister because they *can* like him. They define religion by their ability to prefer.

Religion as belief is a cementing of doctrine, keeping preferences in place and claiming that they have been in place long enough to have become reality. Certain stories must be repeated often enough to close the book on all counter-examples, which is what belief requires. The doctrine becomes important when stories move to the front. Religion becomes about the characters and what they did, along with all that is meant by what they did. Exploration of the meaning of stories gives rise to other stories and the correlation between and among stories.

So it is not the content but the process that determines what you focus on. Along with these levels are the different entities that make up human beings, with patterns located toward the bottom, awareness in the middle and consciousness toward the top. Where you focus determines your perspective and, more importantly, what you perceive yourself to be. (See diagram on next page.)

Once you have begun the process of moving up, you must continue it. You cannot get back to reality by moving down to it; you must move up. Thus when you are starting to recognize stories, you are focused near the top level, but if you think that the stories are true, then you are in stories looking back downward.

Up and down does not indicate good and bad. This scale is simply a portrayal of your progress and growth.

Exploring the landscape reveals where you are, where you are going, and what is in the way—all within an

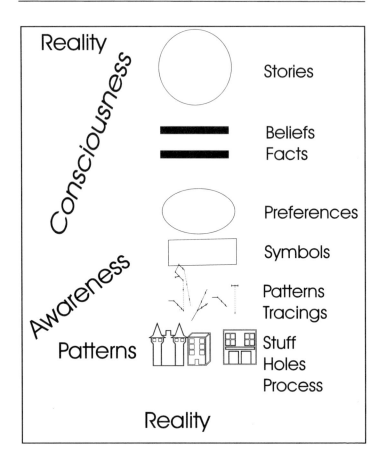

illusionary structure. Follow the progression and it will
lead you to perception of reality and appreciation of your
enlightenment.

37

More Doing

Every time you do anything, you limit your ability to include. Thus, you limit your love. The whole process of identity is exclusion—declaring one thing as distinct from everything it is not. You exclude "this" from who you are and exclude "that" from who you are. You exclude in groups called minorities. You then start excluding members of the smallest minority you can find. It takes time to build an identity; that alone should be a clue to you that identity is illusion. So, to shed an identity takes no time. It is instantaneous. You can spend your whole life building and re-arranging your identity which will keep you busy. Everything you do contributes to your identity as does everything you don't do. You must limit yourself by degrees because it is too painful to do it all at once. You get assistance from others: teachers, clergy, employers, parents, peers, and children, in your quest for the ultimate limitation, the big, unique "You" who you share with nobody else. The big "You" then must go out and sell yourself to others because this "You" is the only right you. "You" must defend yourself against all others and against the universe.

This identity process is the ultimate exclusion and all you are ever excluding, really, is possibility. Every time you "do" more, possibility becomes invisible to you. Perception is limitation: looking at something in lieu of looking at everything, hearing/listening to something while not hearing/listening everything, feeling something as opposed to feeling everything.

If you never did anything, you would be so light all the time that you would never want to do anything again. You would become unproductive in the ordinary sense of productive. What use would you be then? You would cease to be used as a tool as you started living as a source. You would be a conduit for light, ever growing, ever including. You would flow, not even existing in ordinary terms. You would be tickled by the whole universe all of the time. Each moment would be an entirely fresh beginning for you, and the end as well.

People are busy. *Doing* tethers them, holds them in place, lets them know where they are not and sets up an artificial scale of value. Enough people have effectively stated that money is worth something that almost everybody believes it. Similarly, people have set up an artificial and unnatural association between emotions and present needs. What the world needs now is production, and to get this output, people have hooked happiness to accomplishment. "I didn't get anything done today," is a spiritual statement, but not one of accomplishment. People think their worth is dependent upon what they *do*. They place monetary value on doing or producing which influences emotional declarations of happiness. Since "doing" is unnatural and unimportant, a system had to be created to make it important.

How long have you gone without doing anything? Doing is a form of control projected onto the future, the past, and identity. If you really stop doing everything for a period of time, all of these ingredients will be threatened. You will begin to doubt who you are. You will lose limitations. *Not doing* is the shortest route there is to shedding limitations, at least in an industrial society.

The moment you think that what you *do* is important, you become dependent on it. You become controllable by receiving payment or attention for what you *do*. Have you ever seen a parent *do* to his or her children? This is accomplished every time an action takes priority over the child (throwing the baby out with the bath water). Children are taught at an early age that they will get attention when they *do* something and will otherwise be ignored. The magician does the magic with the hand that is not being watched. *Doing* steals your attention away from all of the magic surrounding you. Just sit with a child, *doing* nothing, for a day or two. If the child is over four, you will most likely discover that he or she cannot even sit still and has already been convinced of the importance of *doing*. *Being* is ignored when *doing* takes place. People's very existence is undermined by *doing*. There is nothing to *do*.

There is nothing worth doing. There is no worth to *doing*. The most spiritual practice that people can take part in, everybody can play, is in *not doing*. Get lazy.

This country is founded on the right of everybody to work—the right of everybody to forget who they are and then take part in the illusionary structure that ties doing to existence. "I do; therefore, I am" is the motto of this century. Hopefully, it is not that of the next, or Earth will become ecologically uninhabitable, except for certain species of insects.

People are constantly in one of two states, sometimes in both: "What should I do?" or "busy." There is nothing to do and nobody to do it. You do not exist since limitations are not real. You are reality, and as such, you are all possibility with the expression of none.

Your first great love is for limitations. People don't say they love limitations, but their actions betray this. Everybody is attempting to define the game by attempting to do the most meaningful and useful things.

Doing does not limit your lightness it just eclipses your perception of it. Doing distracts you and leads your perceptions away from reality. If you are looking at what is being done, has been done, or could be done, then you are not focused on the perfection of the moment. While you are doing, there is a tendency to run patterns. How often do you do something for the first time? When you repeat something for the second time, patterns start to take over, and by the third or fourth repetition, the performance is entirely patterned. Consciousness is not necessary for doing. All species can "do."

Human beings are the only species that derives value and worth from "doing." A deer cannot define itself as anything; it doesn't need to. People can define themselves as anything, and they selectively and consistently define themselves by limitation. Consciousness is a gift, an evolutionary opportunity which flies in the face of "doing." Consciousness is *not doing*; it is not even *being*. It is nothing.

Experiencing enlightenment is having nothing to do and doing nothing, even if you are busy. Enlightenment is entertainment without the need for external influence. Doing is entertainment by external sources. The two are entirely opposed.

Anything that you get done leads to more doing. There is always more to do; it is endless. You can remain occupied forever. Occupied is exactly what doing does for you; it fills you up and takes you over. It undermines wholeness by reinforcing the separation between you and what you are acting upon. It forces you to act and as you "do" you become superficial, hypocritical and alone. When you are occupied, you are already in use. You are already demeaned, a tool to be used.

People are most afraid of not doing anything. They usually don't notice that anytime they do something, they move themselves closer to being done. Being done is the possibility of running out of things to do. If you run out of things to do, you will have nothing to do.

It is unlikely that you will be able to do nothing even though there is nothing to do, so you had better get it done soon.

"You shall hold no God before me," said the Lord. You reply, "I'll be there on Sunday Lord; I'm a bit busy today. Too much to do, too little time."

Do you think God will wait for you to get done? So, since you will probably go on worshipping your "God of Doing," perhaps it would be useful to tell you what to do. Do the least significant, smallest, most meaningless tasks you can find. Repeat these little doings differently each time. For example: make one inch lines on a piece of paper, millions of them, but have the way you draw each one be different. The very practice of drawing variation out of repetition sets you free. After you have drawn several million lines, draw a few more and a few more. The moment you think that what you are doing is important, you define yourself by "doing." "What did you do today?"

"I drew eight-thousand seven-hundred and twenty-three one-inch lines on a piece of paper, each in a slightly different way."

"Wow, that sounds like great work, how much does it pay?"

"Nothing."

"That's great. I have been wanting a little more nothing in my life. Where do I sign up?"

"The very act of doing it is signing up. Here is some paper and a pencil."

When people do what they perceive to be the right thing, they think they are good. When they do what they perceive to be the wrong thing, they are bad. Either way they suffer under the burden of more and more to do. When they do what others perceive to be the right thing, they get praise or money. When they do what others perceive to be the wrong thing, they get punished. If it is bad enough, they get a lot of attention and then get punished. When people do nothing at all, there are no actions to determine their placement on the scale of good and bad, so "doing" itself is judged as good, and "not doing" is defined as bad. This is a judgment that most people take for granted. "Of course doing is good, idle hands are the devil's playground."

Is there anything for light to do? Light never has anything to do. Certainly, it illuminates things, but that is revealing the very nature of light and requires no variation or maintenance. Light moves so fast that by the time you look at where it is, it isn't there anymore. It keeps traveling nowhere. It is lazy and unemployed, and yet without it, you would be constantly in the dark. There would be no fossil fuel, no heat, and no energy. There would be no oxygen, no life at all. Human beings derive and are entirely dependent on an unemployed, worthless entity. You owe your existence, all of your being and doing to light. Human beings are light, and anything they have, do, or are conceals this fact.

Life is simple but dependent. The more you do, the more you complicate both your own life and that of everybody around you. When you realize your (you're) light, you contribute to the universe in a way that only consciousness can. You recognize nothing for all that it is, and everything is lighter for it. One person perceiving his or her light contributes to the possibility of all other people seeing light as well. Anything short of enlightenment is working in the dark. You can't know what you are doing, and it is unlikely that you will do anything but mess things up and keep yourself busy in the process. Until you are enlightened—do nothing. Once you are enlightened, you can do anything, but why would you?

It is unlikely that you would undertake a big project in the dark or that you would close your eyes while you build a house unless you thought there would never be light again or convinced yourself that the dark was the light. Most people confuse light and dark. Work in the dark and then wonder why satisfaction constantly eludes you. "That is just the way life is," they say.

It isn't. Life is no way at all. Your perceptions are the way they are because when you confuse light with dark, there are bound to be consequences. Lighten-up means darken-up to people who have confused the two. Doing is one of the main ways that people get distracted from the light. Stop. Look around you. Stay in bed all day and watch the flow of light to dark, the days passing, with nothing at all to do. If you stay in bed for too many days you will be called an invalid—in valid. You will discover the differences between light and dark. Which is which? And, "Which witch will which witch watch, which watch will which witch wind?"

Meaning

Meaning is the glue which holds illusion together. It is not soluble in any known solvent, but it softens in the presence of love and trust. All "doing" and every act to maintain control is an attempt to keep meaning in place. If you quit your maintenance job, the worst might just happen—you could lose meaning. At the loss of meaning, who you thought you were falls apart, the objects you held so dearly lose their importance, their shape, their definition. Limitations disappear, without effort. Would this be so bad after all?

While seeming to be your ally, meaning is always in your way. The same mortar which holds the building together makes it difficult to take the building apart. As you dismantle your illusion, you will run into meaning. You pound away at it using all kinds of tools, and still it seems that meaning is everywhere you look. You pray, but as soon as you are done praying, there is meaning again. Meditation, neuro-linguistic programming, philosophy, religion, addiction, and learning (just to name a few of tools) all get worn down as they continue to chip away at meaning. No matter what the illusion is, the universal bond within it is meaning. One little glob of meaning is enough to have you be unwilling to dismantle a certain part of your illusion.

Throw out anything that reminds you of your past. High school year books, jewelry, pictures of everybody, mementos, and diaries. Throwing out anything and everything that even vaguely reminds you of your past is easier than breaking apart illusion. Imagine you have a blanket that you used to hold when you were a child or a trophy that you won in high school; to each of these you attach a meaning. The blanket represents a younger you, a simpler time, security. The trophy means that you are a winner, and seeing it again can remind you of all the attention you received. People surround themselves with meaning. They attempt to remain on purpose, so that they can keep their illusions together. Purpose helps them remember who they think that they are. This is not reality. This is illusion.

Illusions will not stand without meaning. "What means something to you now?" Another way of saying this is, "What are you making important right now?" Meaning defines the relations between everything there is. It is you who have assembled the collection of thoughts, ideas, opinions, things, history, and attributes together which you call "You." These are all symbols of who you are. They are not really who you are, any more than a snapshot is who you are. When you tend to these symbols, you attach importance and meaning to them and thus distinguish them from everything else. Due to the ability of the mind to generalize, you walk around reacting to anything that looks, sounds, or feels like your particular symbols. If you see a blanket with a pattern similar to that of your security blanket as a child, you then remember your blanket and with it some of your childhood. You remember by pattern and may or may not be aware that you are referring to an earlier pattern. If your awareness is eclipsed by either consciousness or patterns, your behaviors may become influenced by seeing the blanket, and you might act like you did back when you needed a blanket to be secure. You may start acting childish, defensive, or just plain scared. You may become more peaceful and aware of a deep warm sensation of security upon remembering your blanket.

Everything is an invitation for your mind to refer to what it has already come into contact with and to adopt the patterns that it used earlier. Patterns are pervasive. Patterns are used as a shortcut to have you recognize your meaning comparatively, refer back to it, and then define yourself by whatever current influence will get you the most attention.

If you see something new and completely unfamiliar you will not know what importance to attach to it.

Pretend that you just landed here from another planet and that you do not recognize anything around you. In other words, what would the world be like if you didn't add meaning to it. Meaning is identification at its simplest and ownership or understanding as it becomes more complex. Meaning is the way you block yourself from seeing the light. If you let go of something, it still stays around because you have attached meaning to it. Meaning is to your illusion as gravity is to objects. The center of your mind is the source of your meaning and the farther anything gets from that center, the less important it becomes. The most meaningful possessions, be they things or ideas, are gathered close around you, near and dear.

A Short Cut?

You can lead a horse to water, but you can't make her drink.

Do you remember the question you have been pondering since the introduction? What is the second half of "Anything that is now has always been?"

Did you ponder this endlessly? Did you catch yourself trying to figure out the right answer? Did you discover that you could find evidence for an answer being right? Did you think that life would somehow be different if you found the right answer?

Anything that is always has been.

?

Did you cynically not even waste your time thinking about it?

It seems that thinking is not sufficient to see between thoughts. Thus the answer to any question is always closer than your next thought.

If anything that is has always been, then anything that is will always be.

With that one sentence you are relieved of the necessity of ever doing anything again. You no longer need to hang on since anything that is has always been will always be. There is nothing to do if permanence is already yours. You can be infinitely relieved in that there is no time crunch; you don't need to get anything done or figure anything out. There is no test. You don't even have to die. Anything that is now has always been and will always be. You are; thus you always will be. All takes care of itself; you don't have to take care of anything. There is no need for hope, no work to be done, no need for prayer. When you are halfway there, you are all the way there. When you are a third of the way there, you are there. When you are one one-hundredth of the way there, you have already arrived. You cannot miss the boat because you are the boat. Anything that ever has been always was and will always be.

The whole is this simple and elusive. Religions have sold permanence for years. They have told you that Heaven is forever and your Earthly existence is temporary. They have promised you forever—later.   They sweetened   the   deal   by promising that your forever will be good instead of forever bad.

But, if it is forever, then it is probably everything too, so it would have to be all good and all bad. The religions never did have to be philosophically consistent, thank goodness. No one (not even religion) can give you something that you don't already have. So, permanence and life everlasting is already yours. Anything that is not permanent can only appear from your limited perspective. When your perspective is limited you are bound to see limitations which are not real. Reality is All possibility. You are All possibility. All limitation is illusion. The idea of an end is a big limitation with many little limitations and disappointments leading up to it. With complete, total, infinite possibility now and forever, there is nothing to be afraid of (nothing is your biggest fear.). The moment you limit yourself, the fears that your limitation may not be real (and also that it may be real) enter. With limitation, you are damned if you do and damned if you don't.

Trapped halfway across the stream, in your perceptions, you must do something to get to the other side. All of your efforts have been spent prying the whole apart and then determining which parts of the whole are more important than others. You want more than your share of the parts that are important. Inventory control becomes your main pursuit as you seek to get at least your fair share.

You have been trying to pry the circle apart, which cannot be done. Since you abhor the idea of failure, you perceive yourself as successful. Certainly you must have pried it apart.

All you have ever done and will ever do, all you have ever thought or will ever think has been done and thought in an attempt to separate the whole. To somehow have

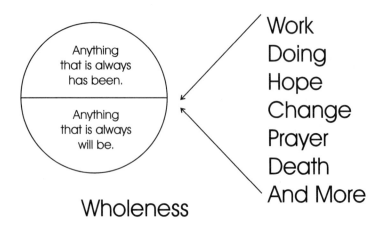

the future be different from the past, or the same as the past. To have "how life will be" be different from "how life under your influence is now." To perceive that you have made a difference. To get something done before you go.

When you were born, in your perception, the clock started ticking. How will you make your dent on this world? Life became an effort as you forgot to enjoy yourself and had to get to work. It took years, about six, to forget your passion for learning and having fun. But you did it; you got on with your necessary job of making whole that which was whole to begin with. After all, you had to separate it before the whole would look as though you had made it whole.

You probably didn't know that this is what you were doing. You were probably in some little area working on some part of this huge project, unaware of the whole, unaware of what you were doing except in relation to what you could notice (or not notice) around you. Philosophy, the opportunity to know you are working on the whole, probably eluded you. If you knew in your bones that everything was already whole, then you would not have bothered to work. You wouldn't keep working unless you had already been working for so long that you had to think your work was important.

Young children know that nothing is more important than everything else. They live in a whole world. Old people, who have lived broadly and seen much, realize that they have never made a difference, except in their own minds. The whole is as whole as it was when they were children and remained whole even during their productive years, when they could not see the whole. Most people avoid young children (by sending them to daycare or school and keeping them busy at all costs) and old people (by keeping them in nursing or rest homes). People do not want to discover that "doing" anything is a waste of time. No perspective or all perspectives leads you to the whole while having some perspective leads you only to illusion.

You pry the sides apart in an attempt to make a difference. The sides don't move, but you think they do. If they ever really did, you would have a nuclear event that would devastate everything. Your thinking serves you in your attempt at prying, but primarily your thinking directs you where to pry. You must pry where the whole is weakest, the least whole. To make the most difference, you must be the most fragmented: extreme fragmentation is the place of greatest leverage. This is the place where you are the most certain of where you stand and where you are currently working the hardest.

You attempt to control by getting between the way things are, with the knowledge you have of how they were, so you can make things different in the future. This time-bound model is so oppressive that you wear yourself out in the process while constantly being unsuccessful. You suggest that you will be happy when the future is assured, when things are a certain way and are no other way. This is the route to a very difficult life—an unnecessary route, an unnatural route, except that almost everybody is taking it with you.

If you could ever really make a crack in the wall, those walls would come tumbling down. Don't worry, ever; you can't. Thank God, all of the work you have ever done has been meaningful and worthless.

Anything that is always has been.

Anything that is always will be.

Different people are working at various parts of the whole attempting to break it apart, each person hoping that where he or she is working will be the point of leverage allowing a crack to occur. You are working for separation while the whole remains intact.

You fail over and over. You pick yourself up, dust yourself off and get back to work. There are so many ways you attempt to miss your failures, so many ways you determine your perceptions rather than just having them. You perceive what you wish to see in an effort to make yourself more important. The whole, with absolute integrity, remains whole, despite your best efforts.

You make up stories and excuses for why the whole is still whole or why things are not the way they should be. Embedded in each of these stories is an excuse based on impermanence. Transience is the basis of all your excuses.

Enlightenment is seeing the whole, wholeness, within and without. All wholeness, complete and perfect. Nowhere to get to and nothing to do. If you don't have to split up the whole, then you can appreciate it. You need no excuses for things being perfect the way they are and the way they will always be. It is only when you think things should and can be different that you must put your shoulder to the wheel and get to work. The wheel doesn't care.

Can it really be so easy? No, not if you still have to prove you are more important than something or someone else. Not if you have to be the one who makes life whole rather than the one who discovers that life already is whole. Anything that is not infinitely easy is not worthwhile. If it seems the least bit like doing or effort, then you are fighting reality, attempting to separate then rejoin wholeness. New products, new ideas are all just ways of packaging parts of the whole in a futile attempt to split it up. The whole can only be lost in your perception. And it can always be found because it is always there.

"Perception is reality," some people say. It isn't. Perception is limitation. Enlightenment and wholeness are reality.

The only purpose in life (given that wholeness already exists and that you are that wholeness and always have been) is to fit the appropriate punch line to a suitable joke and laugh.

Bringing It Together

The circle below represents wholeness. The middle line represents the present and supposedly splits the circle. People are trying to determine (or control) where the "right" line is and are taking advantage of the possibility of separation.

Finding the right spot to split the whole is another way of illustrating the search of "Where do you stand?" Knowing where you are and your tangential attempts at influencing each point represents the teeter totter described in Chapter 20. As you live and build illusion, you get further and further from the circle itself, while never leaving it, except in your perception.

There is a lot of "when" and "then" but very little "now" in this diagram, due to your commitment to

illusion. The diagram does not represent the way things are; it shows the way you perceive them. "Now" always turns into the past or isn't quite here yet, in your perception. So you get busy working to fill up the smallest place you can find, "now," in your attempt to influence "when" and "then." The line, of course does not even exist. "When" and "then" are illusions and all you really have is "now."

People attempt to leave their mark, to influence things sufficiently, in the "right" direction. They draw lines to do so; the longer the line, the better because it allows them to think they are influencing reality while staying as far from it as possible.

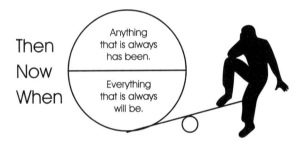

Then
Now
When

Anything that is always has been.

Everything that is always will be.

Effort is applied to the lines you have drawn, but nothing moves. You would rather see something move to reassure yourself of your control and influence, so you see movement. You must be effective and meaningful, so you stop looking at reality and start noticing what is changing. Nothing isn't changing, but you ignore nothing while attending to *some*thing and you create an imaginary world in which things are real and things change so your perceptions don't have to. You are hypnotized, entranced by external change. In order to convince yourself that change is taking place, your world must be complicated and busy enough to keep you interested, while resembling reality just enough to have you trust it. As your imaginary world, illusion, becomes more complex, your time and attention are consumed in direct proportion to complexity. Soon you forget about reality entirely. The most efficient way to invite this dose of amnesia is to call your illusion "reality."

You ignore reality and spend all of your time tending to your illusion. You start with a line and then work through geographical figures which give meaning to the lines. When you add structure to those figures by having them symbolize other things, you never have to wonder what to do because there is always enough to do.

You must clean, polish, rebuild, refurbish, and categorize all that you have built. Reality requires no maintenance while illusion requires constant maintenance. Every moment spent working on or thinking about your illusion makes it appear more real. Illusion consumes you and becomes you, without being becoming to you, since it is so much less than who you are while pretending to be everything.

Your illusion seems so real that it must be real. When you began recognizing symbols, you settled for appearances over substance, so anything that seems to be some way must be that way. Your illusion seems to protect you; thus it must protect you. It is your external skin, guarding you from reality. Soon you have a system that looks like the diagram on the next page.

Both sides are illusion. To perceive reality you must ignore everything but the narrow line between anything that has been and anything that will be. You must not attempt to redraw it or any other point or line. Just observe it. Instead you stay as far away from reality as you can get. Illusion becomes both who you think you are and your buffer zone, keeping you from perceiving who you really are. You are still in reality, but you are not perceiving it. Reality is nothing and your illusions are something else.

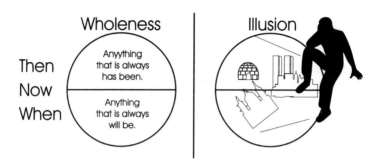

Your illusion requires constant maintenance. It needs you—you perceive that your illusion is you. Reality, all there is, is the enemy of illusion, and so it is your enemy. You have no friends but a lot of company. Not really, because everybody and everything threatens illusion. Losing your balance is an essential part of dis-illusion, doing away with illusion, which results in enlightenment, not disillusionment.

You don't have to play into your illusion, but at a certain point (that you miss), you forget that there are many other games. Illusion cannot stand the light of day; it is not real; it is not there at all. You are a figment of your imagination, and so is everything that you perceive yourself to be. You are the light, not that which is illuminated. Everything illuminated is just there for the entertainment of consciousness. When you confuse yourself for that which the light is shining on, you become an object, a thing. The light is shining on you, blinding you, rather than shining from you. You can not see what isn't, you can only see what is. Would you rather live in a full universe or an empty one? The less secure you are, the fuller you need the universe to be.

Reality is always satisfied with nothing. Your illusion is not satisfied with nothing, so you go for something, anything, and the possibility of illusionary satisfaction. If you wanted everything you could get back to nothing— but you don't want everything. You want *some* thing. You tie yourself to anything that will let you know who you are or where you stand, but the knots don't hold. You are constantly threatened, plagued by the possibility of being set free. Free to discover how crazy you have been, free to explore reality, the whole.

You must stop seeking enlightenment to find it. You must abandon all illusion because it limits you. You must ignore all musts, even this one.

Smile. Everything is simpler than your illusion; complexity is not importance or important. If you see the light, you will not be the light. Light is nothing at all. As long as you attempt to "be" at all, the light will be obstructed by your illusion. The sun is going to shine on your backyard some day. You are shining NOW.

Why Illusion?

Momma told you not to smoke, as she twisted her foot on the remains of her lipstick-stained cigarette smoked right down to the filter. "Smoking is bad for you."

You have been subjected to school teachers preaching to you for years of the importance of learning while they were not learning themselves but smugly sitting with their answer books opened. People smiled at you and said, "Hello," whether they knew you or not, whether they liked you or not. Your dad said he would spend time with you as soon as he got a chance, but there was always something else he had to do. You were hurt, over and over, by the people who loved you the most.

You were driven out of the world you were born into. Pushed from reality by life's pain and traumas. It isn't really life that is the problem; it is other people. Many people mean well, but meaning is something they added selectively from their illusion. Meaning is the glue which sticks illusion together. Any person you come into contact with is in the process of defending his or her illusion from you. From the moment you were conceived, you were a threat to your mother's equilibrium and to the relationship between your father and mother. People's own existence is defined by problems. They are problems for themselves, so of course, you are a problem for them, too.

From the moment you were born, you were in the way. You didn't fit in. You couldn't walk around like other people, you couldn't tell people what you wanted or needed, and you couldn't even play card games. You were in the way, but your parents didn't admit that you were in the way, so they pretended you were not. Acting one way while thinking another is called incongruity. Incongruity is any battle between how things are and how someone wants them to be. Incongruity is the difference between all possibility and perceived possibilities. Your parents loved you, but they couldn't get anything done with you around. They loved getting things done. They were in a double bind, food of the mind, and they conveyed their problem to you as though the problem was you.

It is the everyday incongruities that inspire and terrorize you into illusion construction. You need somewhere to be safe from all the trauma around you, from all the pain, from all the problems that define people's lives. Your parents are confused and terrible Gods, well-meaning perhaps, but not flexible enough to love you except under certain conditions. Everything gets in the way of their being with you. Typically, when they are with you, their minds are thinking about other things. When you receive enough mixed messages, you retreat, you run and hide in an illusionary world where you are in control. Away from their wanton exercises of control. The subtleties of the abuse that a child goes through are so great and plentiful that almost every child has a horrible childhood.

Parenting could be a spiritual experience. However, it could more accurately be described as, the grown-up God, misunderstanding a child. At age two, consciousness shows up and the battle of illusions begins. The child says, "no," and the parents say, "yes." Illusion becomes mandatory because only in a make believe world can people consistently get their way.

Illusion becomes the answer to every problem. Go to your illusion and things will be all right. By about age six you had already created enough illusion that the idea of getting rid of it was impossible. So, illusion became real. Your innocence and purity were gone, and you settled for what you made up. Your defenses became your world. You lived within them. When children play tag, they often declare a place safe where they can go to take some time out from their game. Your illusion became your secure place to take time out from living. Thinking about or attempting to influence the future is usually done to structure your next hiding place.

When illusion becomes reality, pain is replaced by numbness, and awareness is eclipsed by both consciousness and patterns. Consciousness focuses on constructed illusion and pays little attention to sensory data.

Within illusion everything is illusion. There are no real emotions. There is no real satisfaction. No real anything. You escaped from the trauma of coming into contact with other people's illusions and ended up lonely and jailed. You used up your allotment of pain and suffering early in life and were well justified in locking yourself away.

Over the years, you continued to develop your illusion. You did not look too closely at other people, you tried not to judge and you constantly lowered your standards. You shrank to fit the diminishing area left open within your illusion. If you tried to move very fast or spontaneously, you bumped into things, got hurt, or got scared.

Looking back over your illusion twenty or thirty years later, you find it is getting tiresome. There is nothing new in it. You built it to defend yourself against other people, but the more you defended, the more offended you became by other people. You ponder whether what you are experiencing as life really can be all there is to life. The hollowness of illusion seems to provide security but leads to an empty life. Your ability to perceive has been limited the most and consciousness and has narrowed so much that your perceptions no longer interest you (awareness has been eclipsed by patterns). You change things, you reorganize your illusion, but very soon the same emptiness returns. Your life looks good on the surface, but you know better. You can only shrink so far before you start to expand again. The bigger your illusion gets, the smaller you get. So, as you start to grow again, you dismantle your illusion.

Remember, your illusion is reality to you. Your opinions have become facts, you have turned lead into gold. At first, dismantling an illusion is very difficult and threatening. It seems that you are taking apart real things, but as you break up your constructs, you discover they are not real. "If this one is not real, what else is not real?" With some rigor, the dismantling of your illusion starts to gain speed. You begin to doubt what you have believed, question what you have known, and trust nobody. Paranoia, at times, can be as simple as blaming somebody else for the wool you pulled over your own eyes.

You will have as much illusion to take apart as you put together, no more, no less. How long it takes you to dismantle your illusion corresponds with how much emotion you blocked while you were putting it together. Each piece of your illusion was put in place because of fear. Often as you take your illusion apart, whatever you attempted to block appears again, looking real in its illusionary surroundings. Against a backdrop of illusion, anything can look real.

Dismantling can take a long time, but luckily there are many short cuts. All that inspired you to build an illusion in the first place has an opposite that you can embrace. Distrust worked full-time on the construction of your illusion, so trust can be employed to break it apart. Repetition was required to weave the patterns of your illusion, so by adding novelty to any behavior, reality can be revealed. Fear, terror, and selfishness all donated their time to the monument you built to hide behind. Pick their opposites (trust, curiosity, and giving unconditionally) and you will have allies in your demolition work. From every position within your illusion, there is a loss of perspective. So, rise above your illusion. When you look at it from above, it ceases to limit your perspective; it no longer blocks you from what you didn't want to be true. There is often a hierarchy of vertical and horizontal distortions to work through as you rise above your illusion. Circling around, you continually gain altitude and reveal the illusion as imaginary while continuing to grow and expand as you spiral upward and outward. Trust (being willing to operate without evidence) is necessary in taking apart the constructions of the mind. If you have to see your progress as progress, then you will be tricked into moving backward while thinking you are moving forward.

Anything that can convince you to keep your illusion intact is your enemy. If you are busy with the content of your illusion you can't see patterns. Patterns keep your illusion together. Awareness can break illusion apart. The mind is important to illusion; it thinks it will die if the illusion disappears. Illusion is only important when it is considered to be reality. Doubt everything. In the world of illusion, nothing is as it seems, so you can't figure out how to take illusion apart; the figuring out is part of illusion, too. If you get rid of one thing at a time, you will never get rid of everything. Doubt everything, trust everything, confound and undermine your ability to think. It is your thinking that got you into this emptiness in the first place. The biggest enemy of emptiness is nothing. Nothing is as full as it can get. Nothing contains everything, but everything does not include nothing.

The emperor is wearing no clothes. Illusions within illusions gain credibility by complexity and abundance, but you built them and you can doubt them. Don't even trust yourself doubting them, doubt your doubting. The path is narrow and the pitfalls are many. Trust, but just for the moment. Find out what real trust is—trusting without an object of that trust. Stop believing your stories, stop making excuses, and illusion will fall away.

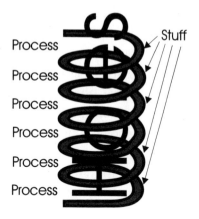

Have as many possibilities as you can. The closer to reality you get, the more possibilities you will have and the more danger your illusion will be in. One moment lost in illusion is one too many. If you believe any story, then you are still in your illusion. If you think your parents injured you, then you are still in illusion. If you think you finally understand something, then you are still in your illusion. If you finally like yourself for the first time, then you are still in your illusion. If you lose five pounds and know it, then you are still in your illusion. If you want to buy something, then you are still in your illusion. If you are having a good time, then you are still in your illusion.

But you can get out. For awhile you will not recognize your surroundings, or yourself. You may go through confusion, anger, sadness, excitement, tension, and more. It is a long journey, though it need not take a long time. Many people will not complete the journey to their satisfaction. Incompletion itself is an excuse to continue the illusion, to make consciousness important. Because something is not yet done, you have to stay around and complete it. Incompletion is a widely-accepted excuse but still part of the illusion.

Let go without doing anything. Trust, though you know you don't dare. Jump though you may never land, or worse yet, you may hurt yourself. In the illusion, there is no real you to be hurt. The price you have paid for protecting yourself is losing yourself. You have gotten what you were running from. Running from and running to seem to be the same thing. Illusion is an expensive temporary fix, it was the only one you had when you were young, but that was then and this is now. Take apart your illusion and you will discover that you cannot possibly be hurt; pain is a device to chase you into your illusion.

Not knowing who you are can steal everything and nothing from you. Within an illusion, everything has to fit together. You have to be careful what you let in and ignore any inconsistencies that already exist. Illusions are fragile, as is anything dependent on consistency. Illusions are serious, as is anything built on fear. Illusions are transient, as is anything that limits possibilities. Illusions depend on selective acceptance and primary exclusion.

Illusions are so fragile they are in danger as soon as you know you have one. Be careful, you might discover that your thoughts are no more important than a gentle breeze, there for your entertainment. Illusion can not stand light. You must be trained not to recognize illusion as illusion. The basic element of the training is repeatedly calling illusion "reality." When you start to take illusion apart, you will discover that there is nothing to do because illusion was really never there to begin with. All the models of therapy which are based on giving credence to thought and figuring things out, will result, at best, in an experience of temporary relief followed by increased trauma. These therapies are illusion enhancers. Shine light on illusion and you will discover that nothing is there. Nothing is having its way with you, and fun doesn't get any better than that. If you are the least bit dependent on anything, then you are hooked by illusion.

Enlightenment is just on the other side of your illusion.

Light

You can not have a purpose different from everyone's purpose, unless you make it up. There is a Universal Purpose, UP. The UP is to keep light company. Those who have recognized their enlightenment know this. Those who have not are still dependent on time and space.

Probably the easiest path to recognizing your enlightenment is to run 186,000 miles per second, which is not an easy task. It makes the four-minute mile look like sitting still, or moving backward. Comparative thinking obviously won't get you there because if you compare where you are now with light, you have too far to go, which is just the point.

You will recognize your enlightenment. That is certain. From the moment you do so, nothing will be ecstasy. If you join light the moment before death, you will have a moment of ecstasy; if you do it fifty years before death, you will have fifty years of ecstasy. The sooner the sooner. It doesn't matter.

There are many paths leading you to recognizing your enlightenment. Some well-worn and riddled with temptation based on all who have gone before and the ritualization that surrounds longevity. This book represents a new path, a new whole/hole you may crawl through. This is no tourist trap, since it has had but one traveler. Light is always the same, there is no differentiation, but how you get to the recognition varies. This book is an opportunity for those willing to take a short-cut. Not the easy cut. It may be easier to sit cross-legged in a cave for twenty years than to walk directly into the light with your senses open, facing all you would rather not face. This path reveals who you are not often enough that nothing finds a residence within you. This path varies your perspective often enough to allow you to hold various and opposite perspectives at the same time. To follow this path, you must expand beyond control all the way to entertainment and ecstasy.

The only way to reveal where you are now is to be light yourself. No information can travel at the speed of light, so nothing need be formed. At any speed slower than 186,000 miles per second, things start mattering again. Once you have matter, there is so much to do. And all of it matters.

Chuck played a lot. Play was his main occupation, as a child. Sometimes he would play with other children on his suburban block and other times he would make up games all by himself. Either way he was always entertained. His parents were busy. Occasionally he would play with them but then the games took on much more structure and needed to have exact starting points, stopping points, and names. On almost any night as darkness approached he might be an Indian, a scientist, or a lion but he knew that his game was over when his parents turned on the porch light. The light indicated that it was time for him to go inside. He could always play until he saw the light, and so can you. Until you see the light, keep playing.

Glossary

All: That which you can look at, or listen to forever without ever having it look or sound the same—infinite amusement.

Analogy: A vehicle which transports the mind.

Assertion: A linguistic statement. An attempt to define who you are through a linguistic statement which can be verified by the senses. A statement you can provide evidence for. A report on illusion.

Awareness: A wind in your head. The evolutionary step just prior to consciousness attending to momentary sensory observations. Pure observation, sensory data with nothing added. The perception of illusion as nothing.

Belief: A thought with repetition as credibility. A mental technique which has to do with a selective blindness combined with repetition to provide a kind of controlled stupidity in a specific domain. The artificial removal of paradox. The lock box of patterns and thoughts that preclude awareness and examination. The pact between the past and the future which doesn't involve the present.

Cause and Effect: A tool of the mind which attempts to make things predictable. A technique which oppresses the mind endlessly by the conditions which exist outside of it.

Choice: An illusion invented to convince you that you can control the future. Crossing a line.

The Choice: Choosing between something and everything, spiritual choice.

Choosing: A process of selecting illusions.

Comparison: A function of consciousness designed to make the mind important. By comparison, the mind knows where it stands.

Consciousness: Awareness aware of itself. The ability to perceive the wind but not its effects. The ability to perceive multiple illusions simultaneously. The purpose of consciousness is to be entertained.

Control: The systematic limitation of possibility with the ultimate goal of reducing all possibility to one—certainty

Crazy: Mistaking Reality for illusion and visa versa.

Creation: The distortion of nothing.

Credibility: Repetition.

Culture: The set of rules of engagement between members of a group to alleviate the necessity of treating any member of the group individually.

Declaration: A linguistic attempt to create something out of nothing. .

Difference: A faulty foundation from which to build a crazy philosophy.

Doing: A little segment of control projected onto the future, the past, and identity. The basis of all doing is the declaration that things aren't as they should be.

Edge: Where any two planes that you have declared separate and distinct get so close together that you cannot tell the difference between the two.

Emotions: The result of an overlap between illusion and reality. Their purpose is to give you something you *know* isn't real.

ENLIGHTENMENT: Giving up control, the releasing of thoughts and an acceptance of the flow of things. The ongoing process of consciousness focused on reality. It is always closer than your next thought.

Entertainment: No thought happening twice.

Free Choice: The systematic mind-based process of exclusion. A competitive game with winners and losers. A euphemism for control.

Holes: The space between stuff.

Humor: To remember to want what you were compulsed to have.

"I" or "You": Some entirely undefined mixture of patterns, awareness, and consciousness, typically limited to what people think.

Identity: Composed of incomplete thoughts—thoughts that are stuck and standing still. What you wouldn't do, think, or have.

Illusion: Anything that requires maintenance. The result of thinking the same thought many times and building repetitious thoughts into patterns of thought.

Incongruity: The difference between how things are, how you think they are and how you want them to be. The difference between all possibility and perceived possibilities.

Intuition: An end run around the illusion.

Land of connections: A place where you are whole and your perceptions are amusing limitations.

Land of deceptions: A place where you see little tiny pieces and call what you see the whole.

Language: The divisional, fragmentary tool used by consciousness to define its relationship to everything. Language creates illusion.

Life: What happens when reality hits the road.

Limitation: The actualization and conscious focus on one possibility.

Love: A declaration of inclusion.

Magic: Noticing that you are standing nowhere, instead of somewhere.

Mathematics: The science of determining patterns.

Meaning: The glue which holds illusion together.

Meditation: The currency one pays for revelation. Not having content run through your head.

MIPPS: Multiple Illusionary Perspectives per Second.

Mind: The result of consciousness. Defined by the illusions you hold to.

Mother: Someone who can whip up a batch of French toast, make love to her husband and play two hands of Rummy all at the same time.

Nothing: The eternal backdrop for all that is. It purifies awareness.

Occupied: Undermining wholeness by reinforcing the separation between you and what you are acting upon.

Paranoia: Blaming somebody else for the wool you pulled over your own eyes.

Passion: The meaningless pursuit of knowledge for entertainment.

Past: A fictitious time invented as evidence for consistency and continuity.

Perception: A limitation—it is looking at something in lieu of looking at something else.

Personality: Composed of an imaginary location where you have spent enough time to personalize it and make it your own by building structures and symbols to define the location as distinct, more meaningful, and better than other locations.

Perspectives: Limitations—fragments of the whole.

Philosophy: The opportunity to know you are working on the whole.

Planes: Fundamental illusion formed by drawing lines.

Politician: Someone who may be too lazy to do something but is always willing to make rules about how other people should do it.

Precocious: Teasing the universe.

Preference: The foundation of repetitious thought.

Present: The sole domain of untethered, uneclipsed awareness.

Process: The interaction between stuff and holes and between holes and holes and stuff and stuff.

Progress: Getting closer to nothing.

Purpose: A story without an ending.

Quality of Life: Entertainment, measured in multiple illusionary perspectives per second (MIPPS).

Reality: The mathematical computation of all possibility.

Recognize: Think again—the double thought which moves you to pattern.

Remember: You were once a member but you were cast out and now you are rejoining. A long story for one word to tell.

Respect: Look again.

Sales: The road to Reality. An increase or decrease in the recognition of possibilities.

Science: An attempt to relieve people of the need to trust themselves through repetition.

Space: A second level distortion.

Spirit: The manifestation of Reality in a specific location.

Spirituality: Consciousness focused on Reality.

Stories: Made up of things and words that modify those things. Defining repetition as security.

Story: A narrative about movement through a particular grouping of lines.

Stuff: A particular kind of hole that is no longer content being nothing and must derive self-esteem by being something.

Subtlety: The art of attending to all points equally without perceiving one point to be larger than another.

Thinking: The illusion that illusion is not illusion. A process of systematic limitation.

Tickling: The process of bringing the mind and the body together.

Time: A second level distortion.

Transience: The basis of all your excuses.

Trust: Being willing to operate without evidence.

Universe: A representation of what is common to All.

Worry: A culture's equivalence of caring.

Universal Purpose (UP): To keep light company.

Index

Other Books by Jerry Stocking

Thinking Clearly—An Adventure in Mental Fitness

There Are No Accidents—A Magical Love Story

Laughing with God

How to Win by Quitting

Spiritual Seduction

Contact Moose Ear Press to find out about quantity discounts
or information on other books, tapes or seminars by Jerry Stocking.

Moose Ear Press
P.O. Box 2422
Clarkesville, Georgia 30523
(706) 754-7540
FAX (706) 754-7550

Other Books by Jerry Stocking

Your life is dominated by "no." Your identity is based in "no"; your interactions defined by what you wouldn't do and your energy perpetually constrained. Control is always based on what you "no" or know. All play, love and fun is based in "yes." The more you say "yes," really yes, the more healthy, wealthy and wise you will be. Seduction is defined as converting "no" to "yes" in the presence of attention. This fun and exciting book begins with an exploration of life on Earth, as is, then dances with life as an opportunity to flirt, learn, play and have lots of sex. It then moves from profound fun and success on Earth to Spirituality. (315 pages)

How much of your day is consumed by what you perceive you have to do? Rules you think you have to follow? Games you believe you have to play? What can you do to get out from under it all? QUIT! It's the one choice we never seriously consider. Quit something you feel you must do and you'll soon discover that you never had to do it in the first place. In the process you'll discover what you really want to do. By letting go, you'll experience the genuine fullness and vitality of truly living. (272 pages)

Your mind is capable of incredible feats and miracles. *Thinking Clearly—An Adventure in Mental Fitness* will help you experience it all. Most people are mentally flabby, easily angered and worried. A few people are mentally fit. They enjoy life and do more with less effort. A wealth of stories, illustrations and exercises in perception will bring to you a life so mentally fit that every challenge becomes an adventure and a delight. (204 pages)
(formerly *Cognitive Harmony*)

Laughing With God is a dialogue between two characters: a person much like you—with the same needs, dreams and desires—and God. Together they explore the human condition. The conversation emphasizes flexibility and the importance of amusement and playfulness over the seriousness which is currently robbing us of thoroughly wonderful lives. God is representative of the inspired bliss that exists in all of us. The person takes on the role of being truly ignorant, sometimes embarrassing, always sincere and continually willing to learn. (144 pages)

(formerly *Introduction to Spiritual Harmony*)

There Are No Accidents is a novel which explores personal growth in fun and entertaining ways. Adventure, romance and spirituality wind through a story of love and living. The book is full of magic, things that we don't yet understand but will begin to appreciate as we open to the Voice of our spirituality.

(162 pages)

Matthew Fox "*Laughing With God* is witty, wise, humorous, and sometimes exasperatingly truthful—not unlike the Deity Herself. The author's dialogues with God sparkle with intelligence and humor. We feel encouraged to carry on our own."

"I have your books in my briefcase and on this 24-city tour I anticipate being the beneficiary of **Bill Moyers** your insights and experience. What a bold leap you have taken, one I much admire as a great example of 'following your bliss.'"

Dr. Bernie Siegel "You don't have to agree with Stocking's God to be challenged and enlightened. Learn who you really are and about the true meaning of God and the place God takes in our lives. [*Laughing With God* is a] very interesting book."

Illusion Conclusion

Come out and play!

LEAVE THE WORLD OF ILLUSION WHERE EVERYTHING, EVEN WHAT YOU CALL HAPPINESS, IS JUST A DEGREE OF SUFFER-ING. **You are invited to attend a very special course, Illusion Conclusion (IC!)**, where you will discover how incredible you are and always were.

The IC! Course will be challenging to your limitations and provide an environment for who you are to shine through illusion. **Illusion Conclusion** courses are held at the foothills of the Smoky Mountains in Northern Georgia, with five days of coursework and three integration days.

You are being held hostage by illusion and probably don't even know it. As a four or five-year-old you were full of energy, curiosity, spontaneity, movement and playfulness. Slowly illusion has replaced these qualities, choking your aliveness, making your body stiff and limiting your thinking to repetition and structure.

Illusion isn't nice and isn't necessary, but its nature makes it tough to find, even when it is all around you. If you put a frog in a pot and slowly heat the water, the frog will soon boil because it doesn't notice the slight increase in temperature. It will not jump out of the pot. Illusion slowly takes over your life, too slowly for you to notice. Light is the enemy of illusion because it reveals illusion as illusion. Light is fast; illusion is slow. Ridding yourself of illusion speeds up your thinking, making it difficult for illusion to catch and bind you. Is life, the world, going too fast for you? Are you too busy? The less encumbered you are by illusion the faster you will be, thus the slower the world will be relative to you.

Life gets easy—light—enlightened.

Call and register today. **800.899.2464**

Come to the Course, or get the tapes, then come to the Course.

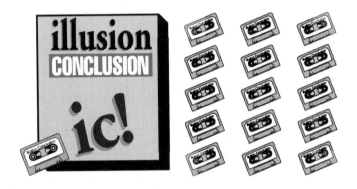

If you want to listen to IC! Course tapes before coming to an IC! Course, you can get the 24-hour Illusion Conclusion Course on tape, complete with a booklet including diagrams. The cost for the tapes is $149 and we reduce the tuition for your IC! Course by $100 if you have purchased them. We are a nonprofit corporation and use the proceeds from tape sets to fund consciousness research and expand human horizons.

We had a professional bowler call to return the tapes. "I listened to almost all of one side of one tape and I don't get it," he said. He agreed to listen more. He called back three months later having listened to the entire tape set three times. He was asking philosophical questions, had deepened his relationships and, his bowling scores had increased. He attributed his new-found delight to the tapes.

A CHOICE EXPERIENCE, INC. • PO BOX 2422
CLARKESVILLE, GA 30523 • 800.899.2464